IMAMATE AND LEADERSHIP

LESSONS ON ISLAMIC DOCTRINE

(BOOK FOUR)

SAYYID MUJTABA MUSAVI LARI

TRANSLATED BY:
HAMID ALGAR

IMAMATE AND LEADERSHIP

LESSONS ON ISLAMIC DOCTRINE

(BOOK FOUR)

SAYYID MUJTABA MUSAVI LARI

TRANSLATED BY:
HAMID ALGAR

IMAMATE AND LEADERSHIP

LESSONS ON
ISLAMIC DOCTRINE

(BOOK FOUR)

SAYYID MUJTABA MUSAVI LARI

TRANSLATED BY:
HAMID ALGAR

Jacket Design by: F. Farhang

August 2002

August 2000

Musavi Lari, Mujtaba, 1935 - Imamate and Leadership/ Mujtaba Musavi Lari; Translated by Hamid Algar.- [S.l: s.n], 2002.
287 p. (Lessons on Islamic Doctrine; book four)
Cataloging based on CIP information.

1.Imamate. 2.Islamic Leadership - Imams (Shiites).
I.Algar, Hamid, 1940 - .
II.Title.

BP222 .M87.04952 297.44
M78-27721

Contents

About the Author

Sayyid Mujtabā Mūsawī Lārī is the son of the late Āyatullāh Sayyid 'Alī Asghar Lārī, one of the great religious scholars and social personalities of Iran. His grandfather was the late Āyatullāh Ḥājj Sayyid 'Abdu 'l-Ḥusayn Lārī, who fought for freedom in the Constitutional Revolution. In the course of his lengthy struggles against the tyrannical government of the time, he attempted to establish an Islamic government and succeeded in doing so for a short time in Lārestān.

Sayyid Mujtabā Mūsawī Larī was born in 1314/1935 in the city of Lār where he completed his primary education and his preliminary Islamic studies. In 1332/1953, he departed for Qum to continue his study of the Islamic sciences, studying under the professors and teachers of the religious institution, including the main authorities in jurisprudence (*marāji'*).

In 1341/1962, he became a collaborator of *Maktab-i-Islām*, a religious and scientific journal, writing a series of articles on Islamic ethics. These articles were later collected into a book published under the title *A Review on the Ethical and Psychological Problems*. Twelve editions of the Persian original of this book have been published, and it has also been translated into Arabic, Bengali, Urdu, Swahili, Hausa, French, and English, under the title, *Youth and Morals*.

In 1342/1963, he travelled to Germany for medical treatment, and returning to Iran after a stay of several months, he wrote a book called *Western Civilization Through Muslim*

Eyes. The book includes a comparative discussion of Western and Islamic civilization, and in it, the author seeks to prove, by way of a comprehensive, reasoned, and exact comparison, the superiority of the comprehensive and multi-dimensional civilization of Islam to that of the West. This book has recently been reprinted for the seventh time. In 1349/1970, it was translated into English by a British Orientalist, F. G. Goulding, and it aroused much attention in Europe. Articles concerning the book appeared in several Western periodicals, and the BBC arranged an interview with the translator in which the reasons for translating the book and the reception accorded it in England were discussed. The English version of the book has up to now been printed three times in England, eight times in Iran, and twice in America.

About three years after the publication of the English translation, Rudolf Singler, a German university professor, translated it into German, and the version he produced proved influential in Germany. One of the leaders of the Social Democratic Party informed the translator in a letter that the book had left a profound impression upon him, causing him to change his views of Islam, and that he would recommend the book to his friends. The German translation has now been reprinted three times.

The English and German versions of the book were reprinted by the Ministry of Islamic Guidance for wide distribution abroad through the Ministry of Foreign Affairs and the Islamic Students' Associations abroad.

At the same time that the first printing of the German translation was published, an Indian Muslim scholar by the name of Mawlānā Rawshan 'Alī translated it into Urdu for distribution in India and Pakistan. This Urdu translation has now been reprinted five times.

This book has also been translated into Japanese, Spanish, Arabic and French languages.

Sayyid Mujtabā Mūsawī Lārī has also written a pamphlet on *Tawḥīd* (divine unity), which was translated in England under the title, *Knowing God*, and published several times in

America. It has also been translated into Spanish, Russian, Polish, Norwegian and Urdu languages.

In 1343/1964, he established a charitable organization in Lār with the purposes of propagating Islam, teaching Islam to rural youth, and helping the needy. This organization remained active until 1346/1967. Its main accomplishments were the dispatch of students of the religious sciences to the countryside to teach Islam to children and young people; providing thousands of school children with clothing, books and writing equipment; building a number of mosques, schools, and clinics in towns and villages; and the provision of miscellaneous services.

Sayyid Mujtabā Mūsawī Lārī pursued his interest in Islamic ethics, writing new articles on the subject. In 1353/1974, a collection of these articles, revised and supplemented, appeared in book form under the title, *The Role of Ethics in Human Development*. The book has now been reprinted six times, and the English translation is underway.

In 1357/1978, he travelled to America at the invitation of an Islamic organization in that country. He then went to England and France and after returning to Iran began writing a series of articles on Islamic ideology for the magazine *Soroush*. These articles were later collected in a four-volume book on the fundamental beliefs of Islam (*tawḥīd*, divine justice, prophethood, imamate, and resurrection) under the title *The Foundations of Islamic Doctrine*.

This four-volume work has been translated into Arabic, some parts of it having already been printed three times. The English translation of the forth volume of this work forms the present book. Urdu and Hindi translations are also underway; four volumes of the French translation have already appeared.

In 1359/1980, Sayyid Mujtabā Mūsawī Lārī established an organization in Qum called Office for the Diffusion of Islamic Culture Abroad, later renamed, Foundation of Islamic Cultural Propagation in the World. It dispatches free copies of his translated works to interested persons throughout the world. It has also undertaken the printing of a Qur'ān for free distribution among Muslim individuals, institutions and religious schools in Africa, and distributes English, French, Russian and Spanish translations of the Qur'ān.

بسم الله الرحمن الرحيم

In the Name of God, Most Gracious, Most Merciful

Lesson One
The Place of Leadership* in Islam

The Imām is, with respect to the masses composing the *ummah*, the leader and exemplar from whose intellectual power and insight those travelling toward God benefit, whose conduct and mode of life they imitate, and to whose commands they submit.

Imāmate has a broad and comprehensive sense that includes both intellectual authority and political leadership. After the death of the Prophet, the Imām was entrusted with the guardianship of his accomplishments and the continuation of his leadership, in order to teach men the truths of the Qur'ān and religion and ordinances concerning society; in short, he was to guide them in all dimensions of their existence.

Such leadership, exercised in its true and proper form, is nothing other than the realization of the goals of Islam and the implementation of its precepts, precepts established by the Messenger of God; it bestows objective existence on the ideal of forming a community and codifying a law for its governance. Imāmate and leadership are sometimes understood in a restricted sense to refer to the person who is entrusted with exclusively social or political leadership. However, the spiritual dimension of man is connected intimately with the mission of religion, and the true and veritable Imām is that

---

* By 'leadership' here is implied the conception of Imāmate. An Imām is an infallible person designated by the Prophet as his successor by God's command.

exalted person who combines in himself intellectual authority and political leadership; who stands at the head of Islamic society, being enabled thereby both of convey to men the divine laws that exist in every sphere and to implement them; and who preserves the collective identity and the human dignity of the Muslims from decline and corruption. In addition, the Imām is one whose personality, already in this world, has a divine aspect; his dealings with God and man, his implementation of all the devotional, ethical and social precepts of God's religion, furnish a complete pattern and model for imitation. It is the Imām who guides the movement of men toward perfection. It is therefore incumbent on all believers to follow him in all matters, for he is a living exemplar for the development of the self and of society, and his mode of life is the best specimen of virtue for the Islamic community.

Most Sunnī scholars are of the opinion that Caliphate *(khilāfah)* and Imāmate *(imamāh)* are synonymous, both signifying the heavy social and political responsibility bestowed on the caliph, who attains his position of guardianship for the affairs of the Muslims by election. The caliph both solves the religious problems of the people and assures public security and guards the frontiers of the country through the exercise of military power. The caliph (or Imām) is therefore at one and the same time a leader of conventional type and a ruler concerned with the welfare of society, whose ultimate aim is the establishment of justice and guarding the frontiers of the country, it is for the sake of these aims that he is elected.

According to this concept, the qualifications for leadership are governmental competence and capacity for rule. On the one hand, the leader must punish errant and corrupt individuals by implementing the penalties God has decreed; hold in check those who would transgress against the rights of others; and repress rebellious and anarchic ruffians. On the other hand, by acquiring the necessary military equipment and organizing a powerful army, he must both protect the frontiers of the Islamic state against all aggression, and also confront, with *jihād* and armed struggle, various forms of *shirk* and corruption and factors of ignorance and unbelief if they prevent the progress or the implementation of true religion and the dissemination of *tawhīd* by way of propagation and guidance powers proves impossible.

In this view of things, it does not present a major problem if the leader or ruler has no background of erudition with respect to God's ordinances, or even if he has strayed beyond the boundaries of piety and polluted himself with sin. Anyone can lay claim to the title of successor *(khalīfah)* to the Prophet who undertakes the tasks he used to fulfil. It is not offensive if some oppressive tyrant establishes his dominance over Islamic society by trampling the rights of the people, shedding their blood and exercising military force, calling himself the leader of the Muslims; or if some two-faced politician assumes the office of successor to the Prophet, and then proceeds to rule over people, despite his lack of spiritual and moral qualities, cancelling all notion of justice and equity. Indeed, not only is it impermissible to oppose him; it is necessary to obey him.

It is on the basis of this view of the matter that one of the great Sunnī scholars expressed himself as follows concerning the caliph:

"The caliph cannot be removed from office on account of contravening God's laws and commands, transgressing against the property of individuals or killing them, or suspending the laws God has decreed. In such a case, it is the duty of the Islamic community to set his misdeeds aright and to draw him onto the path of true guidance."[1]

However, if such an atmosphere predominates in the institution of the caliphate, with the caliph having no sense of responsibility, based on his own religiosity, toward Muslim society, how can those who wish to reform the situation constantly watch over the deeds of a corrupt leadership, evince the appropriate reaction on every occasion, and purge Islam of deviation? Can rulers be persuaded by mere advice to change their ways?

If God had wished to entrust the destinies of the

community to unworthy rulers, to impious and selfish oppressors, it would not have been necessary for him to bestow messengerhood on the Prophet or to reveal the ordinances needed for the stability of society. Did those caring, self-sacrificing and noble souls who throughout the centuries rebelled against evil and oppressive rulers act contrary to God's will?

Dr. 'Abd al-'Azīz al-Dūrī, a Sunnī scholar, writes as follows:

"At the time the sovereignty of the caliphate was being established, the political theory of the Sunnīs with respect to this institution was not based simply on Qur'ān and *ḥadīth*. Rather it rested on the principle that Qur'ān and *ḥadīth* must be understood and explicated in accordance with whatever events subsequently occurred. Thus every generation left its mark on the theory of the caliphate, because that theory assumed a new shape with each new occurrence and was colored by it. An obvious example is the case of Qāḍī Abu 'l-Ḥasan al-Māwardī, who served as chief judge under the caliph. When writing his book *al-Aḥkām al-Sulṭāniyyah* he kept the concerns of the caliph in mind, at a time when the caliphate was at its most degenerate. He employed all his mental powers to reconcile the views of earlier jurists with the situation existing in his own time and the developments that were occurring then. His sole talent was in eschewing any kind of free and original thought. He wrote:

"'It is permissible for an unfit individual to be the leader even if a fit individual is also to be found. Once someone has been chosen, he cannot be removed simply because there is someone better and more fitted available.'

"He admits and vindicates this principle in order to justify rule by numerous unfit caliphs. It is possible, too, that he wished to refute Shī'ī views on the subject. The theological and credal view he puts forth serves no other purpose for the Sunnīs but to justify the political developments of the day. The only aim was to justify whatever might be grouped under the heading of *ijmā'* (consensus)."[2]

Such are the intellectual foundations of those who regard themselves as followers of the *Sunnah* of the Prophet and the guardians of religion and the *sharī'ah*. They denounce as rejecters and traitors to the *Sunnah* of God's Messenger a whole host of Islamic thinkers and social reformers, followers of the Imāms of justice, the proofs of God and the guides of mankind.

If rulers who are strangers to the spirit of Islam and trample underfoot the laws of God, have the right to rule over the believers; and if the *ummah* of Islam is obliged to obey such rulers, being forbidden to take them to task in order to reform the caliphate or to disobey their orders — what then becomes of the religion of God?

Can the Islamic conscience accept this as a proper form of loyalty to the *sharī'ah* of the Prophet? Is not the inevitable result of this mode of thought the granting of unlimited rights to the powerful and oppressive tyrants that have ruled throughout history?

By contrast, the Imāmate in the view of the Shī'ah is a form of divine governance, an office depending on appointment just like prophethood, something God bestows on exalted persons. The difference is that the Prophet is the founder of the religion and the school of thought that proceeds from it, whereas the Imām has the function of guarding and protecting God's religion, in the sense that people have the duty of following in all dimensions of their life the spiritual values and mode of conduct of the Imāms.

After the Messenger of God, the Islamic *ummah* stood in need of a worthy personage who would be endowed with the knowledge derived from revelation, exempt from sin and impurity, and capable of perpetuating the path of the founder of the *sharī'ah*. Only such a personage would be able not only to watch over the political developments of the time and to protect society from its deviant elements, but also to provide people with the extensive religious knowledge which spring from the fountainhead of revelation and derive from the general principles of the *sharī'ah*. The laws derived from revelation would thus be preserved, and the torch of truth and justice held high.

Imāmate and caliphate are inseparable, in just the same way that the governmental functions of the Messenger of God cannot be separated from his prophetic office. Spiritual Islam and political Islam are two parts of a single whole. However, in the course of Islamic history, political power did become separated from the spiritual Imāmate, and the political dimension of religion was separated from its spiritual dimension.

If Islamic society is not headed by a worthy, just, Godfearing person, one unsullied by moral impurity, whose deeds and words serve as a model for people; if, on the contrary, the ruler of society himself violates the law and turns his back on the principles of justice — there will be no environment capable of receiving justice, and it will not be possible neither for virtue and piety to grow and ascend, nor for the aim of Islamic government to be accomplished, which is none other than orienting men to the Supreme Principle and creating a sound environment for the dissemination of spiritual values and the implementation of a law based on divine revelation. The moral conduct of the ruler and the role of government have so profound and powerful an effect on society that 'Alī, the Commander of the Faithful, peace be upon him, regarded it as more influential than the educative role of the father within the household. He thus said: "With respect to their morals, people resemble their rulers more than they resemble their fathers."[3]

Since there is a particular connection and affinity between the aims of a given government and the attributes and characteristics of its leader, attaining the ideals of Islamic government is dependent on the existence of a leader in whom are crystallized the special qualities of a perfected human being.

In addition, the need of a society moving forward toward its own perfection for leadership and governance is a natural and innate need, and in just the same way that Islam has made provision for the individual and collective needs of man, material and moral, by codifying and ordering a coherent system of law, it must also pay heed to the natural need for leadership in a fashion that accords with man's essential disposition.

God has provided every existent being with all the tools and instruments it needs to transcend the limitations of weakness and lack and advance toward its own perfection. Is it then possible that man who is also nurtured in the embrace of nature would somehow be excepted from the operation of this inviolable rule and be deprived of the means of spiritual ascent?

Could it be said that a Creator Who has lavished generosity on man for the sake of his bodily development might deprive him of the most basic means needed for his spiritual elevation, that He might grudge him this bounty?

At the time of the death of the Messenger of God, the Islamic nation had not reached the cultural or intellectual level that would have permitted it do continue its development toward perfection without guardianship and oversight. The program that Islam had established for the development and elevation of man would have remained soulless and incomplete unless the principle of Imāmate had been joined to it; Islam would have been unable to play its precious role in the liberation of man and the blossoming of his talents.

Fundamental Islamic texts proclaim that if the principle of Imāmate is subtracted from Islam, the spirit of the laws of Islam and the progressive, monotheistic society based on them would be lost; nothing would remain but a lifeless form.

The Prophet of Islam, peace and blessings be upon him and his family, said: "Whosoever dies without recognizing the Imām of his time dies the death of the *Jāhiliyyah*."[4]

The reason for this is that during the *Jāhiliyyah* — pre-Islamic era of ignorance — the people were polytheists; they knew nothing of either monotheism or of prophethood. This categorical declaration by the Prophet, peace and blessings be upon him and his family, shows the importance that he assigned to the Imāmate, to the degree that if someone fails to place his spiritual life beneath the protective cover of a perfected ruler he is equivalent to one whose whole life was spent in the *Jāhiliyyah* and then went unredeemed to his death.

Lesson Two
The Position of the Messenger of God with Respect to the Future of Islam

The Most Noble Messenger, peace and blessings be upon him and his family, was well aware that after he had departed for the proximity of his Exalted Lord, the community would lose its unifying foundation, fall into a whirlpool of division and dissent, and be full of struggle and disorder.

The newly established Islamic community was composed of the migrants – including the Banī Hāshim, the Banī Umayyah, 'Adiyy and Taym – on the one hand, and the Helpers *(anṣār)*—subdivided into the Aws and Khazraj tribes—on the other. Once the matchless leader that was the Prophet had departed, ambitions arose on every hand, and instead of being concerned with the interests of Islam, men sought to capture leadership and rule for themselves, wishing to transform divine leadership into tribal rule. The varying aspirations and tendencies that arose left no firm, unifying bond in place among people, a profound tragedy that the Prophet had foreseen and to which he had alerted his followers: "My *ummah* will divide into seventy three factions, only one of which will attain salvation, the other factions being destined for hellfire."[5]

The greatest blow that was struck against the unity of Islam after the death of its founder, sowing the seeds of dissension among Muslims, was the difference of opinion relating to the question of rule and leadership. It led to wars, rebellions and bloody struggles, sundering the unity of the

Muslims and scattering their unified ranks.

If indeed the Prophet had not made some provision for the painful situation — a situation he foresaw —; if he had not attempted to prevent the emergence of the vacuum that would have threatened the very existence of Islamic society, quitting this worldly stage without any plan for safeguarding his *ummah* from misguidance, would this not have created great problems with respect to government and the administration of affairs? The gravity of future problems was, moreover, apparent even without the receipt of communication from the Origin of Revelation and unseen agents.

How is it possible to imagine that Most Noble Prophet, peace and blessings be upon him and his family, should have neglected nothing in the proclamation of his message but paid no attention to the future course of Islam and its culture, to the guardianship of the truth, and the preservation of both religion and society, entrusting all this simply to the hand of fate and whatever circumstances might later arise? Was it possible that he should not select a captain to steer the ship of the *ummah* away from the dangerous waves of dissension that he expected it to encounter?

Those who say that the Prophet did not delineate any form of government to succeed him, remaining silent on the subject and leaving his crisis-stricken *ummah* at a loss what to do — how can they attribute such inappropriate silence and such irresponsible laxity to one whom we know as the Universal Intelligence? It must also be borne in mind that his death did not come suddenly; he realized in advance that he was about to leave the world. In his sermon of the Farewell Pilgrimage *(hijjatu 'l-wadā')* he had proclaimed to the people that he was about to depart from their midst, and that he would not be standing with them at the same place the following year.

Islam was then young, and a long path lay ahead of it if it was to come to fruition. The standard bearer of its movement had committed himself to uprooting all traces of the *Jāhiliyyah*, and to erasing from the hearts and souls of the people any of its residue that might persist. He was threatened on two fronts. Internally he was threatened by the Hypocrites who had penetrated the ranks of the Muslims through outwardly ranging themselves beneath the banner of prophethood and were striving repeatedly to defeat the Prophet. In the ninth year of the Hijrah, when he had departed on the Tabūk campaign, he became anxious on account of their intrigues and plotting, and in order to prevent the occurrence of any untoward event he named 'Alī, peace be upon him, as his deputy in Madīnah. Externally he was threatened by the two great empires, Byzantium and Persia, and there was the constant fear that at any moment either of those great powers might attack the center of the Islamic movement.

It is evident that confronted with such grave problems the Prophet was bound to place responsibility for the preservation of the *ummah* in the hands of a person or persons who had the capacity for it, in order that the Islamic call might remain firm and protected.

The first caliph felt a sense of responsibility for the future of the Islamic state and was unwilling for it to be threatened by a vaccum in the leadership. He did not leave the *ummah* to its own devices, and while on his deathbed instructed the people as follows: "I appoint 'Umar b. al-Khaṭṭāb as commander and ruler over you; pay heed to his words and obey him."[6] The caliph thus regarded it as his right to designate his own successor and to enjoin obedience to him on the people.

The second caliph likewise realized the need to act quickly once he had been fatally stabbed. He ordered a six-man council to be convened, which implies that he did not grant the Muslims the right of appointing the caliph themselves, otherwise he would not have assigned the task to this council.

The Commander of the Faithful, 'Alī, peace be upon him, accepted the responsibility of the caliphate under extraordinarily complicated and disturbed circumstances, for he was fearful that popular disorder might lead to a wholesale relapse into *Jāhiliyyah*.

Taking all this into consideration, is it at all possible that the Messenger of God, peace and blessings be upon him and his family, should have overlooked the depth of the danger or the sensetiveness of the situation, despite the fact that society had only just emerged from *Jāhiliyyah*, and that he should not have drawn up a plan to confront the dangers he anticipated after his death?

It would indeed be impossible to find any acceptable explanation for a failure on the part of the Prophet to concern himself with this matter. Likewise, it is unimaginable that he should have shown no concern for the future of the summons he had launched, not caring what might become of it after his death.

On the contrary even on his deathbed and while sorely vexed by the pains of sickness, the Prophet was concerned for the *ummah* and full of anxiety for its future, to the degree that it completely preoccupied his whole being.

During those sensitive and critical moments, when everyone was in a state of shock and bewilderment and some of the Companions *(ṣaḥābah)* including 'Umar b. al-Khaṭṭāb were gathered around his bed, the Prophet said: "Bring me paper and an inkpot; I wish to write instructions for you so that you never go astray."[7]

This effort of the Prophet, peace and blessings be upon him and his family, preserved in a tradition on the authenticity of which all are agreed, is clear testimony to the fact that the Messenger of God, precisely at the time that he was spending the last moments of his luminous life, was concerned for the future of Islam and was giving thought to the dangers that would arise after his death. He wished to lay down a path for the future in order to preserve the *ummah* from deviation and society from degeneration, for he understood these matters better and more profoundly than anyone.

A matter that deserves particular attention is the question of successorship in heavenly religions and laws, for all the prophets of God selected deputies and successors in accordance with revelation. For example, Ādam, Ibrāhīm (Abraham), Ya'qūb (Jacob), Mūsā (Moses) and 'Īsā (Jesus), peace be on them all, selected their successors, all of whom are known to us by name.[8]

The Most Noble Messenger, peace and blessings be upon him and his family, said: "Every prophet has a legatee *(waṣiyy)* and an heir *(wārith)*, and 'Alī is my legatee and heir."[9]

Since according to the Qur'ān the norms of God are fixed and unchanging, it follows that the Prophet of Islam must also act in accordance with this immutable divine norm by presenting his own deputy and successor to the Islamic *ummah*. This indeed is what happened. In conformity with God's command and as required by prophethood and the need to perpetuate the message of Islam and implement its goals, he selected his legatee, thus making its duty clear to the *ummah*. All of this represents a belief that originates in the Book of God.

Muslims are unanimous in believing that the Prophet of Islam, peace and blessings be upon him and his family, never made any mention of Abū Bakr or the two caliphs that followed Abū Bakr as his caliphs and successors, nor is there any indication of their caliphate in the Qur'ān and the *Sunnah*. The caliphate of Abū Bakr is thus a simple historical event, not an indisputable religious belief, so that every Muslim has the right to express an opinion on the matter in accordance with his own understanding, as simple logic requires.

Lesson Three
The Proclamation of 'Alī's Leadership by the Prophet

After the death of the Most Noble Messenger, peace and blessings be upon him and his family, and the departure of that great leader from the midst of society, the interests of Islam and the *ummah* made it imperative that a distinguished and worthy leader, a being overflowing with knowledge and piety, should assume the governance of the newly emergent Islamic movement which needed continued instruction. This was necessary in order to guarantee the continuity of Islam, to safeguard it from deviation, to prevent the *ummah* from falling back into its former reprehensible social and moral habits, and to reinforce as much as possible the Islamic socio-political order.

To leave the question of leadership to a community that had only recently escaped the fetters of *Jāhiliyyah* and from whose spirit and soul the traces of *Jāhili* beliefs had not yet disappeared, would not have sufficed to secure the lofty aims of the Prophet or to protect the religion from the danger of negative forces.

The only path was then for a worthy personality, erudite in all matters concerning the message, equipped with intelligence and extensive religious knowledge, possessed of a luminous faith and exempt from error just like the founder of Islam, should gather the reins of affairs in his hands in order to pursue with care and subtlety the task of training and educating men and solve the problems and questions concerning the *sharī'ah* that might arise during the period of his governance.

Historical evidence shows that the Messenger of God, on his return from the Farewell Pilgrimage, fulfilled this need on the eighteenth day of Dhu 'l-Ḥijjah by designating his legatee and successor in accordance with divine command, thus showing the people the path to be followed for the *ummah* to gain felicity.

In the tenth year of the Hijrah, which was also the last year in the life of the Beloved Prophet, peace and blessings be upon him and his family, he decided to participate in the great Islamic gathering that was to be held in Makkah. Once it became known that the Prophet was setting out for the Ka'bah, throngs of Muslims from near and far set out in the direction of Madīnah in order to have the honor of travelling with him, to learn the pilgrimage rites from him, and to perform that great ritual of Islam directly in his presence.

Finally the great caravan set out, composed of the Migrants *(muhājirūn)*, the Helpers *(anṣār)*, and the other Muslims who were leaving Madīnah in the company of their leader, and they advanced towards Makkah. After entering the city, they began their acts of worship at the Ka'bah. During those days the city of Makkah witnessed one of the most glorious of Islamic ceremonies, performed by thousands of Muslims who were gathered around their leader like the thunderous waves of an ocean. The Prophet too was proud in front of his Lord that on such a day he was able to see the results of his unremitting efforts and toil.

After that year's pilgrimage had been completed — the pilgrimage known as the Farewell Pilgrimage — the Prophet left the House of God together with the great crowd of pilgrims *(ḥujjāj)*, estimated by historians to have numbered between ninety and one hundred and twenty thousand, and prepared to return to Madīnah. The caravan traversed several valleys and arrived at a waterless plain known as Ghadīr Khumm.[10] It was then that the messenger of revelation came to the Prophet and ordered him to halt. The Prophet stopped the caravan and waited for the stragglers to catch up with the main body.

This sudden halt in that torrid landscape beneath the burning midday sun astonished the weary travellers, but it was not long before Jibrīl (Gabriel) the trustworthy angel of revelation conveyed to the pure soul of the Prophet a heavenly message — the categorical and clear command of the Creator that he should appoint and announce his legatee and successor:

"O Messenger of God, convey to mankind the command that God has sent you. If you do not do so, you will not have conveyed the prophetic message. God will protect you from the harm men might cause you." (5:67)

Close attention to the content of this verse demonstrates to us the important truth that the proclamation of this particular divine message was of such importance and gravity that if the Prophet were to shrink from conveying it, it would be equivalent to his refraining from fulfilling his entire prophetic mission, while conveying it to the *ummah* was tantamount to the completion of that mission.

In the verse, the Most Noble Prophet, peace and blessings be upon him and his family, is reminded of the extraordinary significance of the task that has been assigned to him, and he is guaranteed protection from any dangers that might result from proclaiming the message.

At the same time, not more than a few days were left in the glorious life of the Prophet, peace and blessings be upon him and his family, for he died seventy days after the event of Ghadīr Khumm. All that he had achieved in the course of twenty three years since the beginning of revelation, all that man needed for his guidance and felicity, was now at the disposal of mankind. Only one particular matter remained, the proclamation of which would complete his prophetic mission and bring his task to complete fruition.

It was in addition probable that while fulfilling the instructions he had received the Prophet would be attacked or harmed by evil wishers, and in order to reinforce his determination God informed him that He would protect him and guard him against being harmed.

The content of those instructions must have been particularly sensitive in order for their fulfilment to have been coterminous with the entirety of the Prophet's mission and for the failure to proclaim them to have damaged and diminish prophethood itself. Moreover, the Arab mentality prevailing at the time tended to regard the aged persons of each tribe as best suited for positions of leadership and not to consider younger persons as qualified; this feature hardly constituted a favorable climate for the proclamation of God's command.

The spirit of the Prophet was also troubled and surely pained by certain bitter memories. He had not yet forgotten the negative attitude of certain narrow minded people to the appointment of Usāmah and 'Attāb b. Usayb as commanders, for when he appointed the former as commander of the army and the latter as commander of Makkah, some of the Companions raised their voices in protest.

All of these constituted factors that made the declaration of 'Alī b. Abī Ṭālib, peace be upon him, someone as young as thirty three years of age, a formidable and even intimidating task for the Prophet.

In addition, many of those who had now joined the ranks of the Muslims and entered the circle of the Prophet's Companions, had earlier fought against 'Alī, peace be upon him, which further increased the delicacy of the situation; their hearts were troubled by the memory of those events and fanned the flames of hatred within them.

Despite all those unfavorable circumstances, the divine will decreed that the best and most exalted personage who through the grace of God had attained the highest spiritual station next to the Prophet should be appointed as his successor, so that by the designation of this great man to lead the *ummah*, the universal message of the Prophet should be completed.

According not only to Shī'ī scholars of *ḥadīth* but also certain Sunnī scholars as well,[11] the Qur'ānic verse in question was revealed on the day of Ghadīr Khumm, the day on which the Prophet, the veracity of whose speech is guaranteed by

God Himself, received the divine command, by way of revelation and in accordance with wisdom, to expound the last and most essential foundation of Islam by presenting 'Alī, peace be upon him, to the people as his successor.

Yes, that personage whose being had never been polluted by polytheism or sin, whose entire life had been devoted to disseminating the teachings of religion and promoting Islam, who was a complete reflection of the Messenger of God — he was the one fitted to preserve the laws and norms of religion, to assume the leadership of humanity as it advanced toward perfection and salvation. It was his form alone that was worthy of putting on the garb of Imāmate and leadership.

The time for the noon prayer arrived, and the great throng that had descended at Ghadīr Khumm performed the prayer behind the Prophet.[12] Then the Prophet advanced to the middle of the crowd that filled the whole plain in anticipation of an historic event, in order to implement the categorical command of God. He mounted a pulpit that had been improvised from camel litters, in order for everyone to be able to see and to hear him.

He then began to deliver his address, in powerful, clear and compelling tones, so that everyone was able to hear him or at least be aware of what was transpiring.

After praising and thanking God, to whom alone belong absolute power, wisdom and vision, and whose governance, knowledge and perception are immune to defect and decline, he said:

"O people, I will soon be responding to the call of my Lord and departing from your midst. I will be held to account, as you too will be. Will you not bear witness that there is none worthy of worship other than God, the One and Unique? Do you not testify that Muḥammad is His servant and messenger? Are not paradise, hellfire and death all realities? Is it not true the day of requital and resurrection will definitely come, and that God will restore to life those who lie buried in the ground?"

The voice of the multitude arose in response: "Indeed we

bear witness to all of that."

Then he continued: "Now that the Day of Requital lies before us, and you believe in the raising of the dead on the Plain of Resurrection and that you will enter the presence of your prophet on that day, pay heed to the manner in which you treat the two weighty *(thaqalayn)* and precious legacies I leave you as I depart for the hereafter.[13]

"That which is the greater of the two is the Book of God. It is in your hands as well as His, so lay hold of it firmly lest you fall into misguidance. The lesser of the two legacies is my progeny and the people of my household. God has informed me that my two legacies shall never be separated from each other until the Day of Resurrection.

"O people, do not turn away from these two legacies. As long as you have recourse to them, you will never go astray — the Book of God and my family."[14]

At this point, the Prophet, peace and blessings be upon him and his family, called 'Alī, peace be upon him, to his side. He took hold of his hand and raised it up high, thereby presenting him with all his qualities and attributes to the gathered throng. Then the Messenger of God asked: "O people, who is more deserving of the believers than their own persons?" They answered: "God and His Messenger know better." He continued: "For whomsoever I was his master, 'Alī is now his master."[15]

"O God, love whomsoever loves 'Alī, and be the enemy of whoever is 'Alī's enemy.[16] O God, aid whoever aids him and humble his enemies.[17] O God, make him the pivot of truth."[18]

After completing his speech, the Prophet requested the people to convey what he had said to those who were absent.

The one who was thus installed in the seat of Islamic leadership on that day, in accordance with divine command and by virtue of the Prophet's declaration, who was entrusted with the guidance of the *ummah*, was 'Alī. The most worthy and renowned man in the Islamic community, he who was a treasury of knowledge and an incarnation of virtue, had been selected as the leader of the Muslims, and by proclaiming the important matter of Imāmate and caliphate the Prophet had given a decisive and binding command to the *ummah*.

The assembled multitude had not begun to disperse when the agent of revelation revealed this verse to the Prophet:

"*Today I have perfected for you your religion, completed for you My bounty, and chosen Islam for you as religion.*" (5:3)[19]

According to al-Ya'qūbī, "This verse, revealed at Ghadīr Khumm, was the last verse to be revealed to the Most Noble Messenger, peace and blessings be upon him and his family."[20]

The Prophet left the place where he was standing, while all around the sound of *takbīr* was to be heard as the pilgrims expressed their warm and enthusiastic feelings towards 'Alī, peace be upon him. People came up to him in groups and congratulated him on his appointment as leader, addressing him as their master and the master of every believer, man and woman.

The well known poet Ḥassān b. Thābit who was present on that occasion, composed and recited to the people, with the permission of the Prophet, an eloquent ode in honor of the auspicious event.

The verse just cited, which declares how God has on this day perfected His religion and completed His blessing, permits us to understand the full significance of what had transpired. A momentous happening must have occurred for the Qur'ān to qualify it in such terms, for the Islam that God has chosen and approved was the Islam of that day: the religion of truth had attained its perfection through the appointment of 'Alī, peace be upon him, and God's blessing to mankind had been completed through his selection as the legatee *(waṣiyy)* of the Prophet, peace and blessings be upon him and his family.

Both universally accepted *ḥadīth* and reliable books of history to which Shī'īs and Sunnīs alike refer emphasize that this verse was revealed at Ghadīr Khumm on the day that the Prophet, peace and blessings be upon him and his family, had entrusted 'Alī, peace be upon him, with the responsibility of governing and leading the *ummah* after himself. *Sūrah al-Mā'idah*, to the early part of which this verse belongs, is the last *sūrah* to have been revealed to the Most Noble Messenger, peace and blessings be upon him and his family, in the unanimous view of the exegetes. This means that its revelation took during the last days of his blessed life, and no further command was revealed to him thereafter by his Lord.

The view held by some that the verse refers to the beginning of his prophetic mission, meaning that it was on that day that God's religion was perfected and His blessing completed, is baseless, and utterly incompatible both with the historical facts and the correct interpretation of the verse. The day on which the mission of the Prophet began was the beginning of the divine blessing, not its culmination, an extremely important difference. What is at issue in the verse is the completion of the blessing and the perfection of religion; now that this matter has been accomplished, Islam is chosen and approved as religion for mankind. Neither history nor *ḥadīth* can support the opposing view.

The momentous scene that Ghadīr Khumm witnessed and the task that the Prophet, peace and blessings be upon him and his family, fulfilled on that day had long lasting consequences for the history of Islam. Apart from those who are prisoners to fanaticism and mental stagnation, no historian who is concerned with the recording of events and the preservation of historical fact can ignore what took place on that day or conceal the matters that are connected with it. During the early centuries of Islamic history, the day of Ghadīr Khumm was well known and accepted as an auspicious occasion, and there are many indications that all Muslims participated in celebrating it.

Thus the well known historian Ibn Khallikān describes the eighteenth of Dhu 'l-Ḥijjah as the Day of Ghadīr Khumm,[21] and al-Mas'ūdī mentions the night of the same day as the night of the festival of Ghadīr Khumm.[22] Abu Rayḥān al-Bīrūnī, the famous Iranian scholar of the fifth century, includes the festival of Ghadīr Khumm among the festivals that the Muslims celebrated in his time.[23] In his *Maṭālib al-Su'ūl*, the Shāfi 'ī scholar Ibn Ṭalḥah writes: "The day of Ghadīr

Khumm is a festive day and an historic occasion, for it was then that the Messenger of God, peace and blessings be upon him and his family, clearly and explicitly nominated 'Alī, peace be upon him, as Imām and leader of the Muslims after him."[24]

Now let us see what the Messenger of God meant by the word "master" *(mawlā)* when he said: "For whomsoever I was his master, 'Alī is now his master." Does it mean one who has prior rights of disposition, as the concomitant of the absolute governance of one person over another, or simply a helper and friend?

By referring to the Qur'ān we can see that the first meaning is the correct one, for God says of the Prophet: "*The Prophet has a greater claim to the souls of the believers than the believers themselves.*" (33:6) In addition, there are many places in the Qur'ān where the word *mawlā* occurs with the meaning of *walī* or ruler.[25]

The one who has a greater claim on the souls of others than they do themselves must have *a priori* a similar claim to their property, and will therefore necessarily have the right of absolute governance over them, a governance that permits no disobedience to his orders and commands.

The rank that this implies was first granted by God to His Prophet; it was God who endowed him with authority over the lives and property of the believers and gave him prior rights of disposition in every respect.

There are numerous indications and proofs that the meaning of *walī* in the traditions relating to Ghadīr Khumm is identical to *awlā* ("has a greater claim") in the verse we have just cited. Just as the Messenger of God, peace and blessings be upon him and his family, enjoyed absolute governance based on the Qur'ān, so too did the Commander of the Faithful, 'Alī, peace be upon him, have the same rank and attribute, the only difference being that with the sealing of prophethood with the termination of the Prophet's mission, the gate of prophethood was closed. With this single exception, all the offices of the Prophet were transferred to 'Alī.

The first citation that clarifies the meaning of *walī* in the *ḥadīth* is a sentence uttered by the Prophet, peace and blessings be upon him and his family, before he proclaimed 'Alī, peace be upon him, to be his successor. He asked: "Do I not have greater claims on you than your own selves?"

Here, while proclaiming his own authority over the Muslims, after obtaining their assent to the fact that he had greater claims on them than their own selves, he added: "For whomsoever I was his master, 'Alī is his master." The meaning of 'Alī, peace be upon him, being master must necessarily include the sense of *awlā* ("having greater claims"), the same station that the Prophet himself had with respect to the believers. If the Prophet, peace and blessings be upon him and his family, had intended something else, there would have been no reason for him first to gain assent to his own possession of "greater claims". Could the meaning of *mawlā* possibly be a simple friendship that exists among Muslims?

At the beginning of his address to the people, the Prophet, peace and blessings be upon him and his family, said: "Do you bear witness that there is none worthy of worship other than God, the One and Unique, and do you believe that Muḥammad is His servant and messenger and that paradise and hellfire are both realities?"

Could the reason for posing these questions have anything other than preparing the people to accept a principle comparable to those contained in the questions? Was it not the purpose of the Messenger of God, peace and blessings be upon him and his family, to make the people understand that acceptance of the caliphate and successorship of 'Alī, peace be upon him, which he was about to announce was on the same level as those three principles — divine unity, prophethood, and resurrection?

If what the Prophet, peace and blessings be upon him and his family, meant by *mawlā* nothing more than friend and protector, friendship with 'Alī would have been exactly the same as any other friendship prevailing among the believers since the very beginning of Islam as part of Islamic brotherhood. There would have been no need to proclaim it in such a vast gathering, preceded by all kinds of detailed prefatory remarks and gaining the assent of the people to the three basic principles.

Furthermore, the Prophet, peace and blessings be upon him and his family, mentioned his own death before presenting 'Alī, peace be upon him, to that great assembly; he informed those present that he would soon be quitting this transitory realm. By making this statement, he wished in reality to fill the vacuum of leadership that would arise after him by appointing 'Alī, peace be upon him, as his successor. Mere friendship and love for 'Alī, peace be upon him, could not alone have played a crucial role in Islamic society. Would it have been in any way necessary for the Prophet, peace and blessings be upon him and his family, to deliver a lengthy speech under the burning sun to an assembly of one hundred thousand people simply to expound love for 'Alī, peace be upon him? Had not the Qur'ān already proclaimed the believers to be friends and brothers to each other?

In view of all these consideration, it is not rationally acceptable that the Prophet, peace and blessings be upon him and his family, should on that occasion have been speaking simply of love for 'Alī, peace be upon him.

Moreover, after the Prophet, peace and blessings be upon him and his family, had finished speaking, a large number of the Companions came up to 'Alī, peace be upon him, and offered him their felicitations in a stream that continued until it was time for the sunset prayer. Abū Bakr, 'Uthmān, Ṭalḥah and al-Zubayr were among those who offered 'Alī, peace be upon him, their congratulations on being appointed successor. 'Umar was among the first to address 'Alī, saying: "Well done, son of Abū Ṭālib! Congratulation on this appointment; you have become the master of every believer, man and woman alike."[26]

Had 'Alī, peace be upon him, gained any other appointment at that time which might have qualified him for these congratulations? Was not 'Alī, peace be upon him, known until that point as an ordinary Muslim deserving of friendship like any other?

Ḥassān b. Thābit, the celebrated poet of the Prophet, peace and blessings be upon him and his family, was present among the pilgrims, and he understood the word *mawlā* to imply the Imāmate and leadership. He said in one of his poems: "The Prophet turned to the people and said to 'Alī: 'Arise! I make you henceforth the leader and guide of the people.'"

If one studies the whole of the Prophet's speech with an open mind, free of prejudice and preconceived notions, and examines the evidence and indications it contains, he cannot fail to derive but a single meaning from the word *mawlā* as applied to 'Alī b. Abī Ṭālib, peace be upon him: the one who has prior rights of disposition and the right of absolute governance.

If the Prophet, peace and blessings be upon him and his family, did not use the word "ruler" at Ghadīr Khumm when referring to 'Alī, peace be upon him, saying, for example, "after me 'Alī will be your ruler," it is because he generally used the word *amīr* (commander) in the context of military affairs and the organization of the pilgrimage, whereas the word *wilāyah* (authority or governance) was used in connection with the affairs of the *ummah* and indeed he referred to himself as the *walī* of the believers. Not even God referred to the Prophet, peace and blessings be upon him and his family, as a ruler in the Qur'ān, nor did the Prophet ever call himself a ruler or commander in any *ḥadīth*. In fact the Qur'ān says explicitly: "*It is God and His Messenger alone who are your walī, and those who establish prayers and regular charity and bow down humbly in worship.*" (5:56)[27]

In reality, the link between the Prophet, peace and blessings be upon him and his family, to whom is entrusted the supervision of the Muslims, and the Islamic *ummah* is like the relationship of a father with his offspring, for he is responsible for administering their affairs and protecting their interest; it is not a relationship of ruler and ruled.

Likewise, the Prophet, peace and blessings be upon him and his family, did not use the word caliph or successor with respect to 'Alī, peace be upon him, because obedience to a successor becomes incumbent only after the death of the one to whose authority he succeeds, whereas the intention of the Prophet, peace and blessings be upon him and his family, was the obedience to 'Alī, peace be upon him, was obligatory for the Muslims even before he died. He therefore called him the master of the believers, implying his possession of authority both before and after the death of the Most Noble Messenger, peace and blessings be upon him and his family. Based on the *ḥadīth* of Ghadīr Khumm, he was the master of the Muslims, just like the Prophet, and had "greater claims on them than their own selves."

al-Tirmidhī in his *al-Ṣaḥīḥ* first relates this *ḥadīth,* describing it as exalted and remarkable, and then further relates the Prophet, peace and blessings be upon him and his family, to have said: "'Alī is from me and I am from 'Alī; no one other than 'Alī has the right to do anything on my behalf."[28]

al-Ḥākim in his *al-Mustadrak* similarly relates the Messenger of God, peace and blessings be upon him and his family, to have said: "Whoever follows me has obeyed God, and whoever disobeys me has disobeyed God. Whoever obeys 'Alī has obeyed me, and whoever disobeys 'Alī has disobeyed me."[29]

When therefore the Messenger of God, peace and blessings be upon him and his family, proclaims to the Muslims that 'Alī, peace be upon him, has the same authority over the Muslims as himself, so that obedience to him is equivalent to obedience to the Messenger of God, he is in reality proclaiming 'Alī, peace be upon him, to the Muslim community as its overall leader and as the successor to his authority, calling on them to render him obedience.

One of the Shī'ī scholars writes:

"I say in all sincerity that if the Prophet, peace and blessings be upon him and his family, had stood before the people on the day of Ghadīr and said: 'For whomsoever I am his master, Abū Bakr is his master; O God, love those who love him and be hostile to those who are hostile to him,' I would be absolutely certain that the Prophet, peace and blessings be upon him and his family, had appointed Abū Bakr as his successor. Equally I cannot imagine that the vest mass of Muslims would have had any doubt that Abū Bakr had been appointed to the succession. If the Messenger of God, peace and blessings be upon him and his family, had said that Abū Bakr had greater claims on the believers than they did themselves and that adherence to the Qur'ān was a sure protection against misguidance, there would be no room for hesitation.

"I wish to point out that the hesitancy of Muslims in agreeing that the *ḥadīth* of Ghadīr Khumm indicates the appointment of 'Alī, peace be upon him, by the Prophet, peace and blessings be upon him and his family, as his successor does not rest on obstinacy and fanaticism. It derives rather from the fact that they have grown up in a society where it is believed that the Prophet, peace and blessings be upon him and his family, did not appoint any successor. It is difficult for them to reconcile this belief with the clear meaning indicated by the *ḥadīth*."[30]

Of course, one cannot reject the posibility that some of the Companions did not deliberately disobey the Prophet, peace and blessings be upon him and his family, when choosing his successor; they were simply mistaken in their calculations. They imagined leadership and the rule of the *ummah* to be simply a worldly affair, so that it was permissible for them to overlook the one whom the Prophet, peace and blessings be upon him and his family, had selected and choose someone else to administer the public affairs of the *ummah*.

Such a group among the Companions may have imagined that the selection of 'Alī, peace be upon him, by the Prophet, peace and blessings be upon him and his family, was simply one of those matters of social concern on which the Prophet, peace and blessings be upon him and his family, would sometimes consult his Companions. If this is the case, they failed to grasp all the purposes that the Prophet, peace and blessings be upon him and his family, had in mind and the consequences he intended for his choice. Likewise, they were incapable of reflecting on the disastrous consequences their own choice and decision would ultimately entail.

Lesson Four
The Objection of 'Alī to the Decision of the Companions

Some people ask why at the meeting held in the Saqīfah, 'Alī, peace be upon him, did not raise the issue of his appointment at Ghadīr Khumm by the Messenger of God, peace and blessings be upon him and his family, to be his successor. Why, they ask, did he not tell the Migrants and the Helpers that he had been appointed by the Prophet so that nobody had the right to contest the succession with him or to claim the caliphate? Had the thousands of people who had been present at Ghadīr Khumm forgotten what they had witnessed?

The answer is that the Imām did indeed raise the issue of Ghadīr Khumm whenever he deemed it appropriate in order to prove the justice of his claim to the successorship and to object to the decision that had been taken at the Saqīfah, thus reminding people of what had happened. For example, historians relate the following:

"When Fāṭimah, the daughter of the Prophet, peace and blessings be upon him and his family, together with 'Alī, peace be upon him, sought aid from the Companions, they answered, 'O daughter of the Messenger of God! We have given our allegiance to Abū Bakr. If 'Alī had come to us before this, we would certainly not have abandoned him.' 'Alī, peace be upon him, them said, 'Was it fitting that we should wrangle over the caliphate even before the Prophet was buried?'[31]

Similarly, on the day that the six-man council was convened and 'Abd al-Raḥmān b. 'Awf made plain his inclination that 'Uthmān be appointed caliph, the Imām said: "I will set before you an undeniable truth. By God, is there any among you concerning whom the Prophet, peace and blessings be upon him and his family, said, 'For whomsoever I was until now the master, henceforth 'Alī is the master; O Lord, love whoever loves 'Alī and help whoever helps 'Alī,' ordering this to be conveyed to those who were absent?" All the members of the council confirmed the truth of the words he had spoken, saying, "none can lay claim to any of this."[32]

It is an indisputable historical fact that thirty of the Companions testified at the congregational mosque in Raḥbah to what they had witnessed at Ghadīr Khumm. The historians relate that one day 'Alī, peace be upon him, said in the course of a sermon he was delivering at this mosque, "O Muslims, I adjure you by God: is there among you any who witnessed what transpired at Ghadīr Khumm, who heard the Messenger of God, peace and blessings be upon him and his family, proclaiming me to be his successor, and who observed the people paying allegiance to me? Stand up and give witness!"

At this point thirty men out of those present stood up and in a loud voice testified to what they had seen at Ghadīr Khumm.

Another telling of this same incident relates: "Many people stood up to give witness."[33]

This testimony to what had transpired at Ghadīr Khumm was given at the mosque in Raḥbah during the caliphate of 'Alī, peace be upon him, in the thirty-fifth years of the Hijrah, while the proclamation of 'Alī's successorship at Ghadīr Khumm in the course of the Farewell Pilgrimage had taken place in the tenth year of the Hijrah, i.e., twenty five years earlier.[34]

Taking into consideration the fact that many elderly Companions must have died during this quarter century, that many casualties had been incurred during the wars that took place during the rule of the first three caliphs, and that many surviving Companions were not present in Kūfah, being scattered in other cities, the significance of this historic testimony to what had happened at Ghadīr Khumm is obvious. Aḥmad b. Ḥanbal writes: "Only three men did not rise to their feet, althogh they too had been present at Ghadīr Khumm. 'Alī, peace be upon him, cursed them and they were afflicted."[35]

Abū al-Ṭufayl says: "When I left the mosque at Raḥbah I asked myself how the majority of the *ummah* had failed to act in accordance with the *ḥadith* of Ghadīr Khumm. I met Zayd b. Arqam to discuss the matter with him and told him, 'I heard 'Alī, peace be upon him, say such-and-such.' Zayd replied, 'The truth of what he says is undeniable; I too heard it from the Prophet, peace and blessings be upon him and his family."[36]

'Alī, peace be upon him, adduced the *ḥadith* of Ghadīr Khumm in support of his claims on numerous other occasions. He cited it as proof of his Imāmate during the Battle of the Camel, at Ṣiffīn and in Kūfah, as well as in the Mosque of the Prophet, peace and blessings be upon him and his family, in Madīnah on an occasion when two hundred leading persons from among the Migrants and Companions were present.[37]

Apart from this, various factors prevented 'Alī, peace be upon him, from reacting strongly to what occurred at the Saqīfah and caused him to choose the path of endurance and patience instead, a patience he himself described as akin to having "a thorn in the eye and a bone in the throat."[38]

It will be apposite here to cite some passages from the answer of the late 'Allāmah Sharaf al-Dīn to Shaykh Salīm al-Bishrī:

"Everyone knows that the Imām and his friends from among the Banī Hāshim and other tribes were not present at the Saqīfah when allegiance was being sworn to Abū Bakr; in fact, they had not even set foot there, being engaged in the imperative and grave task of preparing the Prophet, peace and blessings be upon him and his family, for burial and being unable to think of anything else.

"The ceremonies of the Prophet's burial were still not over when the people gathered at the Saqīfah completed their business. They gave allegiance to Abū Bakr, swore loyalty to him, and with remarkable farsightedness agreed to confront firmly any development threatening to weaken the state.

"Was 'Alī, peace be upon him, in any position then to argue his case before the people? And was he given any chance to do so once allegiance had been sworn to Abū Bakr? His opponents displayed cunning and political acumen and neither did they shrink from violence. Even in our age, how many people find it possible to rise up in revolt against the government or to overthrow it simply by popular pressure? And if someone has the intention of doing so, will he be left untroubled?

"If you compare the past with the present, you will see that people were just the same as they are now, that conditions then were just the same. Moreover, if 'Alī, peace be upon him, had raised his claim at that time, the only result would have been confusion and disorder, and he would still have been unable to assert his rights. For him, the preservation of the foundations of Islām and of the doctrine of divine unity was an overarching aim. The ordeal that 'Alī, peace be upon him, underwent at that time tried him sorely. Two momentous matters were weighing on him. On the one hand. his explicit designation as caliph *(khalīf)* and legatee *(waṣiyy)* of the Prophet, peace and blessings be upon him and his family, was still ringing in his ears and impelling him to act. On the other hand, the disturbances and rebellions that were arising on all sides served to warn him that the situation in the entire Arabian peninsula might collapse; the people might change their attitudes altogether, leading to the disappearance of Islām. He was in addition threatened by the existence of the Hypocrites in Madīnah who had grown in strength after the death of the Prophet, peace and blessings be upon him and his family. The Muslims at that time were like a flock of sheep stranded by a flood on a dark winter's night, surrounded by bloodthirsty wolves and predators.

"Musaylamah al-Kadhdhāb, Ṭalḥah b. Khuwaylid and Sijāḥ the daughter of al-Ḥārith, together with the rabble that had gathered around them, were exerting themselves to the utmost to destroy Islam and vanquish the Muslims.

"As if all this were not enough, the Persian and Byzantine emperors, as well as the other powerful rulers of the age, were waiting for a favorable opportunity to attack Islam. Many others too, in their hatred for the Prophet, peace and blessings be upon him and his family, and his Companions were ready to use any means in order to avenge themselves on Islam, and they saw in the death of the leader of Islam a favorable opportunity for causing sabotage and destruction.

"'Alī thus found himself at a crossroads, and it was natural that one of his caliber should sacrifice his own right to the caliphate to the cause of Islam and the Muslims. However, even while sacrificing his right, he wished to adopt an appropriate stance to those who had usurped it, one that did not lead to disorder or disunity among the Muslims or create an opportunity for the enemies of Islam. He therefore remained at home and did not swear allegiance to Abū Bakr until he was forced to leave his home and brought to the mosque. If he had gone of his own accord to swear allegiance, he would have effectively relinquished his claim to the caliphate and his partisans would have been left without any argument to make on his behalf. By choosing the path that he did, he accomplished two things: the preservation of Islam and the safeguarding of the legitimate form of the caliphate. He acted thus because he realized that under the circumstances the preservation of Islam depended on his making peace with the caliphs. He was motivated solely by the desire to protect the *sharī'ah* and religion; in fact, in renouncing the office that was rightly his for the sake of God he was acting in accord with the duty prescribed by both reason and religion — giving priority to the more important of two contradictory duties.

"In short, the situation prevailing at the time made it impossible for him either to take up the sword in rebellion or to argue for his rights and criticize the state of affairs in the young Muslim community. Nonetheless, 'Alī and his progeny, peace be upon them, as well as scholars devoted to his cause have always found intelligent and appropriate ways of reminding the Muslim community of the instructions left by the Prophet, peace and blessings be upon him and his family, at Ghadīr Khumm. As all scholars are aware, they ceaselessly propagated the relevant traditions of the Prophet, peace and blessings be upon him and his family."[39]

Lesson Five
The Rank of 'Alī as Indicated in Other Sayings of the Prophet

It was not only at Ghadīr Khumm that the Messenger of God, peace and blessings be upon him and his family, proclaimed 'Alī, peace be upon him, to be the leader of the Muslims and his successor, officially and in the presence of the people. In the third year of his mission, when he was commanded to proclaim his prophethood openly, he appointed 'Alī, peace be upon him, as his successor. It is known that for the first three years of his prophetic mission, the Most Noble Messenger, peace and blessings be upon him and his family, did not make his summons public, instead calling people to Islam in secret. It was in the third year of his mission that he was instructed to invite his relatives to Islam openly.[40]

He thereupon instructed 'Alī, peace be upon him, to invite forty of the leading personages of Quraysh to a banquet, and forty of the Prophet's relatives accepted.

At their very first session, the nonsensical ravings of Abū Lahab, his raging anger and unbridled arrogance, caused the meeting to break up in confusion. The following day, when again everyone was gathered in accordance with the instructions of the Most Noble Messenger, peace and blessings be upon him and his family, first food was served to the guests, and then it was time for spiritual nourishment. The Prophet, peace and blessings be upon him and his family, stood up among his relatives, praised and supplicated the Creator, and said:

"I swear that there is none worthy of worship other than the One God, and that I am His envoy to you and the entirety of mankind. I have brought you the means of felicity in both worlds. My Lord has commanded me to summon you to the religion of Islam, and I give you glad tidings that whoever among you accepts my summons the soonest and aids me in my mission will be my brother *(ākhī)*, my legatee *(waṣiyyī)* and my successor *(khalīfatī)*."

Those words greatly disturbed those present at the gathering, for their pride was offended, and it almost seemed that the voice of truth and the summons of prophethood would remain unheeded. Suddenly 'Alī b. Abī Ṭālib, peace be upon him, arose and cried out: "O Muḥammad, I believe in the oneness of God and your messengerhood and I distance myself from the idol worshippers."

The Prophet, peace and blessings be upon him and his family, ordered 'Alī, peace be upon him, to sit down. He then repeated twice more his earlier proclamation, but those words of truth made no impact on the hearts of those gathered in that assembly. No one apart from 'Alī, peace be upon him, responded to the call of the Prophet, peace and blessings be upon him and his family. 'Alī's acceptance of that summons and his declaration of agreement with the Prophet, peace and blessings be upon him and his family, came at a time when he was just entering manhood. While everyone else sat voiceless and silent, he arose courageously and affirmed his acceptance of the Prophet's call a second time. Thereupon the Prophet turned to the assembly and said:

"'Alī is my brother and legatee and my successor among you. Obey him, follow him, and pay heed to his words."[41]

The reaction of the assembled guests was extremely hostile, for they wished to strip this declaration by the Prophet, peace and blessings be upon him and his family, of its effect, and they therefore stood up and quit the meeting in the most unworthy and discourteous fashion. This event constitutes one of the plainest and most significant chapters in history, and none of the well known historians has ever seen fit to deny its occurrence. Not even the most narrow-minded among them have been able to excise this historic occurrence from their writings.

At that delicate and dangerous juncture, when the Prophet, peace and blessings be upon him and his family, found himself alone in pursuing his great and glorious goal, he needed a helper and ally capable of supporting him powerfully and historically. Such a person could only be one who was prepared to devote himself fully to the Prophet, peace and blessings be upon him and his family, and who had attained the highest degree of sincerity, courage, and obedience to God, so that once he came to exercise the office of successor, he would be a mirror reflecting all the knowledge, wisdom and moral purity of the Prophet, peace and blessings be upon him and his family.

The Prophet, peace and blessings be upon him and his family, knew that although some of his relatives might accept his call and come to embrace Islam, none among them would be prepared to commit himself to active collaboration or to confront the various forces arrayed against him, the idolators of Arabia and the People of the Book. Such a commitment would necessarily involve a protracted and merciless struggle against all sectors of Arab society, for none of them was prepared to tolerate the summons to change their beliefs and abandon their idols. The suggestion that they should do so could not fall to arouse their intense hostility, so that a conflict was completely inevitable, a conflict that would lead to the destruction of the possessions of anyone who allied himself with the Prophet, peace and blessings be upon him and his family.

Someone who was ready to make himself a protective shield for the Prophet, peace and blessings be upon him and his family, under those unfavorable conditions and even to risk him own life had to be an extraordinary individual. Without doubt there was none among the relatives of the Prophet, peace and blessings be upon him and his family, who possessed the necessary qualities apart from 'Alī, peace be upon him, who was indeed destined to demonstrate in the bitter and punishing events that were to occur extraordinary and even unique qualities of heroism and devotion.

The significance of the proclamation made by the Messenger of God, peace and blessings be upon him and his family, on that day is thus clear. It permits us to understand why he undertook to name as his successor and legatee the one and only person who promised him full collaboration.

Taking into consideration the Qur'ānic verse, "*The Prophet says nothing out of mere fancy, and whatever he utters is the fruit of revelation from his Lord,*" (53:3-4) we must conclude that on that very day, during the earliest part of his mission the Prophet, peace and blessings be upon him and his family, clearly and unmistakably appointed 'Alī, peace be upon him, to be leader and guide of the people after his death.

The traditions in which this occurrence is recorded furthermore indicate that the question of succession was the direct prerogative of God and the Messenger, peace and blessings be upon him and his family, and that the people cannot resolve so momentous a matter in accordance with their own wishes. Indeed, the question was of such significance that the Imāmate was proclaimed together with prophethood on one and the same occasion, in a gathering attended by the foremost relatives of the Prophet, peace and blessings be upon him and his family.

Ibn Hishām , the well known historian, writes:

"'Alī b. Abī Ṭālib was the first man to believe in the Prophet, peace and blessings be upon him and his family, to pray together with him, and to affirm the veracity of that which God gave him, although on that day he was a ten year old child."[42]

Anas b. Mālik remarks: "The Prophet began his mission on Monday, and 'Alī embraced Islam on Tuesday."[43]

Ibn Mājah in his *al-Sunan* and al-Ḥākim in his *al-Mustadrak* record 'Alī, peace be upon him, to have said:

"I am the servant of God and the brother of His Messenger. I am the supremely veracious one, and none but a liar shall say the same after me. I made the prayer seven years before anyone else did."[44]

The Most Noble Messenger, peace and blessings be upon him and his family, emphasized on various occasions that the question of leadership of the *ummah* pertained to God alone, and that he played no role in this respect.

al-Ṭabarī records the following in his history:

"A tribal chief by the name of al-Akhnas made his allegiance and obedience to the Prophet, peace and blessings be upon him and his family, conditional on the leadership of the *ummah* being assigned to him after the death of the Prophet. The Prophet, peace and blessings be upon him and his family, responded: 'This is a matter that belongs to God; He will appoint to this office whomever He deems fit.' The chief in question was disappointed and he sent a message to the Prophet, peace and blessings be upon him and his family, saying that it was unacceptable that he should toil and exert himself only to see the leadership go elsewhere."[45]

Can it then be permissible to prefer a leader chosen by the people to the one selected by God and His Messenger, or to place that lofty personage under the authority of someone else, obliging him to obey him and follow his command? The Qur'ān clearly proclaims: "*None has free choice when confronted with the command of God and His Messenger. Whosoever disobeys the command of God and His Messenger falls prey to obvious misguidance.*" (33:34)

When, therefore, God selects a certain person to be the guide and leader of the people, that person is the caliph, even if the Muslim community does not make it possible for him to exercise governmental authority. It is the same as in the case of prophethood: if God appoints a person as prophet, that person is a prophet, even if people do not believe in him and refuse to obey him.

Another precious utterance in which the Messenger of God, peace and blessings be upon him and his family, emphasizes to the Islamic *ummah* that 'Alī, peace be upon him, is their leader and ruler is the *ḥadīth* known as the "*ḥadīth* of the Rank" *(ḥadīth al-manzilah).* The circumstances under which it arose are the following:

One day the Prophet, peace and blessings be upon him and his family, learned that the armies of Byzantium were mobilizing for an attack on Madīnah in the hope of gaining a swift victory. Upon hearing this, he ordered precautions to be taken and with a single order he was able to assemble a large force of Muslims to confront the enemy.

At the same time, a report reached the Prophet, peace and blessings be upon him and his family, that the Hypocrites were also gathering their forces with the aim of causing disorder in the city during the anticipated absence of the Prophet, peace and blessings be upon him and his family, by killing and inciting people to violence.

The Most Noble Messenger, peace and blessings be upon him and his family, appointed 'Alī, peace be upon him, to guard the city on his behalf, and he ordered that he should remain in Madīnah until he returned, administering the affairs of the Muslims. When the Hypocrites realized that their treacherous plans had been divulged, they began spreading idle rumors in the hope of weakening 'Alī's position. They hinted that the Prophet, peace and blessings be upon him and his family, was angry with 'Alī, peace be upon him, and that it was for this reason that he had not been permitted to accompany him on a major military expedition.

'Alī, peace be upon him, was greatly troubled and saddened by the circulation of these rumors, and he hastened to the presence of the Prophet, peace and blessings be upon him and his family, who had already left Madīnah. He told him what had happened, and with a single historic sentence he clarified the special position of 'Alī, peace be upon him, once and for all:

"Are you not content that your relation to me shall be like the relation of Hārūn to Mūsā, excepting only that there shall be no prophet after me?"

At the end of this *ḥadīth* there is a sentence that many Sunnī scholars have recorded in their books:

"It is not fitting that I should depart without your being my deputy and successor."[47]

Sa'd b. Abī Waqqāṣ, who was an obstinate enemy of 'Alī, peace be upon him, mentions the same *ḥadīth* in order to demonstrate his high standing.

When Mu'āwiyah wanted to have the people of Makkah swear allegiance to Yazīd, he convened an assembly of some of the Companions at the place known as al-Nadwah. He began by condemning and criticizing 'Alī, peace be upon him, expecting Sa'd to agree with him at least on this point. But contrary to his expectations, Sa'd turned to Mu'āwiyah and said: "Whenever I recall three luminous moments in the life of 'Alī, peace be upon him, I wish from the bottom of my heart that they had been mine. The first of the three came on that day when the Messenger of God, peace and blessings be upon him and his family, said to 'Alī, peace be upon him, 'Your relation to me shall be like the relation of Hārun to Musā, excepting only that there shall be no prophet after me.'

"The second came on the plain of Khaybar when the Prophet, peace and blessings be upon him and his family, said: 'Tomorrow I will entrust the banner to one who loves God and His Prophet and whom God and His Prophet love. He will be the conqueror of Khaybar, for he never turns his back on the enemy.'

"The third was on the day when the Prophet, peace and blessings be upon him and his family, disputed with the Christians of Najrān. He gathered 'Alī, Fāṭimah, Ḥasan and Ḥusayn, peace be upon them all, around him, and presented them to the divine presence, saying, 'O Lord, these are the people of my house.'"[48]

In the *ḥadīth* comparing his relation with 'Alī to that of Mūsā (Moses) with Hārūn (Aaron), the Prophet, peace and blessings be upon him and his family, had implicitly designated 'Alī as his brother, assistant and general deputy as well as leader of the *ummah,* and the fact that he excepted only prophethood indicates the comprehensive nature of the station he awarded to 'Alī, peace be upon him.

If we refer to the Qur'ān, we will see that God Almighty granted all the requests Mūsā made on him, and it was in accordance with one such request that He appointed Hārūn the helper, assistant, deputy and successor of Mūsā among his people, and even made him a prophet.[49] Since Hārūn was the leader of all the Banī Isrā'īl, the situation of 'Alī, peace be upon him, was analogous. Just like the Most Noble Messenger, peace and blessings be upon him and his family, he was the ruler of all the Muslims, and his acting on his behalf as his deputy when he was not present was therefore entirely natural, a consequence of his comprehensive deputyship. Likewise, the deputyship exercized by Hārūn when Mūsā went to the place of assignation was not temporary in nature.

Someone might be of the view that 'Alī's deputyship was restricted to the period that the Prophet, peace and blessings be upon him and his family, was absent from Madīnah, so that the *ḥadīth* under discussion cannot be taken as having general significance or as evidence that he was the Prophet's successor.

To this we answer that whenever the Prophet, peace and blessings be upon him and his family, left the Islamic capital, he would always appoint someone to act as his deputy. If by comparing 'Alī, peace be upon him, to Hārūn, the Prophet, peace and blessings be upon him and his family, had intended nothing more than the usual appointment of a deputy, restricted in his authority to Madīnah for the period of the Prophet's absence, why did he not use a similar expression for those other favored Companions he would appoint as deputy? Why did he not use the same or similar words to describe the services they rendered?

History provides no evidence that the Prophet, peace and blessings be upon him and his family, uttered these words with respect to anyone but 'Alī, peace be upon him. The simple truth of the matter is that the Prophet, peace and blessings be upon him and his family, made use of the occasion to proclaim the virtues of 'Alī, to appoint him as his successor, and to make plain that he was his sole legatee. If the Prophet had intended to appoint him only as his deputy for a limited time, it would have made no sense for prophethood to be excluded from the prerogatives of his office. The meaning then would have been something improbable like the following: "'Alī, stand in as my deputy for a while until I return, but you will not be a prophet after me." The exception made of prophethood makes sense only if the various powers and attributes of Hārūn should continue to pertain to 'Alī after the death of the Prophet.

Moreover, this expression was used by the Prophet in appointing 'Alī as his successor on other occasions as well, not simply when assigning him deputyship in Madīnah, as history bears witness. For example, in the earliest days of the Hijrah, when the Prophet caused every Muslim to conclude a pact of brotherhood with another Muslim, 'Alī hastened sorrowfully to the presence of the Prophet and said: "How is it that you have assigned every Muslim a brother, but have not chosen anyone to be my brother?" In the presence of a group of Companions, the Prophet then replied: "I swear by the Lord Who sent me with the message of truth, I delayed the matter only in order to make you my brother. You are to me as Hārūn was to Mūsā, excepting only that there shall be no prophet after me. You are my heir and my brother."[50]

This *ḥadīth* demonstrates among other things that the barring of 'Alī from prophethood was not because of any unfitness on his part, but only to the fact that Muḥammad, peace and blessings be upon him and his family, was the Seal of the Prophets. Had prophethood not been sealed with him, 'Alī would doubtless have been a prophet.

The Messenger of God, peace and blessings be upon him and his family, called 'Alī, peace be upon him, his brother on a number of occasions.

Thus we read in the *Sīrah* of al-Ḥalabī:

"After the Prophet concluded pacts of brotherhood among the Companions (for example between Abū Bakr and 'Umar, Usayd b. Ḥuḍayr and Zayd b. al-Ḥārithah, 'Abd al-Raḥmān b. 'Awf and Sa'd b. al-Rabī', and Abū 'Ubaydah and Sa'd b. Mu'ādh), he took 'Alī by the hand and proclaimed, 'This is my brother.' Thereafter 'Alī and the Messenger of God were brothers."[51]

On another occasion, when discussing a matter that concerned 'Alī, his brother Ja'far, and Zayd b. al-Ḥārithah, the Prophet addressed 'Alī as follows: "As for you, O 'Alī, you are my brother and comrade."[52]

On yet another occasion he said: "You will be my brother and companion in Paradise."[53]

Let us now see what is meant by brotherhood in this context.

In order to abolish and obliterate all forms of tribal distinction and privilege which were contrary to the norms of divine justice, the Prophet undertook a number of necessary measures, above all by establishing a special type of brotherhood among the Muslims after the migration to Madīnah. It was his wish to bring a comprehensive brotherhood into being in the Islamic *ummah,* not as an abstract idea but as a palpable and objective reality. By the coming together of two adoptive brothers, who were not linked by any ties of blood or kinship but only by closeness to God and belief in the truths of His religion, the new brotherhood of Islam began to blossom in a practical form. Spiritual brotherhood became the equivalent of genealogical kinship. The links between two adoptive brothers, each hailing from a different tribe and town, contributed moreover to a general expansion of friendship and affection between all the members of the two different tribes, so that a network of deep spiritual and emotional links came into being.

The brotherhood of the Most Noble Prophet, peace and blessings be upon him and his family, and 'Alī, peace be upon him, had come into being no less than ten years before the Hijrah, when the Prophet convened a gathering of his relatives at his house in order to request their aid. The Prophet's purpose in establishing this fraternal link with 'Alī was without any doubt different from the goal of creating closeness between two tribes or the people of two cities that he pursued in Madīnah, not least because no such gap or difference separated him from 'Alī. They were already related to each other as cousins and firm, strong ties already existed between them.

The reason for the brotherhood between the Prophet and 'Alī must therefore have been spiritual and intellectual affinity, a mutual inward attraction. It was 'Alī who more than anyone else resembled the great founder of Islam with respect to his spiritual qualities and knowledge, his devotion and insight. The brotherhood of the Prophet with 'Alī had therefore a special significance that extended beyond this world to the plain of resurrection and the realm of the hereafter. Thus al-Ḥākim records in his *al-Mustadrak* the following remark addressed to 'Alī by the Messenger of God, handed down by two separate authentic chains of transmission: "You are my brother in this world and the hereafter."[54]

One day when Abū Bakr, 'Umar and Abū 'Ubaydah were present, the Prophet placed his hand on the shoulder of 'Alī and said: "O 'Alī, you are the first person who accepted Islam and believed in me; you are to me as Hārūn was to Mūsā."[55]

Once 'Umar saw a man insulting 'Alī b. Abī Ṭālib. 'Umar told him: "You are a hypocrite, for I heard the Messenger of God say to 'Alī, 'Only 'Alī is to me as Hārūn was to Mūsā, excepting only that there shall be no prophet after me.'"[56]

A point to be noted in this tradition is that since the Arabic particle *innamā* (only) implies exclusivity, the Prophet cannot have meant 'Alī's deputyship to be temporary, for he also appointed others as his deputies from time to time. 'Umar's words also imply that he understood the Prophet's declaration to make 'Alī his equal in all respects except prophethood, for he told the man who insulted 'Alī, "You are a hypocrite." His hypocrisy was indeed worse than open unbelief.

However high be the rank of a believer, to insult him entails neither unbelief nor hypocrisy. 'Umar and many of the Companions used to insult each other, but no one ever interpreted this kind of behavior as entailing unbelief or hypocrisy. However, insulting the Prophet, peace and blessings be upon him and his family, does indeed entail unbelief, and it can therefore be said that 'Umar b. al-Khaṭṭāb understood the words of the Prophet to mean that 'Alī, peace be upon him, had the same rank as the Prophet himself.

The *ḥadīth* of the Ark *(ḥadīth al-safīnah)* is one more of the well-known and universally accepted traditions found in the books of celebrated Sunnī scholars that establish the worthiness of the Prophet's family for assuming the leadership and direction of the Islamic *ummah.* Abū Dharr al-Ghifārī relates the Prophet to have said: "The People of my Household are for you like the Ark of Nūḥ (Noah). Whoever embarks on it will be saved and whoever turns away from it will be drowned."[57]

With these words the Prophet depicts clearly the rank of his family and their fundamental role in guiding mankind and giving direction to the Islamic *ummah.* He warns against the perilous consequences of abondoning the lofty and salvific persons of his house, a course that will lead whoever chooses it to darkness and misguidance.

The sense of comparing the People of the House *(Ahl al - Bayt)* to the Ark of Nūḥ is that whoever follows their guidelines in fulfilling his religious duties and whose acts conforms to their commands is guaranteed salvation from the awesome punishment that awaits on the Day of Judgement. Whoever rebels and disobeys, who distances himself from that axis of orientation, is like the one who sought refuge from the dreadful tempest on the mountaintops instead of in the Ark of Nūḥ. The only difference is that the latter met his death by drowning, while the former will be submerged in the torment of hellfire and eternal perdition.

The Most Noble Messenger, peace and blessings be upon him and his family, said in description of the People of his House:

"The People of my House are like the stars that help men find their way on sea and dry land and deliver them from misguidance and errance."[58]

He said further: "Whoever seeks refuge with the People of my House will be safe from misguidance and ruin, and whoever opposes them will fall prey to discord and divergence and join the party of Satan."[59]

From the traditions just cited can be deduced also the dimensions of the House, for whoever is exposed to the possibility of committing error and sin, of deviating from the clear guidelines laid down by the Prophet, peace and blessings be upon him and his family, will never be able to save others from falling into the pit of misery and misguidance or to bring about that radical change in modes of thought, feeling and social organization that is needed to ensure eternal felicity.

It would be possible to object against the Shī'ah or to condemn them for the path they have elected only if their obedience to the People of the Prophet's House were inspired by something other than his instructions and recommendations. Such, however, is not the case.

When the first caliph appointed the second caliph as his successor, what word or sentence did he use? Did he use more than one sentence to indicate that the office of caliphate and leadership of the Muslims that he had exercised now fell to the lot of 'Umar? By contrast, there are numerous expressions and sentences from the Prophet, clear and explicit in meaning, concerning 'Alī; do they not suffice to prove his leadership and succession? The words of the Prophet are far clearer and more explicit than those used by the first caliph; are they not enough to prove at least the claim of 'Alī to religious leadership? Fairminded and intelligent people can judge for themselves.

The scholars and leading figures of the Sunnī community have regarded it as necessary to follow the views and teachings of the founders of the four schools of Sunnī law, even though there is no *ḥadīth* from the Messenger of God, peace and blessings be upon him and his family, enjoining such obedience. We can therefore discern no adequate reason for these same scholars to ignore the teachings of the People of the Prophet's House, in the face of his clear declaration that the Qur'ān and the People of the House will remain inextricably linked until the Day of Judgement.[60]

What is even more remarkable is that some of the founders of the four legal schools were themselves students of the People of the House and benefited from their erudition. A leading Sunnī scholar remarks:

"All Islamic scholars, irrespective of the school to which they belong, are unanimously agreed on the accomplishments and learning of Imām al-Ṣādiq, peace be upon him. Sunnī Imāms who were his contemporaries studied with him and derived knowledge from him. Mālik learned from him, as did some of the contemporaries of Mālik such as Sufyān b. 'Uyaynah, Sufyān al-Thawrī, and many others. Abū Ḥanīfah, whose lifetime more or less corresponded to that of Imām al-Ṣādiq, peace be upon him, studied religious knowledge with him and regarded him as the most learned man of the age."[61]

Ibn Ḥajar, another Sunnī scholar, relates Imām al-Shāfi'ī to have said: "The Household of the Prophet is my means of salvation, and they are my means of drawing near to the Prophet. It is my hope that for their sake the record of my deeds will be given into my right hand on the Day of Judgement."[62]

Again al-Shāfi'ī said: "O People of the Prophet's House, love for you has been made obligatory by God through mention in the Qur'ān. Sufficient cause of pride it is for you that whoever fails to invoke blessings on you in his prayer will fail to have his devotions *(ṣalāt)* accepted."[63]

Unlike the views of the *mujtahids* who founded the four Sunnī schools, there is no contradiction or divergence among the teachings of the People of the House, for they were not engaged in independent reasoning on the ordinances of religion. Their teachings are identical with those of the Prophet, peace and blessings be upon him and his family, of which the Imāms of the People of the House were infallibly aware. The utterances of the Imāms cannot therefore be placed on the same level as the views of the founders of the four Sunnī schools.

In view of all this, how can it be justified to ignore and neglect the teachings of the People of the House?

Lesson Six
The Relationship between the Qur'ān and the Progeny of the Prophet

The *ḥadīth* concerning the "two weighty trusts" known as *ḥadīth al-thaqalayn* is one of the most widely accepted and authoritative of all the traditions narrated from the Prophet, peace and blessings be upon him and his family, and it has also been recorded in the principal Sunnī books of tradition. It possesses the highest degree of authenticity and acceptance. The text is as follows:

"I leave among you two precious and weighty trusts, on being the Book of God and the other my Progeny. These two legacies will never be separated from each other, and if you lay firm hold of them you will never go astray."[64]

Certain Sunnī scholars even add the following sentence at the end of the *ḥadīth*: "'Alī is always with the Qur'ān and the Qur'ān is with 'Alī; they too will not be separated from each other."[65]

Ḥadīth scholars attribute the transmission of this tradition to roughly thirty Companions of the Prophet.[66]

According to numerous *ḥadīth* scholars and historians, Shī'ī and Sunnī alike, the Prophet, peace and blessings be upon him and his family, never failed at different times in this life, including its difficult last moments, to draw people's attention to the profound link between these two great and authoritative sources of Islam, the Qur'ān and his Progeny *(Ahl al-Bayt)*, tracing out thereby an entire program for the future of Islam in a single instructive sentence. Small differences are to be seen in the form of the relevant traditions, some being detailed and others concise depending on the occasion, but the content and meaning are always the same: the profound and indissoluble link between the Qur'ān and the Progeny of the Prophet, peace and blessings be upon him and his family, the absolute interrelatedness of the two.

Ibn Ḥajar, a Sunnī scholar, writes:

"We have mentioned earlier different versions of this *ḥadīth*. Some of them relate to the utterances made by the Prophet at 'Arafah in the course of his Farewell Pilgrimage; others to pronouncements made while he was on his deathbed in Madīnah, surrounded by the Companions; another to his address at Ghadīr Khumm; and yet another to statements made while returning from Ṭā'if."

He then adds: "None of these versions contradict each other, for there is no reason why he should not have repeated the same truth on all these occasions, and on others as well, given the great significance that both the Qur'ān and his Progeny possess."[67]

In another tradition known as the *ḥadīth* of the Truth *(ḥadīth al-ḥaqq)*, the Prophet, peace and blessings be upon him and his family, says: "'Alī is with the truth and the truth is with 'Alī; wherever the truth is, 'Alī will incline to it."[68]

We know that the verses of the Noble Qur'ān form a compendium of the divine commands and laws of Islam; the teaching contained in them are a guarantee for man's happiness and salvation. However, the interpretation and exegesis of the Qur'ān have to be undertaken by persons who are acquinted with the language of revelation and who fully possess the necessary competence, in terms of both knowledge and conduct. The Shī'ah therefore believe that those who possess this competence must be identified by the Prophet himself and appointed by him to administer the affairs of the people and guide them. It is they who understand the language of revelation and can properly acquit themselves of the task of interpreting and explicating God's verses. The juxtaposition of the Progeny of the Prophet with the Qur'ān is thus due to the need of the Qur'ān for an exegesis that will set forth its purposes and regulations.

If we look carefully at the content of the *ḥadīth*, we will see that to separate the Qur'ān from the Progeny of the Prophet and to follow the utterances and views of persons unacquainted with its symbols and truths is bound to lead to error and misguidance. The tradition therefore implies that only the Progeny of the Prophet can establish the firm and categorical meaning of the verses in God's Book that are allegorical.

The fact that the Prophet places the Qur'ān and his Progeny side by side indicates that both are advancing in the same direction and toward the same goal: the Qur'ān is a divine law and book, and the Progeny are its interpreters, executors and guardians. To separate and distance oneself from the Progeny is therefore to invite destruction.

The decline and deviance of the Muslims began when such a separation started to occur and men attempted to hold on to each one separately. The thesis, "God's Book alone is enough for us" came to prevail in their religious thinking, leading to the emergence of such schools as the Ash'arī and the Mu'tazilite. It was as if they knew the value of God's Book better than the Prophet himself and better comprehended its significance!

It is possible to understand the Qur'ān and explain the knowledge it contains only by referring to the utterances of those persons upon whom knowledge has been directly bestowed by God, or at least whose knowledge is derived from instruction by a particular source. Such persons can be only the Inerrant *(ma'ṣūm)* Imāms of the Prophet's Progeny.

Ibn Ḥajar also cites the following sentence uttered by the Prophet, peace and blessings be upon him and his family:

"Do not attempt to go beyond these twin trusts (the Book and the Progeny of the Prophet), for that will lead you into perdition, and do not fall short in adhering to them, for that too will encompass your ruin. Do not imagine the People of the Prophet's House to be ignorant, for they are infinitely more knowledgeable than you and understand well the language of revelation."[69]

The Commander of the Faithful, 'Alī, peace be upon him, said:

"You will never remain faithful to your covenant with the Qur'ān unless you recognize who it is that has betrayed his covenant, and you will never lay firm hold of the Qur'ān unless you recognize who it is that has abandoned it. Seek the straight path of fidelity and the means of adhering to the Qur'ān from the people of the Qur'ān, for it is they who keep alive knowledge and learning and uproot ignorance. They it is by means of obedience to whom you become aware of the knowledge they hold. You comprehend their silence from their speech and their outer appearance from their inner state. They never rebel against the command of religion and never fall into dispute. Religion is a silent and veracious witness dwelling in their midst."[70]

What is meant here is that the Progeny of the Prophet are free from sin and pollution and even minor errors, for it is obvious that whatever is indissolubly linked to the Qur'ān until both trusts are brought together before the Prophet, peace and blessings be upon him and his family, on the Day of Resurrection must be followed and obeyed by mankind together with the Qur'ān itself. God cannot command men to obey one who is polluted by error and sin, nor can He create an indissoluble link between the Qur'ān and such a person. Only those who are utterly beyond the reach of impurity can be juxtaposed with the Qur'ān, for those obedience to whose commands God has made incumbent on all Muslims must be free of all defect.

Not content with his other utterances on the subject, the Prophet declared the number of successors *(khulafā')* who would come after him:

"This religion will endure until the Day of Judgement, for as long as twelve persons from Quraysh rule over you as my successors."[71]

"My successors will be twelve in number, just like the

chieftains of the Banī Isrā'īl, all of them from Quraysh and (according to one version of this *ḥadīth*) from Banī Hāshim."[72]

'Abdullāh relates the Prophet to have said: "As long as there are two men left on the earth, leadership will remain among the Quraysh."[73]

This mention of the twelve successors can refer only to the Inerrant Imāms from the Progeny of the Prophet, peace be upon them, for neither were the first caliphs twelve in number, nor were the Umayyad and 'Abbāsīd rulers. More importantly, the crimes those rulers committed, far from assuring the welfare and happiness of the *ummah*, brought about the destruction of religion, so that it is impossible in any way to consider them the successors of the Prophet.

Those who could not deny the authenticity of the *ḥadīth* concerning twelve successors but wished nonetheless to avoid recognizing the Twelve Imāms of the Prophet's Progeny were obliged to offer tortuous explanations that were utterly irreconcilable with the text and content of the tradition, for the first caliphs and the Umayyad and 'Abbāsīd rulers when added together come to a total of some thirty people, so that the total number of claimants to the caliphate from among the Quraysh exceeds the number specified in the *ḥadīth*. If we refuse to interpret the *ḥadīth* as referring to the Imāms of the Shī'ah, we are left with no clear or reliable meaning for it whatsoever.

Shaykh Sulaymān al-Qundūzī, a Ḥanafī scholar, writes the following, in a vein free of all fanaticism:

"According to scholars, the traditions that specify the successors to the Prophet, peace and blessings be upon him and his family, to be twelve in number are well known and they have been narrated by different chains of transmission. It became clear with the passage of time that what the Messenger of God was referring to in this *ḥadīth* were the twelve Imāms from his Progeny. It is impossible to refer it to the first caliphs, for they were only four in number, nor can it be applied to the Umayyads, for they were more than twelve in number, apart from which with the exception of 'Umar b. 'Abd al-'Azīz they were all tyrants and oppressors, and they did not belong to the Banī Hāshim, where as the Prophet had specified that his twelve successors would be from the Banī Hāshim. Jābir b. Samarah mentions that the Prophet spoke this last part of the tradition softly, because not everyone was happy that the caliphate would go to the Banī Hāshim.

"Equally, this *ḥadīth* cannot apply to the 'Abbāsīds, because their number, too, is more than twelve; they did not act in accordance with the verse enjoining love for the family of the Prophet;[74] and they ignored the *ḥadīth* of the Cloak *(ḥadīth al-kisā')*. The *ḥadīth* must, then, refer exclusively to the Twelve Imāms from the Progeny of the Prophet, for they were superior to all others with respect to knowledge, moral virtues, piety and lineage. They were a line who inherited their knowledge from the Messenger of God, peace and blessings be upon him and his family, their great ancestor. This is confirmed by the *ḥadīth* concerning the two weighty trusts and numerous traditions that have reached us from the Prophet."[75]

Lesson Seven
Irresponsible Attitudes of the Companions

Here the following question arises. Given the fact that the Prophet, peace and blessings be upon him and his family, proclaimed 'Alī to be his legatee *(waṣiyy)* and successor *(khalīfah)*, emphatically designation him as the leader of the Muslims both at Ghadīr Khumm and on other appropriate occasions, how did it happen that after the death of the Most Noble Messenger his Companions *(ṣaḥābah)* ignored God's command and abandoned 'Alī, that noble and precious personage, decided not to obey him, chose someone else to be leader in his place, and entrusted the reins of rule to him?

Was there any ambiguity in the words of the Prophet, or were all those different phrases and expressions establishing 'Alī's rank and designating him leader not enough?

A clear answer to this question can be found by examining the events that took place in the age of the Prophet, peace and blessings be upon him and his family. We see that there existed among his Companions elements who, whenever his commands ran contrary to their wishes and inclinations, pressed him to change his mind in the hope of preventing him, by whatever means possible, from carrying out his plans. When they despaired of reaching their goal, they would start complaining.

The Qur'ān warns these people not to oppose the commands of the Prophet in the verse that reads: "*Let those who oppose the commands of the Prophet fear disaster and a painful torment.*" (24:63)

During the last days of his blessed life, the Messenger of God prepared an army to do battle with the Byzantines and he appointed Usāmah b. Zayd to be its commander. This appointment of a young man, despite the availability of older and more experienced men, proved displeasing to some of the Companions, and led to an argument among them. Those who were strongly oppossed to Usāmah b. Zayd asked the Prophet to dismiss him, but he paid no attention to their request and commanded Abū Bakr, 'Umar and 'Uthmān to join the ranks of the Muslim army as it departed from Madīnah. However, they not only disregarded military discipline but also disobeyed the categorical command of the Prophet. Instead of proceeding to the front with the army, they split off and returned to Madīnah.[76]

The disrespectful mumblings of some of the Companions greatly vexed the Messenger of God, peace and blessings be upon him and his family, and with a heart full of pain and concern for his people, he came forth from his house and addressed the people as follows:

"O people, what are these words of yours concerning the appointment of Usāmah that have come to my ears? Just as you are criticizing him now, you once objected to the appointment of his father Zayd b. al-Ḥārithah as commander. I answer by God that just as he was worthy of command, so too is his son."[77]

Even after the death of the Prophet, 'Umar came to Abū Bakr and demanded that he should dismiss Usāmah. The caliph replied: "The Messenger of God appointed him, and you wish me to dismiss him?"[78]

The Prophet's wish and desire during the final days of his life was to empty Madīnah of the leaders of both the Emigrants and the Helpers. He therefore has Usāmah's army prepared for battle and gave the command for *jihād*, ordering the army to advance in the direction of the Syrian border. Insistently he asked the foremost of the Companions to leave Madīnah and fight under the banner of Usāmah, retaining only 'Alī to stay at his bedside. This remarkable act on the part of the Prophet was very significant. However, those Companions failed to comply with his instructions, and they withdrew from the army commanded by Usāmah.

Throughout his life, the Prophet never appointed anyone as commander over the head of 'Alī, peace be upon him; it was always he who was the standard bearer and commander.[79] By contrast, Abū Bakr and 'Umar were to be simple soldiers in the army of Usāmah, and the Prophet personally ordered them to serve under him when he appointed him commander at the battle of Mu'ta. Historians are unanimously agreed on this point. Likewise, at the Battle of Dhāt al-Salāsil, when the army was commanded by Ibn al-'Āṣ, Abū Bakr and 'Umar again served as simple soldiers. This contrasts with the case of 'Alī b. Abī Ṭālib, whom the Prophet, from the beginning of his mission until his death, never made subordinate to anyone, an extremely significant point.

History will never forget the time when the Most Noble Messenger, peace and blessings be upon him and his family, was on his deathbed, his state becoming progressively more grave. He felt that the last strands of his life were being plucked apart. He therefore decided without further delay to put his final plan into effect and said: "Bring me paper so that I can write for you a document to prevent you from ever going astray."[80]

Just as he had clarified the question of leadership in numerous speeches and utterances, he wished now, one final time, to address this weighty matter, described by the Qur'ān as the completion of religion, by enshrining it in an authoritative written document to remain among the Muslims after his death. Thereby the door would be closed on any future deviations from his orders. But those same people who in defiance of his orders had refrained from going to the front were now watching the situation carefully with the intention of implementing their plans at the first possible opportunity. They therefore refused to permit writing utensils to be brought to the Prophet.[81]

Jābir b. 'Abdullāh says:

"When the Messenger of God fell sick with the illness that was to end in his death, he asked for paper in order to write down for his *ummah* instructions that would prevent them from ever going astray or accusing each other of having gone astray. Words were exchanged among those present in the Prophet's house and an argument ensued in the course of which 'Umar uttered words that caused the Prophet to order him to leave the house."[82]

'Ubaydullāh b. 'Abdullāh b. 'Utbah relates Ibn 'Abbās to have said:

"During the final moments of the life of the Messenger of God, peace and blessings be upon him and his family, a number of people were present in this house, including 'Umar b. al-Khaṭṭāb. The Prophet said: 'Come, let me write for you a document that will prevent you from ever going astray after me.' 'Umar said: 'Sickness has overcome the Prophet; we have the Qur'ān, which is enough for us.'

"Then disagreement arose among those present. They began to argue with each other, some saying, 'Quick, have the Prophet write a document for you so that you will never go astray after him,' and others repeating the words of 'Umar.

"When the arguing and nonsensical talk reached its pitch, the Prophet, peace and blessings be upon him and his family, told them all to leave."

Thus it was that, as Ibn 'Abbās says: "The great misfortune arose when their noisy disputing prevented the Messenger of God from writing his testamentary document."[83] He then adds sorrowfully: "The tribulations of the Muslims began on that very day."[84]

In the discussion that took place between Ibn 'Abbās and the second caliph concerning the caliphate of 'Alī, the caliph said: "The Prophet wanted to declare 'Alī as his successor, but I did not allow it to happen."[85]

Some Sunnī historians and *ḥadīth* scholars have written that when the Prophet decided to write a document that would prevent the Muslims from going astray 'Umar said: "The Messenger of God has become delirious." Others, however, in order to soften the offensiveness of his words, maintain that he said: "Sickness has overcome the Prophet; you have the Book of God at your disposal, which is enough for us."[86]

It seems that the Most Noble Messenger, peace and blessings be upon him and his family, was unaware of the importance of the Book of God and they were better informed than him on this point! Was it necessary to accuse him of mental derangement if he wished to draw up a written document specifying who was to lead the *ummah* after his death? If indeed the Prophet's decision could be attributed to the failing of his mental powers as a result of illness, why did the second caliph not prevent Abū Bakr from drawing up a comparable document during the last moments of his life, or accuse him of being deranged? 'Umar was present at the side of Abū Bakr and he knew that Abū Bakr intended to designate him as ruler in his testament, so naturally he wanted the document to be signed.

If 'Umar truly thought the Book of God to suffice for the solution of all problems, why did he immediately hasten to the Saqīfah after the death of the Prophet, together with Abū Bakr to ensure that the question of the caliphate should be resolved in accordance with their ideas? Why did they not at that point refer exclusively to the Book of God and make no mention of the Qur'ān, even though the Qur'ān had already settled the matter?

al-Ṭabarī writes the following in his history:

"When Shadīd, the emancipated slave of Abū Bakr took into his hand the command Abū Bakr had written for 'Umar to become his successor, 'Umar said to the people, "People, pay heed, and obey the command of the caliph. The caliph says, 'I have not failed you in providing for your welfare.'"[87]

The expression of personal opinions running counter to the orders of the Prophet, peace and blessings be upon him and his family, continued after his death, culminating in the changing of certain divine decrees in the time of the second caliph and on his orders. Instances of this are to be found in reputable books by Sunnī authors.[88]

For example, the second caliph said: "Let them never bring before me a man who has married a woman for a set period, for it they do I will stone him."[89] The fact that he prohibited temporary marriage *(mut'ah)* proves that this type of union was common among the Companions and other Muslims at the time, for otherwise it would not have been necessary for him to order them to desist. Now if the Messenger of God, peace and blessings be upon him and his family, had forbidden this form of marriage, the Companions would never have had recourse to it and there would have no need for 'Umar to threaten people with stoning.

The second caliph himself admitted: "There were three things that were permissible in the time of the Prophet which I have forbidden and for which I exact punishment: temporary marriage, the *mut'ah* pilgrimage, and reciting 'Hasten to the best of deeds' *(ḥayya 'alā khayri 'l-'amal)* in the call to prayer."[90]

It was also he ordered that in the call to prayer *(adhān)* at dawn the phrase, "prayer is better than sleep" *(aṣ'ṣalātu khayrun mina 'n-nawm)* should be recited.[91]

According to the *Sunan* of al-Tirmidhī someone from Syria once asked 'Abdullāh b. 'Umar about the *mut'ah* pilgrimage. He replied that it was permissible. When the man remarked that 'Abdullāh's father had prohibited it, he answered, "If my father has forbidden something which the Prophet, peace and blessings be upon him and his family, permitted, should we abondon the *Sunnah* of the Prophet and follow my father?"[92]

Ibn Kathīr similarly records in his history: "'Abdullāh b. 'Umar was told that his father had prohibited the *mut'ah* pilgrimage. He said in reply: 'I fear that a stone will fall on you from the heavens. Are we to follow the *Sunnah* of the Prophet or the *sunnah* of 'Umar b. al-Khaṭṭāb?'"[93]

During the time of the Prophet, peace and blessings be upon him and his family, as well as the caliphate of Abū Bakr and the first three years of the caliphate of 'Umar, if anyone were to divorce his wife three times on a single occasion, it counted as a single repudiation, and was not therefore final.

However, 'Umar said: "If such a repudiation is made, I will count it as a threefold (and therefore final) repudiation."[94]

The Shī'ah believe that such a repudiation *(ṭalāq)* counts only as a single repudiation, and Shaykh Maḥmūd al-Shaltūt, erstwhile rector of the Azhar, regarded Shī'ī jurisprudence *(fiqh)* superior in this respect as well as many others.[95]

No one has the right to tamper with revealed ordinances, for they are divine and immutable, not even the Prophet himself. The Qur'ān says: "*Were Muḥammad to attribute lies to Us, with Our powerful hand We would seize him and cut his jugular vein.*" (69:44)

However, we see that unfortunately some of the Companions awarded themselves the right of exercising independent judgement *(ijtihād)* with respect to certain ordinances, changing and modifying divine law in accordance with their own notions.

The second caliph introduced class differences into Islamic society during the time of his rule, increasing racial tensions between the Arabs and the Persians.[96] He established a discriminatory system of distributing public monies, awarding more to those who accepted Islam early on than to those who embraced it later; more to Qurayshite Migrants than to non-Qurayshite Migrants; more to the Migrants than to the Helpers; more to the Arabs than to the non-Arabs; and more to masters than to their clients.[97]

Toward the end of his life 'Umar himself came to recognize the negative effects of his policy and he said: "If I remain alive this year, I will establish equality in Islamic society and abolish discrimination. I will act in the way the Messenger of God, peace and blessings be upon him and his family, and Abū Bakr both acted."[98]

The foregoing indicates the arbitrary attitude that some of the Companions assumed with respect to the commands of the Prophet. In certain cases where those commands did not correspond to their personal inclinations, they tried either to avoid implementing them or to change them completely. The fact that they ignored the unmistakably authoritative utterances of the Prophet on the day of Ghadīr Khumm or that they behaved similarly with respect to other matters after his death, should not be regarded as either surprising or unprecedented, for they had already given an indication of their attitudes during his lifetime.

In addition, it should not be forgotten that in every society most people tend to remain indifferent to political and social matters, choosing to follow their leaders and those who seize the initiative. This is a clear and undeniable fact.

However, there were respectable and independent minded people who did not change their position after the death of the Prophet. They did not approve of the election that took place at the Saqīfah, and they separated themselves from the majority in protest against the introduction of the consultative concept into Islamic government. Although they were more or less compelled to remain silent, they remained loyal to 'Alī b. Abī Ṭālib, peace be upon him, as leader. Among the outstanding personalities belonging to this group were Salmān al-Fārisī, Abū Dharr al-Ghifārī, Abū Ayyūb al-Anṣārī, Khuzaymah b. Thābit, Miqdād b. al-Aswad, al-Kindī, 'Ammār b. Yāsir, Ubayy b. Ka'b, Khālid b. Sa'īd, Bilāl, Qays b. Sa'd, Abān, Buraydah al-Aslamī, Abu 'l-Haytham b. al-Tayyihān, as well as many others whose names are recorded in Islamic history. Some scholars have listed two hundred and fifty Companions of the Prophet, complete with names and descriptions, as belonging to this class.[99]

al-Ya'qūbī mentions in his history Abū Dharr al-Ghifārī, Salmān al-Fārisī, Miqdād b. al-Aswad, Khālid b. Sa'īd, Zubayr, 'Abbās, Barā' b. 'Āzib, Ubayy b. Ka'b, and Faḍl b. al-'Abbās as being among those who remained loyal to the cause of 'Alī, peace be upon him.[100] Qays b. Sa'd even went so far as to argue with his father over the question of the caliphate and he swore never to speak to him again because of this views.[101]

These are some of the earliest Shī'īs; they supported 'Alī's right to the leadership because of the clear injunctions in the Qur'ān and the *Sunnah*. They remained unswerving in their views until the end. During the period of the first three caliphs the number of Shī'īs in fact rose, all of them being outstanding and virtuous personalities, their names being linked to piety and purity in the books of history and biography where they are mentioned. Among them were men such as Muḥammad b. Abī Bakr, Ṣa'ṣa'ah b. Ṣūḥān, Zayd b. Ṣūḥān, Hishām b. 'Utbah, 'Abdullāh b. Budayl al-Khuzā'ī, Maytham al-Tammār, 'Adiyy b. Ḥātim, Ḥujr b. 'Adiyy, Asbagh b. Nubātah, al-Ḥārith al-A'war al-Hamdānī, 'Amr b. al-Ḥumq al-Khazā'ī, Mālik al-Ashtar, and 'Abdullāh b. Hāshim.

Lesson Eight
Does the Qur'ān Provide an Unconditional Guarantee for the Companions?

The praise to be found in the Qur'ān for acts of the Companions that had already taken place can in no way be taken as proof for the justice of their conduct or their freedom from corruption and deviation throughout the entirety of their lives. It cannot be imagined that their deeds would always and under all circumstances be synonymous with justice and truth, for the pleasure of God Almighty and man's resulting attainment of eternal bliss are contingent on the maintenance of faith and consistently righteous behavior for the whole of one's life. If these two attributes are forfeited, the inevitable result will be deviation and corruption, with regard to both belief and action, and however brilliant be one's past, it will be utterly unable to secure one's eternal felicity.

The Most Noble Messenger, peace and blessings be upon him and his family, who instructed the whole of mankind in piety and the qualities of true humanity, who was the supreme monotheist and exemplar of moral virtues, who was never polluted with polytheism or sin — even he was addressed thus in the Qur'ān:

"*If you assign partners to Almighty God, all your deeds will count for nothing and you will be among the losers.*" (39:65)

It is obvious that the Beloved Messenger, possessing as he did the quality of inerrancy, was not separated from God for even an instant. The purpose of this Qur'ānic warning must then be to prevent the Muslims from falling prey to arrogance and their intentions from being polluted by hypocrisy. Every individual must exert himself to the utmost, drawing on all his powers and capacities, to the very last moment of his life, in order to earn the pleasure of his Lord, remaining firm and steadfast in his commitment.

The Qur'ān says concerning that great prophet Ibrāhīm and his progeny: "*If they tended to polytheism, their deeds would lose all validity.*" (6:88)

Likewise, the Qur'ān also says: "*God does not love the oppressors*" (3:57) and "*God is displeased with the wrongdoers.*" (9:96)

History makes it plain that by no means all of those who are known as Companions were in fact pious and righteous people. This can be deduced, for example, from a tradition of the Most Noble Messenger, peace and blessings be upon him and his family, recorded in the *Ṣaḥīḥ* of al-Bukhārī:

"On the Day of Resurrection I will be standing beside the pool of Kawthar, waiting for those who will come to me. I will see some of them separating and moving away from me, and I will ask, 'Are they not from among my Companions?' I will be told, 'Yes, but you do not know how they turned back to their previous ways after your death.'[102]

There is a comparable *ḥadīth* in the *Ṣaḥīḥ* of Muslim:

"People will come up to me beside the pool, in a manner visible to me. When they are brought before me, they will be ashamed. I will then say, 'O God, are these my Companions?' I will be told, 'You do not know what they did after your death.'"[103]

al-Taftāzānī, the well-known Shāfi'ī scholar, writes:

"The clashes, disagreements and battles that took place among the Companions have been recorded in books of history, and narrated by trustworthy authorities. It can therefore be deduced that some of the Companions must have deviated from the path of justice and truth and become polluted with oppression and wrongdoing. The reason for their deviation, wrongdoing, and oppression, was the feelings of hatred, obstinacy, and envy they nurtured, their hunger for leadership and rule, their addiction to pleasure and lust. It cannot be assumed that all the Companions were free of sin and impurity."[104]

If the followers of certain schools of thought in Islam do not have high regard for some of the Companions *(aṣ-ḥāb)* or the Followers *(tābi'īn)* and criticize them in a number of respects, this cannot justify cursing them or calling their Islam into doubt. Competing views on this subject must not be allowed to degenerate into mutual hostile wrangling, and there is no justification for condemning as unbelievers any of the followers of the Messenger of God, peace and blessings be upon him and his family, for even some of the Companions themselves did argue with each other most vehemently. Thus at the Saqīfah some called out for Sa'd b. 'Ubādah to be killed; Qays b. Sa'd b. 'Ubādah came to blows with 'Umar; and Zubayr declared that he would not return his sword to his sheath until everyone had sworn allegiance to 'Alī, whereupon 'Umar insulted him and called out for him to be seized, resulting in Zubayr's beating.

'Umar's behavior to Miqdād at the Saqīfah, the way in which 'Uthman dealt with Ibn Mas'ūd, 'Ammār b. Yāsir and Abū Dharr al-Ghifārī, as well as many other incidents, are all examples of the strife and disputation that took place. Differing views concerning certain of the Prophet's Companions cannot therefore serve as justification for cursing any Muslim or declaring him an unbeliever, nor can they be allowed to damage the unity of all Muslims.

In any event, the Sunnīs themselves do not in practice regard all the Companions and Followers as worthy of respect. After all, those who killed 'Uthmān were either from the Companions or from the Followers, and Khālid b. al-Walīd killed Mālik b. Nuwayrah, who was a Companion.

Among the Companions there were exalted personages who attained the utmost degree of faith, piety, and devotion, over whose hearts and souls God Almighty ruled; their whole beings resonated with purity and truthfulness. However, there were others in the corners of whose spirit still lurked the traces of *Jāhīlī* customs and modes of thought; they remained attached to the customs of the past. There were even elements whose acceptance of Islam after the conquest of Makkah was based on the calculation of personal interest. However, the powerful influence and awe inspiring presence of the Prophet forced them to conceal their inner desires and inclinations, and it was only after his death that they were able to return to the habits and customs of the *Jāhiliyyah*.

To approve undiscriminatingly the mode of conduct of all the Companions, to deny that any of them was guilty of evil deeds, and to assert that they were without exception persons of righteousness, is incompatible with the *Sunnah* of the Messenger of God, peace and blessings be upon him and his family.

One cannot therefore seek salvation among the Migrants and the Helpers or claim that he may gain eternal felicity by means of attachment to either of these groups. The attainment of that goal depends on the maintenance of certain conditions until one departs through death's gate.

Sunnī scholars nonetheless maintain that all the Companions of the Prophet were entitled to exercize independent judgement *(ijtihād)* and are thus to be excused for whatever errors they may have committed, or even rewarded for them. Whatever offense they may have committed is thus justified. The triumph of this mode of thought made it impossible for any objection to be raised and emboldened certain egoistic and ambitious people to commit any crime they desired — people like Mu'āwiyah, 'Amr b. al-'Āṣ, Khālid b. al-Walīd, al-Mughīrah, Sa'īd al-'Āṣ, and Busr b. Abī Arṭāt. Matters reached a point that Mu'āwiyah had the temerity to proclaim: "All property belongs to God, and I am the representative of God; I will therefore dispose of it in whatever way I see fit." No one spoke out against him with the exception of Ṣa'ṣa'ah b. Ṣūḥān, one of the great figures of the Shī'ah; he refuted his claim.[105]

If to be numbered among the Companions of the Messenger of God was a guarantee of righteousness and salvation why did some of them even in his lifetime abandon their beliefs and join the ranks of the misguided, thereby earning condemnation and punishment by the Prophet?

Ḥarqūṣ b. Zuhayr, the leader of the Khārijites at the battle of Nahrawān, was one of the Companions of the Messenger of God, and no one could imagine that toward the end of his life he would suddenly turn and fall prey to misguidance. Yet that is precisely what he did, a miserable ending that had been foreseen by the Prophet in these words: "He will abandon his religion just like an arrow drawn forth from the quiver." Not only did he join the Khārijites; at the battle of Nahrawān he was the standard bearer in rebellion against 'Alī b. Abī Ṭālib, peace be upon him, by whose hand he was ultimately killed.

'Abdullāh b. Jaḥsh was another Companion who left behind the light of Islam. When he migrated to Abyssinia, it might have been expected that like the other Muslims who sought refuge in that land he would remain firm and steadfast in his beliefs and the defense of God's religion. Soon, however, darkness overtook his heart; he abandoned Islam and converted to Christianity.

We conclude then that God's expression of satisfaction with the Companions was conditional on their remaining within the bounds of faith and piety and maintaining their link with God to the very end of their life. If they changed direction and went astray, all of their good deeds were voided, and God Almighty's satisfaction became transformed into anger and wrath. Not only was no unconditional guarantee of God's permanent pleasure not given to the Companions or the common believers of later generations; it was not given even to the Prophets or the Imāms, despite their whole beings overflowing with virtue and blessings for mankind.

Lesson Nine
The Formation of the Caliphal Order at the Saqīfah

The blessed and fruitful life of the Most Noble Messenger, peace and blessings be upon him and his family, each moment of which had been filled with resplendent deeds, had come to an end. The great founder of Islam, the soul of the world, the savior of mankind, had bid farewell to life and departed for the eternal realm. With his departure the link of revelation with this world was severed, and the heavenly manifestations of that blessed being, to describe which is beyond human power, faded away for ever. May God's peace and blessings be upon him and his family.

His immaculate body had not yet been interred. 'Alī, peace be upon him, some members of the Banī Hāshim, and a few Companions were busy washing and enshrouding the body in preparation for burial; they, and they alone, were fully preoccupied with the great blow that had descended and the urgent duty they had to perform.[106]

At the very same time, a group of the Helpers had convened a meeting at a pavilion nearby known as the Saqīfah of the Banī Sā'idah in order to settle the matter of succession to the Prophet in conformity with their own wishes. 'Umar immediately sent a message to Abū Bakr, who at that time was in the house of the Prophet, telling him to join him immediately. Abū Bakr realized that something significant was about to happen, so he left the house and hurried together with 'Umar to the meeting place where the Helpers were meeting, being joined on the way by Abū 'Ubaydah b. al-Jarrāḥ.[107]

Aḥmad Amīn, a well-known Sunnī and Egyptian writer whose stance toward the Shī'ah is negative to the point of fanaticism, writes as follows:

"The Companions of the Prophet, peace and blessings be upon him and his family, were at odds over the question of the succession. It was a sign of their unworthiness that they began arguing over it before the Prophet had even been buried. It was only 'Alī b. Abī Ṭālib, peace be upon him, who did not behave in this fashion, busying himself instead with the washing, enshrouding and burial of the Prophet. The foremost among the Companions were all intriguing over the succession; they had abandoned the body of the Prophet, and no one was present at the burial save 'Alī and his family, or showed any respect for the one who had guided them and brought them forth from the darkness of ignorance. They did not even wait for the burial to take place before they started fighting with each over his legacy."[108]

Different groups were advancing arguments on their own behalf at the Saqīfah. The Helpers claimed to be exceptionally privileged in that they had preceded others in Islam, had enjoyed the respect of the Messenger of God, peace and blessings be upon him and his family, and had struggled hard for the sake of Islam; this, they claimed, entitled them to the leadership. They suggested that the reins of power be entrusted to Sa'd b. 'Ubādah, and had him brought to the Saqīfah even though he was ill.

Similarly, the Migrants claimed that they were the most deserving of the leadership, given the fact that they were from the same city as the Prophet and had abandoned everything for the sake of Islam and the Prophet.

The logic of both groups derived from an essentially tribal spirit, for they were determined to obtain a monopoly on power for themselves, excluding their rivals and condemning them as less deserving.[109]

The discussions wore on and turned into a bitter dispute.

The group headed by 'Umar supported the claims of Abū Bakr, urging everyone to grant him allegiance and threatening anyone who opposed him.

Abū Bakr then rose and began to expound the virtues of the Migrants and the services they had performed:

"The Migrants were the first group to embrace Islam. They despite the arduous circumstances they persevered and refused to abandon monotheism despite the pressures exerted on them by the polytheists. Naturally it should not be forgotten that you, O Helpers, also have rendered great service to Islam and that after the Companions you have primacy over all others." He then added: "We must be the rulers *(umarā')*, and you, our deputies *(wuzarā')*."

Ḥubāb b. al-Mundhir then rose and said: "O Helpers, you must seize the reins of power so firmly that none dare oppose you. If you permit disagreement among yourselves, you will be defeated, with the result that if we choose a leader for ourselves, they will also choose a leader for themselves."

To this 'Umar responded: "There can never be two rulers in one realm. I swear by God that the Arabs will never agree to be ruled by you, for their Prophet was not from among you. Our argument is strong and clear: we are the Companions of the Messenger of God, so who can oppose us, other than those who choose the wrong path or wish to cast themselves into the whirlpool of perdition?"

Ḥubāb b. al-Mundhir stood up again and said: "Pay no heed to what this man says. They want to usurp your rights and to deny you your claims. Take the reins of power into your own hands and banish your opponents, for you are the most worthy to rule. If anyone opposes my proposal, I will rub his nose in the dirt with my sword." Thereupon 'Umar began to tussle with him and kicked him hard in the stomach.[110]

Bashīr b. Sa'd, the cousin of Sa'd b. 'Ubadah rose to support what 'Umar had said. Addressing the Helpers, he proclaimed: "It is true that our record of fighting in God's way and spreading Islam is superior. However, we never had any aim other than God's pleasure and the satisfaction of His

Messenger, peace and blessings be upon him and his family, and it is therefore unfitting that we should boast of precedence over others, for we have no worldly goal. The Prophet was from among the Quraysh, and it is therefore appropriate that his heirs should also be from among them. Fear God, and do not oppose or argue with them."

After a further series of discussions and arguments, Abū Bakr addressed the people as follows:

"Shun dispute and disunity. I desire nothing but your good and your welfare. It is best that you give your allegiance either to 'Umar or to Abū 'Ubaydah."

To this, however, 'Umar countered: "You are more worthy of ruling than either of us, for you preceded us all in following the Prophet, peace and blessings be upon him and his family. In addition to this, your financial resources are greater than those of the rest of us. You were at the side of the Prophet in the cave of Thawr and you led the prayers in his stead. Given all this, who could imagine himself more fitted than you to rule over us?"

As for 'Abd al-Raḥmān b. 'Awf, he expressed himself as follows: "O Helpers, you have indeed many virtuous qualities, which none can deny. We must nonetheless admit that there is none among you comparable to Abū Bakr, 'Umar and 'Alī."

Mundhir b. al-Arqam supported his view: "No one can deny the virtues of those three, and there is in particular one among them whom none will oppose if he assumes the leadership of the Islamic community." By this he meant 'Alī b. Abī Ṭālib, peace be upon him, and a group of the Helpers accordingly began exclaiming in unison: "We will give our allegiance *(bay'ah)* to none but 'Alī."[111]

'Umar recalls that this outcry caused him to fear the emergence of serious dissension. "So I told Abū Bakr to give me his hand for me to swear him allegiance."[112] Without delay Abū Bakr extended his hand. First Bashīr b. Sa'd came forward and grasped his hand as a token of allegiance, and he was followed in this by 'Umar. Then the others rushed forward and gave Abū Bakr their allegiance.[113] While this was proceeding an argument broke out between 'Umar and Sa'd b. 'Ubādah, with the result that Abū Bakr found it necessary to instruct 'Umar to calm himself. Sa'd told his friends to remove him from the scene, so they carried him home on their shoulders.[114]

The crowd that had given allegiance to Abū Bakr accompanied him to the mosque so that others might also pledge him their allegiance. 'Alī, peace be upon him, and 'Abbās were still engaged in washing the body of the Prophet, peace and blessings be upon him and his family, when they heard cries of *Allāhu akbar* coming from the mosque. 'Alī asked: "What is this uproar?" 'Abbās replied: "Something quite unprecedented," and then added, looking at 'Alī, "Did I not tell you that this would happen?"[115]

Abū Bakr mounted the Prophet's pulpit and continued receiving the allegiance of the people until nightfall, without paying any attention to the task of preparing the body of the Prophet for burial. This process continued the following day, and it was not until Tuesday, one day after the death of the Prophet and the pledging of allegiance to Abū Bakr, that the people went to the house of the Prophet to perform the funerary prayers.[116] "Neither Abū Bakr nor 'Umar participated in the burial of the Prophet."[117]

Zubayr b. Bakkār writes: "After the pledging of allegiance to Abū Bakr was all over, a large number of the Helpers regretted what they had done and began blaming each other and mentioning the claims of 'Alī."[118]

The celebrated historian al-Mas'ūdī writes: "After the events at the Saqīfah, 'Alī told Abū Bakr, "You have trampled on my rights, refused to consult with me, and ignored my claims." Abū Bakr's only answer was to say, "Yes, but I was fearful of chaos and disorder."[119]

The meeting that took place at the Saqīfah was **NOT** attended by such prominent personalities as 'Alī,peace be upon him, Abū Dharr, Miqdād, Salmān, Ṭalḥah, al-Zubayr, 'Ubayy b. Ka'b, and Ḥudhayfah, and only three of the Migrants were present.

Should not all the principal Muslims have been invited to

express their views on what was to be done? Was a brief and disorderly meeting, attended by only three of the Migrants, enough to decide on a question on which the future destinies of Islam depended? Did not the gravity of the issue necessitate that it be put before a gathering of the leading Muslims for a final decision to be reached in accordance with their freely expressed views?

What right had those who considered themselves entitled to make a decision have to deprive others of the same opportunity and to disregard them completely? If a certain group citing public opinion as its justification choose a leader or ruler for their society, but does so out of the sight of thoughtful and respected individuals, does their choice truly reflect the wishes of the people? When Sa'd b. 'Ubādah refused to pledge his allegiance, was it necessary to issue an order for his execution?[120]

Historians record that when some of the Banī Hāshim as well as the Migrants and the Helpers refused to pledge allegiance to Abū Bakr, they took refuge in the house of Fāṭimah in order to swear allegiance to 'Alī.[121] A crowd then attacked the house and even entered it in order to disperse the dissidents and, if possible, compel their allegiance to Abū Bakr.[122]

The election of Abū Bakr was so unexpected, hasty and careless that 'Umar remarked later: "It was an accident that Abū Bakr became leader. No consultation or exchange of views took place. If anyone in future invites you to do the same again, kill him."[123]

In addition to this, the fact that the first caliph designated his own successor itself demonstrates that the notion of a consultative government having come into being after the death of the Prophet, peace and blessings be upon him and his family, is entirely baseless. The Prophet issued no directive for such a government to be established; if he had, different groups of people would not have proposed to the first caliph that he designate his own successor to prevent the chaos and disorder that would have engulfed Muslim society because of the lack of a leader.[124]

The caliph responded to this request of the people by saying that if Abū 'Ubaydah were alive, he would have appointed him, for the Prophet had called him "the trustee of the *ummah*." Likewise, if Sālim the client of Abū Ḥudhayfah had been alive, he too would have been worthy of the leadership, because he had heard the Prophet describing him as "the friend of God."[125]

Considering the measures taken by Abū Bakr, how can anyone say that the Messenger of God did not choose a successor before he died?

Likewise, the selection of a successor to 'Umar by a committee he himself appointed was in conformity neither with divine precept nor with the principle of consulting public opinion. If the caliph is meant to appoint his own successor, why turn the matter over to a six-man committee? If, on the other hand, the choice of leader is a prerogative of the people, why did 'Umar deprive people of this right and assign it exclusively to a committee of his own choosing? He also acted restrictively in that he spoke of certain members of the committee in terms that completely disqualified them for the caliphate.

When the Qur'ān expounds the principle of consultation, it orders the Prophet, peace and blessings be upon him and his family, to consult the people in matters affecting them. (3:159) It proclaims, on another occasion: "*The affairs of the believers are to be settled by means of consultation.*" (42:38) What is at issue is consultation concerning social matters, matters that affect the people, not the Imāmate which is a divine covenant. Something that is a divine covenant and pertains to the guidance of mankind cannot be a subject for consultation.

The adoption of the caliphal system in the fashion we have described led necessarily to the exclusion of the Imāms from the realm of rule and leadership.

Lesson Ten
Reliance on Unsound Criteria

The atmosphere at the Saqīfah was such that even if impartial and concerned people had been present they would have been unable to present matters in their true light. The privileges that those gathered there claimed for themselves as their title to the caliphate derived neither from the Book of God nor from the *Sunnah;* not even one of those present mentioned piety, wisdom, moral probity, profound knowledge of the bases and ordinances of Islam, or freedom from pollution by sin, as a qualification for exercising leadership of the Muslims. They totally ignored all the true criteria and attributes required for the office that are intimately connected with the spirit of Islam and the Qur'ān.

This complete lack of attention to spiritual perfection and attainment on the part of those who were laying claim to Islamic rule in that decision making body was particularly regrettable.

When the Helpers were gathered around Sa'd b. 'Ubādah, he addressed them as follows: "O Helpers, you embraced Islam more promptly than others, which constitutes a particular virtue, for the Prophet, peace and blessings be upon him and his family, spent years inviting his own people to Islam without more than a small group coming to believe in him and accepting his summons. Even they were unable to defend themselves, so God Almighty showed you His favor and enabled you to become the defenders of Islam. In the battles and struggles that followed, He caused your superior strength to prevail and to compel the polytheists to surrender. As a result of your efforts the Prophet was strengthened and his enemies were crushed. When he departed this world, he was content with you, and you were the light of his eyes. So lay firm hold of the leadership, for none is more worthy of it than you."[126]

If there had been any concern for the welfare of Islam and the Muslims, thought would have given instead to continuing in the way of the Messenger of God. In place of these criteria, primacy would have been accorded to comprehensive knowledge of the *sharī'ah,* understanding the cultural dimension of religion and the various needs of Islamic society, and freedom from the taint of sin and moral pollution, and one possessing all these attributes would have been chosen as leader entitled to obedience. All the discussions that took place and the arguments that were put forward displayed on the contrary a complete lack of attention to the spiritual and ethical dimensions of succession to the Prophet, so that we find the Helpers vaunting their wealth and their numbers. If they made no reference to more fundamental matters, it was because they had a very small portion of the spiritual and sapiential riches of Islam, nor did they see themselves to be free of pollution by sin. They were thus unable to base their concept of government on exalted values.

Even Abū Bakr confesses that he is neither superior to the rest of the people in terms of knowledge or spiritual accomplishment nor immune from the commission of error and sin. Thus he says:

"O people, I may fall prey to error, just as it is possible that I will make no mistakes. If you see me deviating from the right path, compel me to return to it. For the Prophet, peace and blessings be upon him and his family, was inerrant but I am not; I have a satan that besets me."[127]

'Umar recounted to Ibn 'Abbās the reasons why he regarded 'Alī, peace be upon him, as more qualified for the caliphate: "I swear by God that if your friend 'Alī assumes the caliphate, he will cause the people to act in accordance with the Book of God and the *Sunnah* of the Messenger and will lead them to the straight and clear path of religion."[128]

When Abū 'Ubaydah b. al-Jarrāḥ learned from 'Alī of his refusal to swear allegiance to Abū Bakr, he turned to him and said: "Abandon the leadership of Islamic society to Abū Bakr for the time being. If you remain alive, everyone will come to see that you are the worthiest of all for that post, for your virtues, strong faith, extensive knowledge, early commitment to Islam, and close relationship with the Messenger of God, peace and blessings be upon him and his family, are evident to all."[129]

The Commander of the Faithful, 'Alī, peace be upon him, spelled out for the Companions the distinguished qualities that are needed in the ruler of the Islamic *ummah*, qualities he himself possessed:

"O Migrants, do not remove from the family of the Messenger of God, peace and blessings be upon him and his family, the government that he himself founded, and do not transfer it to your own households. I swear by God that we, the People of the House, are fitter for this task than anyone else. There are among us persons who have complete comprehension of the concepts of the Qur'ān, who are fully aware of the roots and branches of religion and acquainted with the *Sunnah* of the Messenger of God, peace and blessings be upon him and his family, and who are quite capable of administering Islamic society. It is they who can prevent the occurrence of corruption and divide the spoils of war justly among the Muslims. As long as such persons exist — and they are to be found only in the family of the Prophet — others have no legitimate claim. Beware of your wishes and desires lest you go astray and fall into misguidance, turning away from justice and truth."[130]

He also once asked Abū Bakr in conversation: "What are the qualities a leader should possess?"

He answered: "A desire for the people's welfare, faithfulness to his undertakings, justice and equity in his conduct, a knowledge of the Qur'ān, the *Sunnah,* and the principles of judgeship — these are among the qualities that are needed. In addition, the ruler must refrain from deceit, have no concern for the life of this world, hasten always to aid the oppressed, and regard impartially the rights and claims of all." Then he fell silent.

'Alī thereupon remarked: "Further qualities needed are primacy in embracing Islam and being related to the Messenger of God." Abū Bakr responded that these two might also be regarded as necessary qualifications. 'Alī then asked Abū Bakr: "Tell me by God, do you see these qualities in yourself or in me?" He answered: "All that I have mentioned is to be found in you."[131]

Abū Dharr was not present in Madīnah at the time of the Prophet's death, peace and blessings be upon him and his family, and by the time he returned there Abū Bakr had been firmly established as caliph. He remarked: "With what a slight thing you have contented yourselves, while abandoning the Family of the Messenger of God. If you had entrusted rule to them, not even two people would have opposed you."[132]

A certain narrator relates the following concerning Miqdād b. 'Umar: "One day I went to the Prophet's mosque and I saw a man kneeling on the ground. He was sighing as deeply as if he had lost the whole world and saying to himself, 'How strange that the Quraysh have taken the caliphate out of the hands of the Prophet's family!'"[133]

This the way Salmān al-Fārisī commented on the caliphate of Abū Bakr: "You have installed an old man as caliph, while casting aside the Family of the Prophet. Had the caliphate gone to them, not even two people would oppose you, and you would have enjoyed the fruits of this tree in peace and in plenty."[134]

It is related that one day Ibn Musaṭṭaḥ left his house to visit the tomb of the Prophet. Standing there, he recited verses to the following effect: "O Prophet, important events and discussions have transpired since you left us. If you were among us, none of these problems would have occurred. But you have left us, and we are now like parched barren land, deprived of rainfall. Affairs are in disarray. O Prophet, look upon them and bear witness to what they do!"[135]

'Alī b. Abī Ṭālib, peace be upon him, that lofty personage whose profound piety, exemplary Islamic behavior and humane attitudes make of him a model of true Islamic leadership, addressed to God the following words that welled up from the depths of his heart:

"O Lord, You are my witness that I do not seek the caliphate for the sake of exercising rule or adding to my wealth. My aim is to uphold the dictates of religion and bring order into the affairs of the Muslims, so that the oppressed will gain relief and the divine laws and ordinances, now forgotten, be implemented anew."[136]

If an exceptionally lofty personage, one free of sin and adorned with esoteric knowledge, is present in Islamic society, and has moreover been designated by the Messenger of God, peace and blessings be upon him and his family, as his legatee and successor, it is totally unnecessary and inappropriate that a council be formed in order to select a ruler and leader. In the time of the Prophet, no one imagined that his task was simply to transmit the divine message and that as far as governmental matters were concerned, a council ought to be convened to choose either the Prophet or some other individual as ruler, on the basis of public opinion. Given the presence of one who was in direct communication with the principle of all being and the world of revelation, the question of discussing who should be the ruler did not even arise.

The situation was no different after the Prophet. Given the presence of his legatees who outstripped all others in their awareness of God's decrees and who were utterly beyond the reach of all error and sin, why should anyone else have been sought out to take the place of the one who had brought the Qur'ān? Government is after all a part of the Imāmate. The presence of an inerrant Imām means that no one else is fit to rule, in just the same way that when the Prophet was alive no one else was entitled to assume the responsibility of governing the Muslims and administering their affairs.

The celebrated Sunnī scholar Ibn Abi 'l-Ḥadīd writes: "We recognize no difference between 'Alī, peace be upon him, and the Most Noble Prophet, peace and blessings be upon him and his family, apart from the rank of prophethood and the receipt of revelation that the latter enjoyed. All other lofty qualities and exalted attributes were common to both men."[137]

Shaykh Sulaymān al-Ḥanafī, another Sunnī scholar, relates 'Abdullāh b. 'Umar b. al-Khaṭṭāb to have said: "Whenever we talked of the Companions of the Messenger of God, we would say that Abū Bakr was the foremost among them, followed by 'Umar and 'Uthmān in that order." Someone then asked 'Abdullāh: "What then was the rank of 'Alī?" He responded: "'Alī could not be compared to the Companions. In fact he did not count as one of them, belonging rather to the Family of the Prophet; he was his brother and peer."[138]

Even supposing the logic of the Companions to be acceptable, the claim of 'Alī b. Abī Ṭālib would still be the strongest. He preceded all others in accepting Islam, embracing the faith in the most unfavorable circumstances, at a time when none of the relatives of the Prophet, peace and blessings be upon him and his family, were prepared to believe in him. Similarly, his close relationship and kinship with the Prophet was firmer than that of anyone else. It was in the house of the Messenger that he opened his eyes on the world and under his supervision that he grew up. The very depths of his being were intermingled with the truths of Islam. He was the son-in-law and cousin of the Prophet and he always participated in the arduous struggles against the enemies of Islam. Who then can be more fitted than him for the leadership of the Muslims? Despite all this, that position of leadership was awarded to somebody else.

When we examine history discover the roots of the Companions' behavior, we see that the relations of the Quraysh with the Banī Hāshim were by no means as friendly as they should have been. The lack of harmony was apparent even during the lifetime of the Most Noble

Messenger. Sometimes certain members of Quraysh would criticize and find fault with the Banī Hāshim, causing grief to the Prophet.[139]

Since the Quraysh were unable to bear the caliphate going to the Banī Hāshim, they decided to prevent this from coming about.[140] al-Ya'qūbī writes in his history: "'Umar told Ibn 'Abbās: 'I swear by God that your cousin 'Alī b. Abī Ṭālib is more deserving of the caliphate than anyone else. However, the Quraysh cannot bear seeing him in that position.'"[141] This matter is also recorded by Ibn al-Athīr in his history.[142]

The Most Noble Messenger, peace and blessings be upon him and his family, foresaw how the Quraysh would treat his family: "After my death my family will suffer massacres and numerous hardships."[143]

With profound sorrow he also told 'Alī: "Some individuals harbor in their hearts a hatred for you that they will not display until after my death."[144]

We may thus establish a connection between the events that occurred after the death of the Messenger of God, peace and blessings be upon him and his family, and the attitude of many of the Companions to 'Alī, peace be upon him, on the one hand with dislike felt for the Family of the Prophet by the Qurayshi Migrants on the other hand.

This negative attitude on the part of the Quraysh goes back to the beginning of the Prophet's mission. Although they were well aware of his truthfulness, trustworthiness and honesty, they refused to accept his summons of faith. The Quraysh thought that if they were to accept his messengerhood, the Banī Hāshim would come to prevail over all the other families of Quraysh. So strong were the feelings of jealousy this prospect aroused that they decided to act coercively against him, blockading him and his close relatives and not shrinking from any form of pressure or intimidation. In the end, they drew up a plan to assassinate him, and their conspiracies compelled him to quit his city and homeland. Even then they did not sit quite; they had recourse to military measures, mobilizing all their forces in order to annihilate the

Messenger of God and his followers.

Throughout all these trials and struggles, 'Alī was the stalwart ally of the Prophet, his powerful right hand; in the bloody battles that ensued, many of the leading Qurayshites, filled as they were with hatred and resentment, were brought low by him. The Quraysh thus regarded him as responsible for the deaths of their leaders, their sons and their brothers, and although they lost all hope of victory over the Prophet after the conquest of Makkah and their military operations came to an end, their desire for revenge on the Banī Hāshim in general and 'Alī in particular never abated, continuing to smoulder within them.

The Commander of the Faithful, 'Alī, peace be upon him, said: "The hatred for the Prophet that lurked in the hearts of the Quraysh found its expression against me, and indeed it will be transferred to my descendants after me. Yet I had no hostility toward the Quraysh, and if I warred against them, it was only in accordance with divine duty and the command of the Prophet, peace and blessings be upon him and his family."[145]

al-Miqdād b. al-Aswad, who regarded the caliphate as rightfully belonging to the one whom the Prophet had chosen — that is, to 'Alī — became agitated when he saw the Quraysh laying claim to something that was not theirs. He said to them, as they were gathered in their council:

"Amazing it is that the Quraysh wish to deny the caliphate to the Family of the Prophet. I swear by God that they do this not for the sake of God's pleasure but for the sake of worldly benefit; they have totally forgotten the hereafter."[146]

To 'Abd al-Raḥmān b. 'Awf, who later planned the swearing of allegiance to 'Uthmān, he said: "I swear by God that you have put aside one who enjoined the right and practised justice faithfully. I swear too that if I had men to help me, I would fight now as I did at Badr and Uḥud." 'Abd al-Raḥmān responded: "These words of yours will sow dissension." al-Miqdād retorted: "He who invites men to the truth and to obey the holders of legitimate authority cannot be accused of dissension. Rather it is those who drown men in falsehood who are the originators of dissension and chaos; they prefer their own desires to justice and truth."[147]

al-Miqdād was a pure and precious Muslim, well known for his piety, asceticism and devotion to Islam.

In his *al-Sunan*, al-Tirmidhī records the Prophet to have said: "Each prophet is given seven choice companions, but I have been given fourteen, and 'Ammār and al-Miqdād are among them."[148]

Islamic government thus fell into the hands of persons who had no divine guarantee exemption from sin, and gradually the caliphate degenerated to such a degree that the whole atmosphere of Islamic society was poisoned, losing all trace of piety, brotherhood and equality, and the spiritual and religious resources of Islam were utterly lost during the Umayyad and 'Abbāsid periods.

After allegiance had been sworn to 'Uthmān, the Banī Umayyah gathered in his house, and Abū Sufyān addressed them as follows: "Are there any strangers among you?" "No," they answered. He continued: "O Banī Umayyah, take the caliphate from the hands of the Banī Hashim as if it were a ball, for there is no reckoning or judgement to be feared in the hereafter; there is no paradise and no hell, no judgement and no resurrection."[149]

'Uthmān dissuaded him from continuing in this vein, so Abū Sufyān, who was blind by this point, set out for the tomb of Ḥamzah, the Lord of the Martyrs, accompanied by a guide. Standing next to the grave, he addressed Ḥamzah: "O Abū 'Ammārah, the government that we conquered by the sword is today a plaything in the hands of our slaves." Then he kicked the side of the tomb.[150]

'Alī asked the person who was reporting to him the doings at the Saqīfah and the discussions of the Migrants and the Helpers: "What privilege do the Quraysh claim entitles them to the caliphate?" He answered: "They say they are the family tree of the Prophet and related to him." 'Alī then remarked: "They make mention of the tree, but destroy the fruit of the tree. If they are worthy of the caliphate because they are branches of that tree, I am its fruit, the cousin of God's Messenger. Why do they oppose me in this matter and why is the caliphate not mine?"[151]

In expounding the exclusive relationship he had with the Prophet, peace and blessings be upon him and his family, and the care that the Prophet lavished on his upbringing, 'Alī said the following:

"You must certainly be aware of my closeness to the Prophet, my kinship with him, and the rank I enjoyed in his sight. When I was a child, he supervised my upbringing in his own house. I touched the body of the Prophet and I can still remember its scent. He would put food in my mouth. He never heard a lie from me nor did he ever see guile and hypocrisy from me. I followed and imitated him in all matters so closely that my footsteps were placed in his. Every day he displayed his noble qualities and virtues to me, thus advancing me to ever higher degrees. He would take me with him to Mount Ḥirā and unveil truths to me. At that time, the only Muslim house was that of the Prophet and Khadījah, and I was the third member of that house. I saw the light of divine revelation and I inhaled the scent of prophethood."[152]

Although the Prophet, peace and blessings be upon him and his family, regarded the matter of government and leadership as dependent on God's will and choice, not even awarding himself any choice in the matter, a group of men made up a set of criteria which they claimed gave them prior claim to leadership. It was as if the question of succession to the Prophet could be resolved by referring exclusively to tribal considerations and unimportant distinctions that were utterly unconnected with the exalted values of Islam.

Muḥammad b. Muslim al-Zuhrī relates: "When the Most Noble Messenger went to the Banī 'Āmir to invite them to Islam, a man by the name of Bayḥarah said: 'By God, if this young man allies himself with me, with his help I can conquer all the Arabs.' Then he turned to the Prophet and asked: 'If we accept all your commands and you conquer your enemies with our help, do you promise that after your death rule will pass to us?' The Most Noble Messenger answered: 'The matter of government belongs to God; He will appoint to rule whomsoever He wills.' The man replied: 'Are we to endanger ourselves defending you against your enemies only to see rule passing to others?'"[153]

Lesson Eleven
Answer to an Objection

There are people who think that if government were to originate with the people themselves, with the members of society choosing their own leader from among qualified persons, relying in their choice on their own desires, perceptive capacities and relative knowledge of the strong and weak points of various individuals, this would be more in accord with freedom and democracy and thus enable mankind to attain its highest ideal. They imagine further that if the people are not permitted to have any share in the choice and designation of their leader and if the office of Imām or caliph is not a fully elected one, the people will see in him simply a ruler who has been imposed on them.

The error underlying this view is the identification of the appointed office of the Imām with tyranny. However, we see that in world politics tyranny comes to prevail as the result of a coup d'etat, a revolution, or a military intervention, and all that counts in a tyranny is the personal views and decisions of the ruler.

However, from the point of view of Shī'ism, there are certain inviolable criteria for the post of Islamic leadership. If someone lacks those criteria, it is impossible for him to lead Islamic society or to be recognized as its legitimate ruler. The rationale for the appointed nature of the post of Imām is that the Lord of the Worlds knows His creation perfectly; He knows the nature of man and his interaction with the world better than any scholar, and is better aware than people are themselves of their own interests. Hence it is that He chooses as the leader and guardian of the Muslims the best and worthiest individual, one who has unique attributes such as complete immunity from sin and a life utterly free from the pull of instinctual desire. The one so chosen by God has himself no right to legislate, and since the Islamic concept of law is based on God's exclusive legislative prerogative, his sole point of reference is God's laws and commands, as they descended by way of revelation into the pure heart of the Prophet, peace and blessings be upon him and his family. In all his programs and plans, the divinely chosen leader draws inspiration exclusively from religion, striving always to implement God's commands as a matter of duty.

When God is the source of all legislation, His laws necessarily embrace all the true interests of man.They are in full accord with his primordial and immutable nature; ensure the fulfilment of justice in public life; and make it possible for man to ascend through the degrees of perfection. It is, of course, true at the same time that these laws may be opposed to man's personal inclinations and his self-interest, and that some may experience God's commands as arduous and in conflict with their temperament.

When the ruler is selected by God, Who is Himself the sole possessor of sovereignty, he will necessarily be free of all taint of sinfulness, disobedience, and oppression, and the only goal he pursues will be the welfare and benefit of society, the guidance of the *ummah*, and the construction of a pure and exalted community based on justice. A government of this type will be utterly incompatible with arbitrariness, oppression, and the usurpation of rights.

If religion lays down certain conditions for rulership and restricts people's right to choose, this in no way contradicts their possession of sovereignty. For society has already given its free consent to a system of rule based on its beliefs and is in fact inwardly devoted to such a system. The principle of popular sovereignty is thus limited by certain conditions that are deemed necessary by the religious beliefs accepted by the people.

Furthermore, in democratic governments, which are elected by majority vote, the ruler is always concerned with either winning the support of popular opinion or with following popular wishes, with no criterion available for measuring the legitimacy of those wishes. For that which determines those desires and inclinations are the circumstances in which a person grows up and which influence his attitudes towards the individual and society, towards history and the laws which he supposes to be the best for his particular society.

What is important for a politician in this system of government is to align himself with the views of the majority of his constituents, irrespective of whether or not his performance in social and administrative matters conforms to the principles of justice. His sole concern is to keep the social and political privileges he has obtained, and he may sometimes trample on the truth in order to avoid endangering his position. Rare are those who have no fear of public opinion and base their decisions solely on the welfare of the society.

A celebrated writer on politics by the name of Frank Cont(?) remarks: "The necessity of obtaining a majority of the votes represents a very serious and grave problem, for in striving after that goal no consideration can be given to ethical matters or to right and wrong."[154]

Nonetheless, this is the mode of government favored by the adherents of liberty in today's world, a system in which truth, justice and conscience are treated as mere playthings. If this indeed be the nature of the system, is it all permissible that the successors to the Prophet, peace and blessings be upon him and his family, should be chosen and exercise their functions in accordance with it? Can, for example, a group of Muslims come together, select a certain individual according to their own criteria, and then trust to him rule over the Muslims?

Can someone who is unacquainted with the culture and the principles of religion and the detailed injunctions of divine law build a fully Islamic society if he is appointed ruler? Can he implement God's laws in society with the necessary care, precision, and trustworthiness? If new, unprecedented circumstances arise, what knowledge or divinely bestowed insight can he draw on in order to derive a specific ruling for those circumstances from the general principles of the *sharī'ah* and then to implement it in the public interest? Furthermore, in systems where the government is chosen by the majority, the views of the minority are ignored, so that, for example, a minority consisting of 49% of the people is obliged to submit to the views and preferences of persons who have come to power against their wishes.

For the opinions of such a large group of people to be ignored is in no way compatible with the principles of justice. Is there any reason for them to regard themselves as accountable to a government elected by the majority? Why should they be deprived of their freedom and their desires be crushed? The argument that the choice of the majority reflects the overall interests of society is unconvincing and fails to establish a duty of obedience and accountability on the part of the minority. The question therefore remains: on what basis is the minority obliged to submit to majority decision and to obey the views and wishes of others?

The laws approved by the majority and imposed on the entirety of the people may sometimes be harmful to society and damaging to its true progress and development.

If truth is indeed truth, it does not become falsehood merely because its followers are few in number or in the minority; and if falsehood is indeed falsehood, it does not become transformed into truth through the support of the majority. It may be that majorty opinion is regularly taken as the principle on which to operate because it is allegedly less prone to error, but no proof exists for the proposition that the wishes of the majority are inherently better or more valuable than the inclinations of the minority, nor for the claim that those wishes possess an intrinsic legitimacy making them the proper source of all legislation and the basis for human life.

Communist countries which claim to implement

democracy within the framework of Marxism belong in the final analysis to the category of despotism, since in them the Communist party possesses absolute sovereignty and imposes its will on the masses.

By contrast, when the selection of the leader is a matter of divine prerogative, acceptance of that leader is equivalent to submission to God's sovereignty, a submission eagerly undertaken, for reason confirms the necessity of obedience to the Creator and man discerns in adherence to divine command the source of happiness and well being in this world and the hereafter. There is no longer any question of minority or majority, because the government is the government of God, before Whom all are supremely responsible as the source of all existence, the origin of man's being and perfection, and the fount of infinite bounty. It is He alone Who is deserving of obedience and Whose ordinances and laws command compliance. His laws are promulgated in accordance with the norms of nature and inspired by a comprehensive awareness of the essence of social relations with the result that they are intrinsically just and bound to secure the benefit, well being and happiness of man. The suspicion can never arise that personal motivation or self-interest on the part of the lawgiver is at work.

A society believing in God has no reason to follow the majority, a majority which might well choose an incorrect path in various matters and the judgement of which might prove erroneous. Many people in whom great hopes were placed and who came to power by overwhelming majority vote swiftly came to inspire despair rather than hope, and anger and enmity rather than love and affection.

It can thus be concluded that the views and inclinations of the majority, the result of experiences that are necessarily fallible, cannot form a basis for solving the problems of humanity or instilling justice into the life of the individual and society, nor can they guarantee the happiness and welfare of man.

Lesson Twelve
Shī'ism in the Course of History

Scholars and researchers have expressed different views concerning the birth of Shī'ism and its first appearance. Others too have attempted to evaluate it, approaching it from the point of view of their respective ideological and intellectual predispositions.

Some people believe that Shī'ism arose after the death of the Messenger of God, peace and blessings be upon him and his family, and that its defining essence took shape when his Companions set about selecting his successor. Thus the historian al-Ya'qūbī writes:

"A number of the Migrants and the Helpers refused to swear allegiance to Abū Bakr, inclined as they were to favor 'Alī b. Abī Ṭālib, peace be upon him! al-'Abbās b. 'Abd al-Muṭṭalib, al-Faḍl b. al-'Abbās, al-Zubayr, Khālid b. Sa'īd, al-Miqdād, Salmān, Abū Dharr, 'Ammār, al-Barā'a, Ubayy b. Ka'b were part of this group."[155]

al-Mas'ūdī, also a famous historian, writes:

"Salmān al-Fārisī was a Shī'ī from the very outset, and 'Ammār b. Yāsir was known as a Shī'ī throughout his life. When 'Uthmān was elected to the caliphate, he remarked: 'It is not the first time you have denied the caliphate to the one deserving it!' Abū Dharr was similarly an outstanding proponent of Shī'īsm."[156]

Another group of scholars place the emergence of Shī'ism during the caliphate of 'Alī b. Abī Ṭālib, peace be upon him, while others suggest that it began to take root towards the end of the caliphate of 'Uthmān. Still others regard Imām al-Ṣādiq, peace be upon him, as the founder of Shī'ism. Some people again imagine Shī'ism to be the result of a wish for revenge nurtured by the Iranians, so that its origins may be considered essentially political.

Then there are those who see in Shī'ism a contingent phenomenon in Islamic society and history, without any strong presence or substance. They imagine it to have gradually expanded in Islamic society as the result of certain social and political developments at a relatively advanced point in Islamic history. There are even those who assert this segment of the Islamic *ummah* to be the brainchild of an imaginary personality by the name of 'Abdullāh b. Sabā', basing on this assumption all their judgements concerning Shī'ism and concluding that Shī'ism is nothing more than an anomaly.[157]

Theories such as this amount to nothing more than obstinate calumnies, perpetrated to conceal the truth; or at the very best they spring from complete ignorance of the true culture of Shī'ism and its rich heritage.

Dr. Ṭāhā Ḥusayn, a well-known Egyptian and therefore Sunnī scholar, writes:

"The fact that the historians make no mention of Ibn al-Sawdā' — i.e., 'Abdullāh b. Sabā' — being present at the battle of Ṣiffīn together with his followers proves at the very least that the whole notion of a group of people led by him is a baseless fabrication. It is one of those inventions that acquired currency when the conflict between the Shī'is and other Islamic groups intensified. In order to underline their hostility, the enemies of the Shī'ah tried to insert a Jewish element into the origins of their sect. If the story of 'Abdullāh b. Sabā' had any basis in historical fact, his cunning and guile could not have failed to show itself at the battle of Ṣiffīn.

"I can think of only one reason for his name not occurring in connection with that battle: that he was an entirely fictitious person, dreamed up by the enemies of the Shī'ah in order to vilify them."[158]

Similarly, Dr. 'Alī al-Wardī, professor of history at Baghdād University, writes:

"Did Ibn Sabā' actually exist or was he an imaginary personality? For those who wish to study the social history of Islam and draw the appropriate conclusions, this is an extremely important question. It is claimed that Ibn Sabā' incited unrest, but no such person ever existed. The whole story is reminiscent of the claim made by the Quraysh at the beginning of the Prophet's mission, peace and blessings be upon him and his family, that he received his teachings from a Christian slave by the name of Jabr and based his preaching on the instruction he received from him."[159]

Muḥammad Kurd 'Alī, another Sunnī scholar, writes:

"Some of the well-known Companions who at the dawn of Islam followed 'Alī, peace be upon him, became known as the Shī'ah. What can be deduced from the written sources is that certain shortsighted people regarded Shī'ism as a collection of innovations and fabrications stitched together by a person known 'Abdullāh b. Sabā' or Ibn al-Sawdā'. However, there can be no doubt that this view of things is pure superstition and fantasy, for this 'Abdullāh b. Sabā' the Jew exists only in the world of the imagination. Any attempt to link the origins of Shī'ism to him must be regarded as a sign of pure ignorance."[160]

In contrast to all the opinions reviewed so far, one group of scholars believe Shī'ism to have been first expounded by none other than the Prophet himself, peace and blessings be upon him and his family, and that it was established in conformity with his command.

Ḥasan b. Mūsā al-Nawbakhtī and Sa'd b. 'Abdullāh write:

"The party of 'Alī b. Abī Ṭālib, peace be upon him, was the first to emerge in the time of the Prophet, peace and blessings be upon him and his family, and it became known as the Shī'ah (=partisans) of 'Alī. It was known that they favored 'Alī for the leadership of the community and that they were his devoted companions. al-Miqdād, Salmān, Abū Dharr and 'Ammār belonged to this group, and they were the first to be called Shī'ī. Use of the word Shī'ah was not new; it had been applied in the past to the followers of some prophets such as Nūḥ, Ibrāhīm, Mūsā, and 'Īsā."[161]

This view is confirmed by numerous Shī'ī scholars, and there are many traditions to the effect that the Prophet, peace and blessings be upon him and his family, applied the name Shī'ah to the companions and followers of 'Alī, peace be upon him.

When discussing the occasion for the revelation of this verse, "*Certainly those who believe in the One God and who do good deeds are in truth the best people in the world*" (98:7), Sunnī exegetes *(mufassirīn)* and traditionists *(muḥaddithīn)* report Jābir b. 'Abdullāh to have said: "One day I came to the presence of the Prophet, peace and blessings be upon him and his family, 'Alī entered the room, causing the Prophet to remark, 'My brother has come. I swear by God that this man and his *shī'ah* (supporters) will be among the saved on the Day of Resurrection.'"[162]

al-Ṭabarī, the well-known Sunnī exegete and historian, also remarks in connection with the same verse that the Prophet used the word *shī'ah* when referring to the supporters of 'Alī.

There is then prophetic authority for designating the followers of 'Alī, those who were particularly devoted to him, as Shī'ah.

We thus see that the word Shī'ah is essentially coterminous with Islam itself, for the Prophet himself used it. If we sometimes use the designation Ja'farī Shī'ism, this is on account of the exertions made by Imām Ja'far al-Ṣādiq to disseminate the culture of Islam and Shī'ism. The struggles for power that were taking place in his lifetime afforded him a suitable opportunity to confront the political conditions of his environment. The various ideas that were gaining currency and the foreign elements such as analogical reasoning and preference that had entered Islamic jurisprudence caused him to embark on a program of teaching and reform.

Muḥammad Fikrī Abu 'l-Naṣr, a well-known Egyptian

Sunnī author, has the following to say with respect to the essence of Shī'ism:

"In its theological principles, Shī'ism has nothing to do with Abu 'l-Ḥasan al-Ash'arī, and in its detailed legal provisions nothing to do with any of the four Sunnī schools of law. For the school established by the Imāms of the Shī'ah is more ancient, and therefore more reliable and more deserving to be followed than the other schools. All Muslims followed their school for the first three centuries of Islam. The Shī'ah school of law is also more worth following because in it the gate of independent reasoning *(ijtihād)* will remain open until resurrection, and because its formation was totally uninfluenced by political factors and struggles."[163]

Abu 'l-Wafā' al-Ghunaymī al-Taftāzānī, another Sunnī scholar, says the following:

"Numerous researchers of the past and the present, in both the East and the West, have expressed erroneous views concerning Shī'ism. People then unquestioningly repeat these views, without adducing the slightest evidence or proof. One of the reasons that has led to Shī'ism being thus unjustly treated is that those who originate and spread such views are unacquainted with the books of the Shī'ah themselves and rely exclusively on the writings of their enemies. Western imperialism has also played a role in this regard by constantly attempting to sow dissension among Shī'is and Sunnīs and propagating unfair and controversial theses in the name of unfettered academic research."[164]

These remarks permit us to grasp well the depth of the distortion that has taken place, the extent of deviation from the truth, as well as the mentality of those who have been inspired by their own impure motives or influenced by political factors. Instead of giving primacy to the interests of the Qur'ān, Islam and the unifying *qiblah* of all Muslims, they compete with each other in sowing dissension and causing disunity; Islam itself is sacrificed to their goals, and the common enemy of all Muslims profits.

It is essential to add the following point, that the

designation Shī'ah in the time of the Prophet, peace and blessings be upon him and his family, did not apply to a group that was seeking to detach itself from the rest of the Muslims. It is simply that a certain number of Muslims in the time of the Prophet considered 'Alī, peace be upon him, superior to all others in his knowledge of the truths of Islam and the values and aims of the Prophet's mission. They were profoundly attached to him on account of his lofty insight and vision, his link to the source of all perfection, and, in short, all his moral and spiritual qualities. He inspired them as a perfect specimen of humanity worthy of their imitation.

It is of course true that the Shī'ah first appeared on the scene as a distinct group after the death of the Most Noble Prophet, peace and blessings be upon him and his family, when the close companions of 'Alī, peace be upon him, refused in the wake of the meeting at the Saqīfah to swear allegiance to Abū Bakr and proclaimed themselves as a party among the Muslims dedicated to defending the clear and unambiguous texts providing for the entrusting of rule over the Muslims to 'Alī.[165] Rejecting the attempt made at the Saqīfah to neutralize his claim and the recourse that was had to the thesis of "the welfare of the Muslims," they separated themselves from the majority and formed a group devoted to him.

In this group were to be found such outstanding Companions as 'Ammār, Abū Dharr, al-Miqdād, Salmān and Ibn 'Abbās, whose sincerity, devotion and commitment had been praised by the Prophet. Thus he said of 'Ammār and his parents:

"Be patient and steadfast, O family of Yāsir, for Paradise is your destiny."[166] "O 'Ammār, glad tidings be unto you, for the oppressors will kill you."[167]

He also proclaimed the kindness and favor God had shown to four great personages: "God has enjoined on me the love of four people, and informed me that He himself loves them." When asked who they were, he replied: "'Alī (repeating the name three times), Abū Dharr, Salmān, and al-Miqdād."[168]

He spoke as follows of the sincerity and piety of Abū

Dharr: "The blue sky has not sheltered, nor has the earth borne, one more honest than Abū Dharr; he lives upon earth with the same ascetic detachment as 'Īsā the son of Maryam."[169]

Referring to the station in the hereafter of three persons, he said: "Paradise longs for three persons: 'Alī, Yāsir, and Salmān."[170]

The Prophet supplicated for Ibn 'Abbās as follows: "O God, teach him the science of interpreting the Qur'ān, make him erudite in all things religious, and establish him as a believer."[171]

These then were the devoted followers of 'Alī, peace be upon him, men convinced that he should have been the immediate successor of the Messenger of God, peace and blessings be upon him and his family, and that the caliphate was his indubitable right.

That which was a matter of dispute and disagreement after the death of the Prophet was the question of succession to the political leadership, not the Imāmate, which included the spiritual dimension of the Prophet's legacy. No one at the Saqīfah had anything to say about choosing an Imām, and the question was not even raised. Was this because nobody had the least doubt concerning 'Alī's supremacy in spiritual matters, or was it that because none of the claimants to the caliphate and the succession was qualified for the Imāmate no one laid claim to it? The truth of the matter is unclear.

For some time then there was no mention of the Imāmate. But after the death of several of the caliphs, the question gradually came to the fore, and some of the caliphs, like Mu'āwiyah, for all his lack of commitment to Islam, began calling themselves Imāms.

The topic discussed in works of theology is the Imām and the Imāmate, while the terms used in books of history and the oral and written statements of Sunnī scholars are caliph and caliphate. 'Alī and his descendants, recognized as the leaders of the Shī'ah are however consistently referred to as Imāms. This reflects the Shī'ī belief that strict and precise adherence to the criteria of religion, unswerving piety, and a whole series of other special qualities, must be present in the person of the Imām.

One of the pupils of Imām Ja'far al-Ṣādiq, peace be upon him, Hishām b. Ḥakam, wrote a book on the subject of the Imāmate in which he set forth its theoretical bases.[172]

In addition to the office of prophethood, which comprised the responsibility for receiving and conveying revelation to mankind, the Prophet was the ruler of the Muslims, empowered over all their affairs. From the moment on that the Muslims established a collective existence, all the societal affairs of the people were regulated by the Prophet: the appointment of governors, commanders, and judges; the distribution of booty; the issuance of orders for war; and so on. He implemented divine commands and ordinances in accordance with the ruling function that was vested in him, and it was the duty of the people to obey his commands and instructions.

Rulership, the administration of society, and the establishment of public order and security were thus part of his prophetic function; prophethood and spiritual leadership on the one hand and leadership and rule on the other were both combined in a single divinely chosen person.

The dispute that occurred after his death related only to leadership and rule, so that those people who aspired to the position of rule after the Prophet never advanced any claim of special communication with God or the receipt of revelation, nor did they present themselves as spiritual leaders or guides. Their whole ideal was to seize the reins of power and administer the affairs of the Muslims, paying attention only to the need of preserving the unified society of Islam from disorder and discord by means of careful strategy and plan.

When the people swore allegiance to Abū Bakr after the death of the Prophet, peace and blessings be upon him and his family, Abū 'Ubaydah proposed to 'Alī, peace be upon him: "Abandon this matter to Abū Bakr. If you survive him, you are worthier of the office of caliph than anyone else, for none can doubt your abundant faith, virtue, and intelligence.

Furthermore, you preceded others in your profession of Islam, and you enjoy the additional advantage of being related to the Messenger of God by blood and by marriage." 'Alī replied:

"O Migrants! I entreat you by God not to remove governance from the Household of the Prophet, and to establish it in your house; do not deprive the People of Muḥammad's House of their station and office."[173]

Lesson Thirteen
The True Nature of the Holders of Authority

After the death of the founder of Islam and the emergence of a whole series of verbal disputes concerning the caliphate and succession to the Prophet, the question of the "holders of authority" *(ulu 'l-amr)* came to the fore as a controversial topic bound up with the various intellectual and political currents of the day. Naturally, the expression had not been foreign to the vocabulary and thoughts of the Muslims in the past; people had been acquainted with it since the very dawn of Islam and used it in their discourse.

We find, in fact, that when the Prophet, peace and blessings be upon him and his family, began proclaiming his mission, messages would pass back and forth between him and the Meccan polytheists in which the word *amr* (authority) was used. Thus the polytheists and unbelievers who were enraged by the appearance of the new religion, sent the following message to the Messenger of God:

"O Muḥammad, do not attack our idols and desist from affronting our objects of worship, for we are ready to submit to you in all you desire." When Abū Ṭālib conveyed this message of the Quraysh to the Prophet, he replied: "If you were to place the sun in my right hand and the moon in my left, I will not abandon this *amr*. I cannot possibly agree; either God will make His religion triumph, or I will die engaged in this struggle."[174]

After the people had finished swearing allegiance to Abū Bakr, Abū 'Ubaydah made this request to 'Alī, peace be upon him: "Now abandon this *amr* to Abū Bakr."[175]

What is meant by *amr* in both these instances is nothing other than governance and rule.

The Noble Qur'ān issues the following command to the Muslims, summoning them to obey the orders and instructions of God, the Messenger and the "holders of authority":

"*O believers, obey the commands of God, the Messenger and the Holders of Authority. When you fall into disagreement concerning your affairs, refer to the commands of the Lord and His Messenger, if you believe in God and the Day of Judgement. This will be better for you than anything else you might imagine, and conducive to a far better outcome*" (4:58).

This verse makes plain the true sources of authority in the various religious and social concerns confronting the Muslims. It first commands the believers to submit unreservedly and unconditionally to the commands of the Creator of the universe and all who inhabit it, for He bestows being on all phenomena and is their master and owner. All forms of leadership must necessarily derive from His sacred being, and all forms of obedience must issue in obedience to Him. Obedience is necessitated and required by the Lord's attributes of ruler and creator, and since God is the origin of all legislation, the source of all commands and prohibitions, the role of the Prophet, peace and blessings be upon him and his family, is in the first place the receipt of divine revelation and conveying to mankind what he is entrusted with conveying.

Next comes obedience to the Prophet who is God's representative among men, a prophet who is divinely protected against error and sin and who never speaks arbitrarily or out of mere fancy. In addition to the divine message and commands that he conveys, he has a specific set of plans and strategies for implementing the ordinances of God's religion. The exercise of government requires the choice of a certain policy that will respond to the needs of society, a policy that in Islam was determined by the great leader of religion who perceived wherein lay the welfare of the *ummah* and issued commands that addressed themselves to current circumstances and were informed by an awareness of what leads to social equilibrium. This type of legislation was delegated to the Prophet by God and derived its efficacy and legitimacy from God, the ultimate master of all.

It is clear from the preceding that obedience to the Prophet, being the result of God's command, may also be regarded as a form of obedience to God, in just the same way that disobedience to him is in reality disobedience to God. This is set forth clearly in the following verse: "*Whoever obeys the Messenger has obeyed God.*" (4:80) The conveyance of any decision taken by the Prophet is therefore equivalent to the promulgation of an order from God.

The third aspect of the Qur'anic injuction concerning obedience relates to the Holders of Authority, obedience to whom God has conjoined with obedience to Himself and Messenger. What is meant by the Holders of Authority are those persons to whom the ruling and governmental functions peculiar to the Prophet have been transferred, to whom the leadership of Islamic society has been entrusted by God and His Messenger, and who are the guardians of the religious and worldly affairs of the people. They are empowered to issue, in the light of God's laws, commands and ordinances for the administration of society, and to oblige people to obey them. The necessity of obeying the wishes of the Holders of Authority is, then, categorical and beyond all doubt; it is only in establishing the criteria for identifying the Holders of Authority that there can be any room for discussion or disagreement.

Now let us see what the Qur'ān means by the Holders of Authority *(ulu'l-amr)*. Can the one who happens to head an Islamic government having seized power over society be regarded as one of the Holders of Authority, in the sense that people are obliged to obey anyone who assigns himself the right to rule, even if he spends his whole life sunken in the darkness of sin and the oblivion of ignorance; is utterly devoid of all spiritual brilliance; is utterly unaware of God's laws and commandments; sacrifices the rights of the people to his own tyranny and lusts; and promotes oppressors and the workers of corruption to positions of power, so that the cries of the oppressed are stifled and the overwhelming majority of Islamic society is imprisoned in the chains of humiliation?

If the expression Holders of Authority be interpreted in such a sense, it would be in stark contradiction with the parts of the verse that precede and follow it. For if the ruler issues a command at variance with God's laws, the first part of the verse affirms that those laws must necessarily be implemented and have priority over all else. Yet the verse proclaims too that the commands of the Holders of Authority are to be obeyed! It is obvious that the Qur'ān cannot enjoin at the same two contradictory things, or both command and forbid the same thing simultaneously.

In addition, wisdom and intelligence cannot accept the notion that it is incumbent to submit to absolutely any ruler, even if he violates God's laws and attempts to banish them from society.

How can one believe that on the one hand God should have mobilized His prophets to implement divine law, establish justice, and propagate the essence of religion, even at the cost of their lives, and that on the other hand He should impose upon people the duty of obeying the wishes of rulers who not only do nothing to protect the *ummah* and advance its religious awareness but even wish to nullify all the strivings of the prophets, trample God's law under foot, and enthrone tyranny and oppression in society?

Can the happiness and salvation of society be attained by following such rulers? Can such a government enable the Muslims to attain power and dignity? Can one ascribe to God the illegitimate and foolish view that such rulers deserve obedience?

Of course it might be possible to restrict obedience to the Holder of Authority to those cases where his edicts conform to the criteria of divine law, making it obligatory for Muslims to oppose him whenever he acts in a sense contrary to it.

However, there are certain difficulties connected with this

view of things that cannot be overlooked or ignored. It is plain that not all of the people can be acquainted in detail with God's laws so that as soon as they encounter some ruling contrary to religion they begin to oppose it. Even if they do protest and take up an oppositional stance, to what degree can they count on success?

When the masses are not equipped with the requisite religious knowledge, how can they adopt the appropriate attitude to the decrees of the ruler, obeying them when they conform to the criteria of religion and opposing them whenever they clash with God's ordinances?

Furthermore, if we accept such a hypothesis, when obeying the decrees of the ruler that conform to divine law we are in reality obeying God's commands, not those of the ruler, so that obedience to the Holder of Authority ceases to be a distinct category of obedience.

Another consideration is that whenever a group or class perceives a law to be contrary to its own interests it will find an opening permitting it to violate or subvert the law in question or openly rebel against it. The sense of obedience will then be noticeably weakened in the people, in the absence of any regulatory instance. As a result the very pillars of society will begin to tremble and order and discipline will ultimately vanish. Our interpretation of the verse cannot, therefore, be made to rest on this hypothesis either.

A further possibility is that the Holders of Authority referred to in the verse are leaders chosen by the people, rulers whose exercise of power is based on public opinion. The text of the verse does not indicate this in any way, for the verse specifies only that obedience to the Holders of Authority is necessary, while remaining silent on how those Holders of Authority are to emerge and take power. The objections that we have raised to the preceding interpretations also apply to this interpretation. Bearing in mind all the different problems to which we have drawn attention, we must lay aside all the interpretations reviewed thus far in our attempt to understand the expression Holders of Authority.

Only one way out of this dilemma remains, a single solution that places us on the straight path to attaining our goal. It consists of recognizing that it is God's prerogative to designate the ruler; He alone selects the one deserving of rule over the Islamic *ummah,* a person in whose exalted character the virtues of the Most Noble Messenger, peace and blessings be upon him and his family, and a profound connection to God are manifest, so that obedience to him becomes a natural corollary to obedience to God and the Messenger.

It is true, of course, that the Prophet of Islam set forth, in the course of his finite lifetime, the general principles of belief and of religious law, so that in this sense he perfected the religion of God. Those general principles are to serve as the foundation and basis for deriving the specific divine ordinances of which mankind will stand in need until the Day of Resurrection. However, what was to be done after the death of the Prophet, peace and blessings be upon him and his family? Did the people no longer need a religious authority to whom they might turn for solutions to their problems, in order to deal effectively, in the light of the Qur'ān and the *Sunnah,* with newly occurring situations and circumstances that had not existed during the lifetime of the Prophet?

Thirteen years in the life of the Messenger of God were spent in struggle against the idolaters of Makkah who were loath that men desirous of truth should hear the liberating message of Islam. He did whatever he could to establish the truth of monotheism and refute idolatry, and he prepared men's minds to receive the rich culture of Islam. No opportunity remained for him to expound God's ordinances in detail, to set forth the norms and obligations of religion. That was left to be accomplished at another time.

Even while in Madīnah, the Prophet was still not free of anxiety concerning Makkah. During the ten brief years of his life there he was confronted with a mass of problems and difficulties. Much of his time was absorbed in dealing with the plots of the Hypocrites and fighting battles against the Polytheists and the Jews, battles in which he participated no fewer than twenty two times. He had therefore little time left over to pursue his true mission, to prepare people for entry into Islamic society.

Was it not therefore necessary that after the death of the Prophet an outstanding personality should assume the task of preserving God's ordinances from distortion and change and of further disseminating Islamic culture in all its branches in a form suited to the conditions of the age? Was there not a need for one whom God had preserved from all error and sin and whose very spirit and soul had been formed by the inhalation of divine light?

The Holders of Authority obedience to whom was categorically mandated by God as conjoint with obedience to Himself and the Prophet, peace and blessings be upon him and his family, must in the very nature of things be free of all pollution by error and sin, since this lofty attribute also characterized the Prophet himself.

In other words, the rulers obedience to whom is of the same order as obedience to God and the Prophet are to be found exclusively in that house which God Himself had purified of all sin and to whom the Prophet had clearly referred in a number of utterances, proclaiming them superior to all others and enjoining the Muslims to love them, to follow them, and to be tied to them.

The deduction of the approprate rulings for the countless situations that were to occur in later times, taking into account the verses of the Qur'ān and the relatively few traditions that were transmitted from the Most Noble Messenger, was by no means an easy task, something that ordinary people could successfully undertake. Verses of the Qur'ān that contain legal rulings and traditions of the Prophet concerning the permitted and the forbidden do not amount together to a total of more than seven hundred.

Taking this into consideration, who had the necessary qualifications of learning to deduce, from this relatively small number of texts, rulings for the constantly increasing problems of Islamic society? Could it be anyone other than someone directly instructed by God acquit himself of this grave responsibility?

Likewise, the elaboration of laws to address matters that change in accordance with temporally and spatially determined circumstances is also part of the responsibility of the Holders of Authority, for they have been given the power to promulgate the necessary ordinances at their own discretion. The fact that no explicit ruling for such matters is to be found in the Qur'ān and the *Sunnah* should not be taken as a sign of deficiency in the *sharī'ah* but on the contrary as an indication of the legislative potential and expansive logic that are to be found in religion.

In objection to all this, the verse proclaiming religion to have been perfected might be cited. However, it does not disprove our argument, for according to well known scholars of tradition, it was revealed on the Day of Ghadīr **after** the appointment of the Commander of the Faithful, 'Alī, peace be upon him, as successor to the Prophet. If we examine carefully the situation prevailing at the time, we will see that the newly established religion of Islam was being threatended with attack by various enemies and the infliction of blows from various quarters.

For this reason, the aims of Islam could not be advanced without the presence of a divinely appointed authority, designated by the Prophet, peace and blessings be upon him and his family, nor could its structure have been maintained in the fashion the Prophet himself desired. The need was met by the appointment of 'Alī as the leader and ruler of the Muslims.

Moreover, the verse concerning the perfection of religion does not imply that detailed divine ordinances dealing with all conceivable concerns have now attained a state of perfection. It is true that on the one hand the revelation of divine command came to an end with the death of God's Messenger, who had been instructed by the Creator in the essential and unchanging needs of man, so that in this sense legislation had been completed. However, we see at the same time that many general ordinances are to be found neither in the Qur'ān nor in the *Sunnah,* and the legal sources and juristic mechanism available at the time were inadequate to provide an answer for all the new situations that were bound to occur, the reason for this being the temporally finite nature of the Prophet's mission. In addition, the successive difficulties with which the Prophet had to deal prevented him from fulfilling some of his basic tasks, so that he was unable to teach men everything he had learned. Many of the Companions and contemporaries of the Prophet were in a state of constant dependence on him, and as long as they lived in his shade, they paid no attention to the need of mastering directly the ordinances and concepts of religion. Although they came to occupy important positions after the death of the Prophet, they were ignorant of many matters pertaining to worship, social transactions, and juridical procedure, in addition to which their grasp of political concerns and the problems of the age was weak. Numerous traditions are to be found in Sunnī books which show that the Companions lacked clear ideas concerning questions of inheritance, judgeship, and penalties.

The very logic of the prophetic message necessitated that the *ummah* should gradually become acquainted with religious guidance over a period longer than that which had elapsed before the death of the Prophet. He therefore entrusted the accumulation of laws and ordinances that he had received by way of revelation to his successor and legatee, the very depths of whose being had been permeated by Islam, and in a short time he inculcated in his spirit and heart knowledge of all the truths and teaching of Islam, thus preparing him for leadership. He assigned to him the task of preserving the authentic culture and knowledge of Islam, for him to convey to the Muslim *ummah* after his death in a manner dictated by the circumstances of the age, and instructing society in its duties, based on his own extensive learning.

What we know of the life of the Prophet and of 'Alī informs us that the Prophet spent many hours alone with 'Alī, instructing him in what needed to be done and the difficulties that lay ahead. Whenever 'Alī asked him a question, he would help him and explain the teachings of religion to him.

So after the death of the great founder of Islam 'Alī was the only direct channel for gaining access to truth, freeing the *ummah* of the need to act in accordance with supposition, doubt, analogy, or arbitrary judgement.

Were these last two to have any place in the judicial and penal system of Islam, it would mean that the *sharī'ah* itself is based on speculation and supposition, and any religion the ordinances of which are subject to doubt and hesitation cannot fail to be weak, unsound and unconvincing.

The *ummah*, then, is in no situation to assume itself the task of selecting a successor to the Prophet, peace and blessings be upon him and his family, rather it is incumbent on him to convey the trust that he has received from God to one who is like him protected from sin and who does not fail for a single moment to protect the religion of God. Were it to be otherwise, personal opinions would take the place of divine commandments and the purpose of the Prophet's mission would be undermined, and God's ordinances would be laid aside.

History itself bears witness that the religious learning and culture of those who assumed the leadership after the death of the Prophet were not at a level that permitted them to answer the question of the day. The events that occurred proved that they were incapable of dealing with serious problems or issuing the requisite instructions. Their lack of religious knowledge caused the laws of God to be diverted from their true course and ordinances alien to Islam to be implemented.

Historians record that five men were once brought before the caliph accused of sexual transgressions. The caliph ordered them to be punished, each with a hundred lashes. The Imām 'Alī who was present objected as follows:

"A different penalty must be applied to each of the five. One is an unbeliever in tributary relation to the Islamic government; since he has violated the conditions of this relation, he must be put to death. The second is a married man; he must be stoned. The third is an unmarried youth; his punishment is to be whipped. The fourth is an unmarried slave whose punishment is half that of a free man. The fifth man is a lunatic, and he is not subject to any punishment."

A married woman pregnant with an illegitimate child was brought before 'Umar, and he commanded that she should be stoned. The Commander of the Faithful, 'Alī, peace be upon him, remarked: "Although the woman is a criminal from the point of view of the law, the child she is bearing is innocent, and it cannot be punished together with its mother." Thanks to this intervention on the part of 'Alī, the implementation of a verdict contrary to justice and religion was avoided.[176]

On another occasion, the caliph gave orders for a madwoman who had committed an unchaste act to be punished. However, Imām 'Alī considered this verdict also to run counter to the criteria of Islam and he proclaimed her innocent, basing himself on a tradition from the Prophet, peace and blessings be upon him and his family, to the effect that three groups of people are free of legal accountability, one of them being the insane. This brought the matter to a close.[177]

Many Sunnī authorities record that whenever 'Umar was unable to solve a problem until he consulted 'Alī, he would repeat to himself: "Were it not for 'Alī, 'Umar would be lost." Sometimes he would also say: "I seek protection against the accurrence of a problematic event without 'Alī being present."[178]

What we have cited here are but a few examples of the issuance of verdicts and judgements that had no connection to God's revelation.[179]

Can we assume that God permitted His laws to be violated on numerous occasions after the death of the Prophet and invalid judgements to supplant them? Or was it rather that in order to protect religion the reins of the *ummah* were intended to be placed in the hands of persons who were throughly acquainted with all the details of revealed law and had the duty of implementing it in Islamic society? Once the duty of obeying the leader or ruler is made contingent on his possessing all the necessary attributes, no contradiction between the desires of the ruler and the commands of God and the Messenger on the other will occur. To interpret the verse on obedience in this fashion will solve all the problems we have reviewed above and free us from the need to resort to all kinds of improbable and untrustworthy notions.

The Qur'ān, in fact, does not permit the grant of obedience to those who prefer their own arbitrary wishes to the commands of God, for it clearly proclaims: "*Do not follow those who have forgotten mention of Me and pursue their own fancies.*" (18:27)

It is self-evident that any command issued in contravention of what God has willed will lack all validity, and that no one has the right to legislate in a sense running contrary to God's law. Both intelligence and conscience dictate, as well as the numerous verses and traditions that relate to the matter, that people must submit only to the law of God and obey His commands exclusively.

The Commander of the Faithful, 'Alī, peace be upon him, said: "The only obedience incumbent on people is to the laws of God and the commandments of the Prophet of God, peace and blessings be upon him and his family! As for obedience to the Holders of Authority, this has been made incumbent because they are immune from sin and in the very nature of things they cannot issue an order that violates or runs counter to God's commands."[180]

Imām Muḥammad al-Bāqir, peace be upon him, said: "The Holders of Authority are the leaders of the *ummah*, from the progeny of 'Alī and Fāṭimah who shall remain in existence until the Day of Resurrection."[181]

One of the companions of Imām Ja'far al-Ṣādiq, peace be upon him, asked him: "Who are the Holders of Authority obedience to whom has been made obligatory by God?"

He answered: "They are 'Alī b. Abī Ṭālib, Ḥasan, Ḥusayn, 'Alī b. Ḥusayn, Muḥammad b. 'Alī, and Ja'far (i.e., himself). Give thanks then to God that He has made your leaders known to you at a time when many people are engaged in denial."[182]

A Companion of the Messenger of God by the name of Jābir once asked him about the meaning of the verse dealing with obedience enquiring "who are the Holders of Authority obedience to whom has been made obligatory on us by God?"

He answered: "The first of them will be 'Alī b. Abī Ṭālib. He will be followed by his sons, Ḥasan and Ḥusayn; then by 'Alī b. Ḥusayn; and then by Muḥammad al-Bāqir, whom you will live to see. When you go to meet him, give him my greetings. He will be followed in turn by Ja'far al-Ṣādiq, Mūsā al-Kāẓim, 'Alī al-Riḍā, Muḥammad al-Jawād, 'Alī al-Hādī, Ḥasan al-'Askarī, and finally the Expected One, the Promised Mahdī. These will be the leaders after me."[183]

One of the companions of Imām Ja'far al-Ṣādiq, peace be upon him, addressed him as follows: "Inform me of those pillars of Islam on the observance of which depends the acceptability of my deeds, and tell me too of those things ignorance of which will not harm me."

He replied: "Bearing witness to the oneness of God; testifying to the prophethood and messengerhood of Muḥammad, peace and blessings be upon him and his family, and belief in that which he conveyed from God; adherence to financial obligations such as the payment of *zakāt*; and allegiance to those to whom God has commanded it, that is, to the Family of the Prophet. For the Prophet himself said, 'Whoever leaves this world without knowing the Imām of his age will have died as people died during the *Jāhiliyyah*,' and God commanded obedience to Himself, the Messenger, and the Holders of Authority."

"The first of the Holders of Authority was 'Alī, peace be upon him, followed in order by Ḥasan, Ḥusayn, 'Alī b. Ḥusayn, Muḥammad b. 'Alī, and this line of authority still continue.

"A world that is devoid of an Imām cannot be set right, and to die without knowing the Imām is equivalent to dying the death of one who lived in the *Jāhiliyyah*. More than at any other time, man needs to know his Imām during the last moments of his life; he will be guaranteed high station if he openly acknowledges his Imām at that time."[184]

The atrocities inflicted by the Umayyad and 'Abbāsid

caliphs on the Muslims in general and even on their leaders in religion were not few in number. They perverted the caliphate into an instrument of voice and immorality and plunged their hands into the blood of the innocent simply to shore up their unjust rule. Despite this, they called themselves Commanders of the Believers!

If God were to recognize the rule of these shameless criminals as legitimate and to impose obedience to them on the Muslims as a duty, what would become of justice, equity, and equality, of the rights of the individual and society?

Would this not make a mockery of the divine commandments that ensure the happiness of mankind in this world and the hereafter and promote its true advancement?

In addition to all the foregoing, it may be remarked that traditions reported by many great Sunnī scholars also interpret the expression Holders of Authority as referring to the Imāms from the House of the Prophet.[185]

The Noble Qur'ān restricts authority over the Muslims to God, the Messenger, and to those who pay *zakāt* while bowing down. Thus it says: "*Authority over you belongs to God and the Prophet and those believers who establish regular prayer and pay their zakāt while bowing down*" (5:55). This verse refers to an occurrence that happened only once, for there is no general injunction in Islam that *zakāt* must be paid while one is bowing; this is neither obligatory nor recommended, and we cannot assume that some people used to do it as a matter of practice.

The event in question is the following. A certain poor man entered the Prophet's Mosque while 'Alī, peace be upon him, was bowing in prayer. The beggar asked him for his help, and 'Alī stretched out his finger toward him, meaning that he should remove the ring and take it. The beggar complied and left the mosque.

At this point the angel of revelation came to the Prophet, peace and blessings be upon him and his family, and revealed to him the verse we have just cited.

Sunnīs and Shī'īs agree unanimously that the verse was

revealed with reference to 'Alī and that he manifested the action that is mentioned in it.[186] The verse then is a concise allusion to 'Alī. Although the verse uses a plural *("those believers who ... pay their zakāt while bowing down")* it refers to a single individual. While the reverse – the use of a singular with the intention of a plural – is not permissible in the Arabic language, the use of a plural with singular meaning is quite common and by no means restricted to this instance. For example, the Qur'ān uses a plural to refer to Na'īm b. Mas'ūd al-Ashja'ī, in 3:172 and to refer to 'Abdullāh b. Ubayy in Surah al-Munāfiqūn, apart from other instances that might be cited.[187]

Considering the admission of Sunnī scholars that this verse refers to 'Alī, no doubt can remain that the leader and ruler of the Muslims after the Prophet, peace and blessings be upon him and his family, was 'Alī, peace be upon him, for here his authority is conjoined with that of God and the Messenger.

Lesson Fourteen
The Guardians of the Frontiers of the *Sharī'ah* and the Realm of Islam

In contrast to present-day Christianity, the credal system of which is based on a purely spiritual and ethical summons to man and the scope of which does not extend beyond the propagation of religion and the attempt to guide mankind, Islam is a system that refuses to confine itself to mere religious rituals.

The summons to purposive activity and struggle, the need to expand and disseminate the message of monotheism, the elaboration of laws and ordinances for both the material and spiritual life of man, as well as the direct participation of the Most Noble Messenger, peace and blessings be upon him and his family, in various battles; — all this indicates that the ideational system of Islam aims at the establishment of a government that with its liberating ideals will permit men to rediscover themselves and choose a truly human form of existence. Further, the government that Islam intends to establish will defend the religion of monotheism with the necessary decisiveness, ward off any aggression against the lands of Islam, and implement God's laws with care and precision.

Such a government, on account of its answerability before God's laws, will never be ready to compromise those laws, however slightly, in the face of pressure and hostility from the enemies of Islam, whatever form that hostility may take; it will never ignore God's commandments nor abandon their implementation.

In general, once religious leadership is separated from the ruling institution and religion remains indifferent to the question of political rule, contenting itself with preaching and admonishing the masses, religion will have no guarantor in society. Even if people are made aware of the teachings of religion by the efforts of scholars and thinkers and try to implement those teachings in their lives, the ruling classes will attempt by various means to prevent the implementation of measures that secure human happiness and especially of the divine commandments that might threaten their hegemony. They will even go beyond that, implementing their own carefully calculated plans to shore up their rule and protect their interests, both in the short term and in the long term.

If therefore religion regards its teachings as the source of salvation and happiness of society, it must give thought to the system of rule, propose a specific system of governance equipped with all the necessary laws and ordinances. Only then will it be able to establish religion in society and clear the way for God's religion to advance.

Both in Islam and in the monotheistic religions that preceded it, particular attention was paid to the establishment of a suitable system of government, an entirely logical concern, for the founders of different schools of religious thought were unwilling to abandon the fruits of their efforts to the vicissitudes of history.

Islamic government – i.e., the administration of the *ummah* on the basis of Islamic law – began with the migration of the Prophet, peace and blessings be upon him and his family, and his arrival in Madīnah; it was then that the system of Islamic government began to take shape.

From the very first day that the Messenger of God laid the foundations of Islamic monotheism, despite the hostility of the corrupt and misguided polytheists whom he had left behind in Makkah, and began expanding the power of Islam in Madīnah in all its aspects, political, economic, geographical and cultural, he entrusted the administration of certain matters to responsible and capable elements so that they might contribute to the advancement of the community.

Throughout the battles and wars that took place in order to remove the obstacles that stood in the way of spreading the truth and to establish justice, new lands would come under the control of the Muslims. The Prophet would immediately, appoint in each of these lands a governor and a judge as well as a teacher whose task it was to teach religion to the people. Protection was also extended to the non-Muslims inhabiting these territories and whatever humane cultural values they cherished.

The Qur'ān recognizes the Prophet to have had the functions of ruler *(ḥākim)* and judge *(qāḍī)*, for it addresses him as follows: "*Judge among them according to what your Lord has sent down to you, and follow not their vain desires.*" (5:48)

The prophets were indeed the founders of divine government on earth, and they constituted the principal resource for the establishment of a righteous government that would serve the broad masses of the people.

The Qur'ān assigns rulership not only to the Prophet of Islam but also to Yūsuf (Joseph): "*When Yūsuf reached maturity We bestowed on him rulership and knowledge; thus do We reward the doers of good.*" (12:22)

The Qur'ān addresses Dāwūd (David) as follows: "*O Dāwūd, We bestowed upon you Our viceregency upon earth, so that you might rule justly among God's creation, not following your vain desires for they would lead you astray from God's path.*" (38:25)

The Islamic laws concerning fixed penalties and the payment of blood money, as well as many other topics in jurisprudence, count as the executive pillars of the Islamic system of government that was founded by the Prophet.

The governmental function of the Prophet had another important dimension, that of creating a suitable environment for the strengthening of the Islamic summons, expounding the divine laws and ordinances for mankind, and inculcating in men the concepts of God's Book so that they might attain the lofty goals that Islam had prescribed.

The Qur'ān says the following with respect to this aspect of the Prophet's task: "*God it is Who raised a great Prophet from among the unlettered Arabs in order that he might recite to them the verses of God's revelation and cleanse them from the pollution of ignorance and evil morals, and teach them the sharī'ah of God's Book and divine wisdom, even though they were previously in the pit of ignorance and misguidance.*" (62:2)

The Prophet was thus the ruler of Islamic society in addition to being a guide and a promulgator of God's ordinances. Whoever wished to be his successor ought, then, to have combined in himself these same two dimensions — rulership of society and the spiritual guidance of the *ummah*. In addition, he had to be the guardian of the credal based of Islam and its ordinances, protecting them from change or distortion and resisting decisively the assaults of unbelief, scepticism and misguidance; one able to solve problems arising from any kind of deviation, and to confront any agggression of the Islamic lands by outsiders. Only thus could the continuity and preservation of Islam be assured amid the myriad dangers it faced.

The best method of preserving the rights of the individual and society is to have a government of the righteous, and the most righteous form of government is without doubt the government of the inerrant *(ma'ṣūm)*, which alone makes it possible to hope for the preservation of the rights of all man. A government headed by one chosen by God is in reality the government of God, and it is only this type of government that makes it possible for man to preserve his true personality, nobility and dignity, and to attain all his rights. Respect for the dignity of man and the establishment of justice are among the fundamental principles of such a government. Impious and arbitrary rulers may often pay lip service to human rights and claim to be the defenders of the dignity of the individual and society, but in practice they drag man's honor in the mud, and their only accomplishment is the enthronement of discrimination and injustice.

There can then be no doubt as to the importance of a just

and virtuous government and the efforts of the prophets to establish such, nor conversely of the damage caused by impious rulers who are unconcerned with the ultimate destiny of society and with enabling men to obtain their rights.

The one who wishes to assume religious leadership and undertake the guidance of the masses as the successor of the Prophet, must bear affinity to him with respect to knowledge, deeds, and manner of thought. He must also have special moral qualities and spiritual attributes, be divinely protected from sin, and be fully cognizant of the truths of religion; only then will he be able to solve whatever problem arises on the basis of truth, justice, and the *sharī'ah*. Islam cannot accept that rule over society and the protection of human dignity should be entrusted to the first person who chances along.

The Noble Qur'ān cites the superior strength and capacity of Ṭālūt (Saul) as a reason for his being chosen as a fit leader of his people: "*He is more fitted to rule because God has chosen him and bestowed on him a surfeit of knowledge and power.*" (2:247)

In just the same way that the Most Noble Messenger, peace and blessings be upon him and his family, exercised two offices, the one who wishes to succeed him must also have his two essential qualities: an inner dimension of connectedness with God which is bestowed by God Himself in His grace, and an outer dimension of leadership and rule. These two are inseparable, and leadership of the *ummah* cannot be based on one of them alone; political and social leadership must go together with spiritual guidance. The Imām has both spiritual and legislative authority, and is thus able to perpetuate the correct mode of administering human affairs that was established by the prophets.

When the fifth Imām was commenting on the belief prevalent at the Saqīfah that the two aspects of the matter can be separated from each other, he cited this verse in which God bestowed on the progeny of Ibrāhīm both spiritual guidance and leadership and the administration of society:

"*Are they envious of what We in our generosity have bestowed on the progeny of Ibrāhīm? We sent the Book and wisdom to the family of Ibrāhīm, and gave them too kingship and rule.*" (4:52)

Then the Imām added: "How is it that they accept the combination of the two aspects in the case of the children of Ibrāhīm, but reject it for the Household of the Prophet?"[188]

Lesson Fifteen
The Imāmate as a Rational Necessity

In accordance with the sound disposition and the pure nature that are innate in him, man is ceaselessly engaged in the struggle to develop and advance towards perfection. Consciously or unconsciously, with a love that quickens his spirit, he moves forward in the direction of the utmost dignity and nobility man can attain. This is a reality that is always manifest in humans; spiritual need impels them to advance ever further along their path in order to approach higher degrees and more exalted values. This evolutionary process passes through various degrees which are firmly and profoundly interlinked.

It is of course true that within man unbridled and unholy desires exist that are hostile to this enterprise, and throughout the course of his forward motion man must constantly battle against the destructive inner forces that threaten to rob him of his powers and sacrifice him to forces of evil.

As long as man exists on the plane of being, this struggle towards perfection will also exist. Its aim and culmination must be clear, and there must exist also in human society an exceptional individual who thanks to his spiritual qualities has penetrated to the inner meaning of all laws, a personage who while fully engaged in the struggle has never once fallen prey to deviation.

Such an individual or personage is what is intended by the term Imām. He is the truly liberated man, the chosen herald of monotheism; in his exalted person all conceivable have been realized and rendered active.

As the vanguard of the humanity, he is the divinely appointed link and intermediary between the world of the unseen and the human race. Without himself needing any intermediary, he is guided directly by God. Like a lamp burning in the heart of the darkness, through the teachings that have come to him from heaven, he enables everyone to rise and ascend to the degree permitted by his spiritual ability and capacity. He employs his intelligence, his faith and his will in order to impel them forward to the most exalted degrees and to guide them to the superabundant source of unity, justice and purity.

Were human society to lack such a divinely chosen person, man would be unable by the efforts of his intellect alone to find his directions, no link would exist between the human race and the world of the unseen, and man's efforts to attain perfection would falter and fail.

It is inconceivable that after equipping man with the urge to attain perfection and bestowing on him the potentiality of ascent to lofty degree, God would not lay before him the path leading there or deprive him of the guide that he needs.

On the contrary, God's infinite grace necessitates that He should demonstrate to man the path for attaining the truths of religion and assist him by placing before him a comprehensive scheme ensuring his welfare in this world and his eternal bliss in the hereafter. This comprehensive scheme, embracing all dimensions of human existence, is precisely what God has conveyed to mankind by means of His chosen messengers.

According to the creed of monotheism, none but God can rule over the created universe. In the world of man, which is but a part of the universe, sovereignty must similarly belong to God. It is true that within the sphere of his acts man has freedom of choice, based on the free will that has been allotted to him, but in order for him to harmonize himself with the universe of which he is a part, he must act in accordance with God's commands and refrain from encroaching on His sovereignty. If he fails to respect the laws brought by the prophets, a disharmony and lack of concordance between man and the universe will arise, and he will inevitably find himself deviating from his intended course.

In just the same way that obedience to revealed law and to the Prophet who may be regarded as the quintessence of all the monotheistic movements in history is the same as obedience to God, the one who wishes to rule monotheistic society as the successor of the Prophet must possess the same inner attributes of communication with God; only then will obedience to him accord with man's purposive advance.

From the time that the Messenger of God, peace and blessings be upon him and his family, founded the government of the righteous and prepared the way for the creation of a pure and luminous society, he undertook also the educative programs he had elaborated. However, since the life of the Prophet was transitory like that of other men, it was necessary that as soon as that great educator had departed, a successor should come to the fore, a righteous and worthy man possessing all the attributes needed to lead the Muslims, who would continue the directive and educative role exercised by the Prophet, in the most desirable or even ideal form.

Embodying all the qualities of a perfect human being, he nurtures the spirits of his followers by means of his superabundant spirituality, and he shows them the way of advancing along God's path towards God, obeying God's commands and turning away from all other than God. Only thus will the straight path remain open, enabling everyone to embark on the road to felicity.

We will understand all of this better once we realize that there is no line of demarcation between this world and the hereafter, and that regulations pertaining to man's bodily life cannot be separated from laws relating to his spiritual existence; a specific guardian has been chosen for both. For this reason the pure and inerrant one chosen by God must gather in his hands the reins of the affairs of both this world and the hereafter, and guard the general and universal interest of Islam against other peoples and nations.

Through the blessed existence of this true leader, this representative of God upon earth, the sole path that exists for attaining true happiness remain open before men. With his spiritual richness and wisdom of conduct, he guides them on the road at the end of which they will find, in the presence of God, all the pure and noble qualities for which they yearn.

It is true that among the Twelve Imāms it was only 'Alī b. Abī Ṭālib who exercised rule, and that for a limited period. The other Imāms never possessed governmental powers, and they were not permitted to use the position of leadership that was rightfully theirs to strengthen the position of the Qur'ān, to expand the culture of Islam, or to develop the identity of the *ummah*. But this was the fault of the people, who failed to make it possible for them to assume power and as a result were deprived of the benefits that might have accrued to them from these unparalleled exemplars of mankind. For in appointing the Imāms, God had established His proof before men; He had presented them with these righteous and exceptional men, chosen ones whose existence was a source of benefit not only for all Muslims but for all of mankind.

In addition to this, it is important to remember that the beneficial effects of the existence of the Imāms were not limited to their exercise of political power; they fulfilled their appointed mission in a variety of other ways. The Imām was responsible for preserving the very truth of religion and for keeping God's religion unsullied by distortion and manipulation. Both God and the Messenger had given him the task of instructing people in the verities of the Qur'ān and the teachings of religion, thus giving proper direction to their lives.

Moreover, the Imām is a channel for God's grace, so that even if people were deprived of the government of justice and equity that the Inerrant Imāms would have created — thanks to their own incapacity and lethargy — they did benefit from the other dimensions of the Imāms' existence and activity. They were the channels of God's grace irrespective of whether or not they were permitted to rule and lead Islamic society. Superabundant virtue flowed forth from their beings, bringing men's potentialities to fruition.

The preservation of the very foundations of religion was intimately connected with the attention paid to the subject by the Imāms, for awareness of their presence among the *ummah* was able to prevent many basic deviations from taking place.

Like an alert and careful observer, 'Alī b. Abī Ṭālib, peace be upon him, followed all that was taking place in his time. Whenever an incorrect verdict was issued, a law was distorted, or an incorrect penalty was about to be applied, 'Alī looked into the matter and gave the necessary instructions. He was stringent and honest in protecting the principles and laws of Islam.

He exercised leadership at all stages of his life. Thus he was always prepared to answer the scholars of other religions who came flocked to Madīnah in order to put their queries before the legatee of the Prophet, peace and blessings be upon him and his family.

It was thanks to the blessed existence of the Imām that Islamic learning — the legal, educational, and social teachings of the faith — were disseminated among the Muslims and the vital commands and ordinances of the Qur'ān became widely known. Even in lands ruled by harsh and savage rulers, at a time when the caliphs were sunk in corruption and transgression and strove to prevent society from imbibing Islamic knowledge, the numerous utterances and traditions of the Imāms, rich in learning and wisdom and pertaining to all aspects of the faith, served to preserve religion and give the necessary guidance to society.

Some of the caliphs like al-Ma'mūn sought to destroy the scholarly credentials of the Imāms by arranging debates and disputations among the scholars of different religions and sects, but the performance of the Imāms in these gatherings served only to reinforce their scholarly prestige.

The Imāms, as heirs to the teachings of the Messenger, bequeathed thousands of *ḥadīth* to the scholars of Islam, *ḥadīth* that originated on various occasions and had the purpose of enlightening society on religious matters and clarifying the credal bases of the faith. They pertained to all the different concerns of jurisprudence, to ethics and moral conduct, and to esoteric knowledge. It was by drawing on these resources that scholars were able to disseminate the Islamic sciences widely in society and to elaborate an authentic jurisprudence as opposed to the various legal currents then in existence.

We will be better able to appreciate the incomparable struggle waged by the Imāms in the service of Islamic culture in all of its branches if we compare the *ḥadīth* of the Sunnīs with the traditions narrated from the Inerrant Imāms. This comparison will demonstrate the profundity of vision, the originality of thought, and the varied knowledge of the leaders of Shī'ism. The Sunnī scholars themselves have benefited to some degree from the knowledge and learning of the Shī'ī Imāms, for consciously or unconsciously they have borrowed a great deal from them in this respect. The Imāms thus vindicated fully their function as the true guardians of Islam.

It was Imām Ja'far al-Ṣādiq, peace be upon him, who introduced philosophy, theology, mathematics and chemistry for the first time. Among his companions, al-Mufaḍḍal b. 'Umar, Mu'min al-Ṭāq, Hishām b. Ḥakam, and Hisham b. Sālim were specialists in philosophy and theology. Jābir b. Ḥayyān specialized in mathematics and chemistry, and Zarārah, Muḥammad b. Muslim, Jamīl b. Darrāj, Ḥamrān b. A'yan, Abū Baṣīr, and 'Abdullāh b. Sīnān, in jurisprudence *(fiqh)*, principles of jurisprudence *(uṣūl al-fiqh)* and Qur'ānic exegesis.[189]

Ibn Shahrāshūb writes:

"From no one have so many traditions been narrated as from Imām Ja'far al-Ṣādiq, peace be upon him. As many as four thousand students derived their knowledge from him, and some of the founders of the Sunnī schools of law also drew on that storehouse of learning."[190]

Among his students were the founders of law schools *(madhāhib)* such as Mālik b. Anas, Sufyān al-Thawrī, Ibn

'Uyaynah, and Abū Ḥanīfah; jurists *(fuqahā')* such as Muḥammad b. Ḥasan al-Shaybānī and Yaḥyā b. Sa'īd; and traditionists *(muḥaddithīn)* such as Ayyūb al-Sijistānī, Shu'bah b. al-Ḥajjāj, and 'Abd al-Malik b. Jurayḥ.[191]

Ibn Abi 'l-Ḥadīd, who is regarded as a great scholar among the Sunnīs, writes the following concerning the genial character of 'Alī b. Abī Ṭālib, peace be upon him:

"What can I say of a person to whom all human virtues have been attributed? Every group counts him as one of their own; every virtue arises from his being; and every science and branch of learning goes back to him. Theosophy, the most noble of all forms of knowledge, is derived from his utterances. The teacher of Wāṣil b. 'Aṭā' who was the leader of the Mu'tazilah, benefited from the instruction of 'Alī by two intermediate generations. Likewise, whatever learning the Ash'arites have, they also owe to 'Alī.

"Without any doubt, the philosophy and theology of the Shī'īs and the Zaydīs also go back to 'Alī. He is the supreme teacher of all jurists, for Abū Ḥanīfah, the founder of the Ḥanafī school, was a pupil of Imām Ja'far al-Ṣādiq, peace be upon him, who had imbibed the learning of 'Alī through transmission by his father and ancestors. Mālik b. Anas, the founder of Mālikī jurisprudence, had a master who was the pupil of 'Ikrimah, who in turn had been a pupil of Ibn 'Abbās, who had derived his learning directly from 'Alī.

"'Umar b. al-Khaṭṭāb would always turn to 'Alī for help in solving difficult questions, and he would often say: 'Were it not for 'Alī, 'Umar would be lost.'

"As for the jurisprudence of the Shī'ah, it goes without saying that it goes back to their first leader. In addition, 'Alī was the master teacher of all exegetes of the Qur'ān. This can be easily ascertained by referring to the books of exegesis and seeing how most of their material springs from him. Even that which is narrated from Ibn 'Abbās ultimately goes back to 'Alī. Ibn 'Abbās was once asked: 'How would you compare your knowledge with that of your cousin?' He replied: 'Mine is like a drop, and his like an ocean.'

"All the great gnostics *('urafā')* attach themselves to 'Alī, and he is in addition the one who founded the science of grammar, having taught its fundamental principles for the first time to Abu 'l-Aswad."[192]

Lesson Sixteen
Who are Those Capable of Interpreting Divine Law?

The laws that scholars have laboriously elaborated and compiled over the ages to meet the needs of different societies have always stood in need of intelligent and alert interpreters when it came to implementation. The laws of Islam, although they rest on revealed norms and divine guidance, are no exception to this rule.

Certain verses of the Qur'ān, which is the fundamental and primary source for deducing anything related to Islam, are not entirely clear in their purport and signification for they do not yield a single, categorical sense. Recourse to exegesis in order to clarify points of ambiguity is therefore necessary.

Furthermore, the Noble Qur'ān sets forth the main lines and general principles of the programs of action Islam proposes in various spheres; it does not go into the details of every law and prescript. If therefore someone wishes to obtain comprehensive knowledge of those programs in their entirety, he cannot content himself simply with the text of the Qur'ān.

The differences of opinion and approach that have arisen with respect to the meaning of certain verses, as well as traditions of the Prophet, peace and blessings be upon him and his family, have played a large part in the distortion and transformation of some of the original concepts of Islam. Interested parties and people tied to the ruling establishment have succeeded in putting forward interpretations that correspond to the interests of the rulers, a phenomenon that happened repeatedly during the Umayyad and 'Abbāsid caliphates. In such a whirlpool of confusion, what needs to be done to prevent the truth from remaining unknown? Does it not appear necessary that recourse should be had to a single learned authority on jurisprudence, one divinely protected against sin, a man of independent opinion, having a comprehensive knowledge of the Book, the heir to the knowledge of the Prophet, in order for him to acquaint us with the original meaning and purpose of the Qur'ān?

An authority who implements the various commands of the Qur'ān in a practical and visible way and who serves as an indisputable marker of the right and the wrong? The clarifications he makes and the deductions he draws, being based on the principles of the Qur'ān and inspired by revealed law, will be decisive for all followers of Islam and capable of ending all differences of opinion; he will be like a compass in the hand of a distraught captain

If we do not have recourse to such qualified interpreters of the Qur'ān, we will fall prey to doubt and confusion, or, by following incorrect interpretations, stray far from the true teachings of the Qur'ān.

Imām Ja'far al-Ṣādiq, peace be upon him, established the greatest center for the teaching of Islam, training a multitude of scholars whose task it was to instruct the people and draw their attention to the dangers posed by the fabricators of *ḥadīth*. His scientific and intellectual activity served to offset the waves of corruption that were unfurling at the time, as well as the erroneous concepts and biased theories the ground for which had been prepared by the political situation of the day.

One day, a group of the companions and students of the Imām, men who bequeathed to the *ummah* a great legacy of knowledge that they derived from him, were gathered in his presence. The Imām addressed Hishām b. Ḥakam who was present among them: "Will you not tell us something about the conversation you had with 'Amr b. 'Ubayd?" He replied: "I would be embarrassed to say anything in your presence." But the Imām insisted, and so Hishām b. Ḥakam spoke as follows:

"I learned that 'Amr b. 'Ubayd had begun to assume some religious responsibilities, establishing a teaching circle in the mosque at Baṣrah. This news disturbed me, and so I set out for the mosque, where I found him sitting, answering people's questions. I approached him and said: 'O scholar, I am a stranger here; will you permit me to ask a question?' He replied that I might, so I asked him: 'Do you have eyes?' 'Amr responded: 'Young man, what kind of a question is this? Why ask about something you can see to be true?' But I persisted, asking him to answer my question. He consented, so I repeated the question. When he answered in the affirmative, I next asked him; 'What do you do with eyes?' 'I see colors and people.' Then I asked; 'Do you have a nose?' 'Yes.' 'What do you do with your nose?' 'I smell things.' 'Do you have a mouth?' 'Yes.' 'What do you do with it?' 'I taste the food that I eat.' 'Do you have ears?' 'Yes.' 'What do you with them?' 'I hear sounds.'

"'Now, do you have a heart?' 'Yes.' 'What do you do with it?' 'My heart is an instrument of weighing and measuring; by means of it I assess the truth or falsehood of whatever knowledge comes to my senses and limbs.'

"Then I asked: 'Can any limb or member dispense with the heart *(qalb)*?'

"'No.'

"'Even if all limbs and members are completely healthy?'

"'Young man, whenever any bodily sense is mistaken in its perceptions or doubts their accuracy, it has recourse to the heart in order to resolve its doubts and gain some measure of confidence and certainty.'

"'So the role of the heart with respect to the members and limbs is, in accordance with divine command, to remove error, confusion, and bewilderment?'

"'Yes.'

"'So the existence of the heart in man is a necessity, without which his members and limbs lose their sense of direction?'

"'Yes.'

"'O Abū Marwān, God has not left your senses and limbs without a guide to rectify their errors and doubts. Is it then possible that He should leave human society, despite all the dissension and ignorance that beset it, to its own devices, without any leader to guide it? A fitting leader who will remove all confusion and error?'

"'Amr remained silent for a while, and then he said:

"'Are you not Hishām b. Ḥakam?'

"'No.'

"'Are you one of his companions?'

"'No.'

"'Where do you come from?'

"'I come from Kūfah.'

"Then he said, 'Indeed you are Hishām,' stood up, caused me to sit where he had been sitting, and remained silent until I got up to leave."

The Imām smiled and said: "From whom did you learn this mode of argumentation?" Hishām replied: "From you." Then the Imām said: "I swear by God that this same argument is to be found in the pages revealed to Ibrāhīm and Mūsā."[193]

Men may therefore gain access to the commands and prescriptions of God only when, after the Prophet, peace and blessings be upon him and his family, the leadership of the Islamic *ummah* is in the hands of a person who is enabled by his proven erudition and spiritual qualities to expound those detailed injunctions which have not been explicitly included in revelation but are nonetheless a matter of practical necessity for human society. In the absence of such leadership, the *ummah* will tend to deviate from the principles of Islam and fail to reach the goal of happiness and the purposes for which it has been created.

After the Prophet, the Immaculate Imāms, committed as they were to leadership and guidance, did everything possible to disseminate the teachings of the Qur'ān, for years on end and in the midst of swiftly changing circumstances, and to show the Muslims how to apply those teachings; they guided and instructed the people in word and in deed. As a result, the aggregate of their teachings came of form a precious treasure of learning that was bequeathed to the *ummah*. Because of its evidential force, this treasure was uniquely authoritative, and because of its scope, it offered the means for solving every new problem that might occur.

Everyone knows that the caliphs who succeeded the Messenger of God, peace and blessings be upon him and his family, knew very little concerning the ordinances of Islam and the religious needs of the people. Abū Bakr, the first caliph, is known, for example, to have transmitted only eighty *ḥadīth*.[194]

al-Nawawī says the following in his *Tahdhīb*: "Abū Bakr transmitted 142 *ḥadīth* from the Prophet, peace and blessings be upon him and his family, 104 of which are cited by al-Suyūṭī in his *Tārīkh al-Khulafā'* and 22 of which are included by al-Bukhārī in his collection."[195]

The religious leader of the *ummah* who is meant in every respect to aid and assist his community and to solve their complex religious problems has so little Islamic consciousness that he finds himself consulting al-Mughīrah b. Shu'bah, an extremely corrupt individual, in order to learn God's ruling concerning the portion of an estate that goes to his grandmother![196]

He even confesses himself, with the utmost frankness, that his religious knowledge is not superior to that of anyone else, and declares to the people that if they see him committing an error they should correct him and instruct him in the proper course of action. For this is what he says:

"I hold in my hands the reins of your affairs even though I am not the best among you. If you see that I am treading the right path, then support me, and if you see me embarking on the wrong course, then guide me back to the right path."[197]

As for 'Umar, he transmitted no more than fifty authentic *ḥadīth* from the Prophet.[198]

In connection with the religious knowledge of the second caliph, it is reported that someone once went to consult him on a problem that he faced. He said: "I need to make a total ablution *(ghusl)*, but I have no access to water; what is my religious duty under these circumstances?" The caliph answered: "You are relieved of your duty to pray."[199] The real duty of such a person is, however, spelled out in the Qur'ān. (4:43 and 5:6)

Five *ḥadīth* are narrated on the authority of 'Uthmān in the *Ṣaḥīḥ* of Muslim, and nine in the *Ṣaḥīḥ* of al-Bukhārī.[200]

Facts such as these serve to demonstrate the degree of religious learning possessed by those persons who assumed the leadership of Islamic society. How then could it be expected that the framework of divine law should remain immune to change and distortion and that Islamic society should advance toward its lofty goals? Whoever carries the burden of leading the *ummah* must possess extensive religious awareness and knowledge in order to answer whatever questions and problems arise, whereas the knowledge that the caliphs had of the authentic law of Islam was extremely limited.

One day, while preaching from the pulpit, the second caliph was criticizing a rise in the amount of dowries customarily given and declared that this increase ought to be prevented. When he descended from the pulpit, a woman objected to what he had said: "Why is it necessary to restrict the amount of dowries? Does God not say in the Qur'ān, '*If you have given one of your wives great wealth by way of a dowry, you must not take back any of it*'?" (4:20) The caliph realized his mistake and begged God to forgive him. Then he remarked: "Everyone is better acquainted with God's commands than is 'Umar." Then he mounted the pulpit again and retracted what he had said.[201]

As for the religious knowledge of the third caliph, it is enough that we should refer to the following event.

"During the time of his caliphate an unbeliever was killed by a Muslim. The caliph ordered the murderer to be put to death. But a group of the Companions of the Prophet, peace and blessings be upon him and his family, who were present at the time informed the caliph of his mistake and reminded him that in such cases the murderer should be condemned to the payment of blood money, as a result of which the caliph rescinded his order."[202]

Is it fitting that the leadership of Islamic society should be in the hands of people who by their own admission are so ignorant of the laws of God's religion, a religion the ordinances of which they are supposed to expound and to implement? Is it at all conceivable that God should entrust all the affairs — in fact, the destiny — of a community that had been nurtured on revelation and established by the most noble of creation to people who were not only unable to propel the Islamic *ummah* forward and to remove the veil of ambiguity from complex and difficult questions, but could not even expound the most elementary concerns of religion or implement the *sharī'ah*?

We leave it those whose intelligences are not fettered by fanaticism or prejudice to judge the matter.

Lesson Seventeen
The Imāmate and Inner Guidance of Man

One of the functions and attributes of the Imāmate *(imāmah)* is to extend inner guidance to man. This is something different from outer guidance in matters of law and the *sharī'ah*; it is a distinct and lofty station bestowed by God on a select and precious few among His creation, men who, themselves strongly drawn and attracted to God and fully aware of all the variations of human behavior and the various degrees of faith and knowledge people possess, can influence their thoughts and inner beings. They illumine the hearts of the *ummah* with inner knowledge and aid them in the refinement of their souls and their inward journeying, always bearing in mind the great multiplicity to which they are subject. It then becomes incumbent on men to follow them and to align themselves with the guidance they provide, thus guarding themselves against falling into the pit of instinctual desires and corrupt longings.

Some of the great prophets, after their determination and steadfastness had been duly tested and their spiritual strength had been fully proven, and they had attained the stage of total certainty, gained this station of inner guidance with which we are concerned.

Likewise, it can be deduced from numerous verses of the Qur'ān that the Inerrant Imām *(Imām al-ma'ṣūm)*, who is situated at the highest rank of spiritual life, is also entrusted with the task of inner guidance, for he is a channel of divine grace which comes to him inwardly from the suprasensible realm.

The Glorious Qur'ān specifies certain conditions for the office of Imāmate: "*We have chosen from among them Imāms who at Our command shall guide men to the right path, for they are patient and steadfast and have certain knowledge of Our signs.*" (32:24)

What is meant here by guidance is inner guidance, not legal guidance, for to guide others in an outward sense by exhorting them to follow the truth is a duty for everyone, according to the command of the *sharī'ah*, and fulfilling it is not contingent on being an Imām, patient and steadfast, or having certain knowledge of God's signs, nor is it necessary to traverse different stages and degrees in order to perform it. However, guidance in accordance with divine command is a station that can be attained only through divine appointment, and is possible only for the one who, when confronted with irksome events and occurrences, passes the divine test implicit in them by displaying exemplary powers of endurance; who consistently resists the pollution of sin and struggles against all forms of lowliness and triviality. Equipped with such virtues, he attains the lofty rank of the certain knowledge of God's signs and the station of Imāmate, which is also the station of inner guidance. The Qur'ān says: "*We have appointed them Imāms in order that they might guide in accordance with Our command*" (21:73), and, in another verse, "*A day on which We shall call forth each group with its Imām.*" (17:71)

When Ibrāhīm had completed all the tasks with which God had tested him, God addressed him as follows: "*I appoint you to the station of Imāmate and the leadership of man. Ibrāhīm then asked: 'Will you also grant this station to my progeny?' God said: 'The covenant of My Imāmate will not be granted to wrongdoers.'*" (2:123)

Several points can be derived from this verse.

First, the Imāmate of Ibrāhīm was connected directly to the manner in which he had confronted the tests and trials of prophethood. After he had displayed his strength by passing through all those stages, God revealed to him that he was to be further honored with the lofty office of Imāmate, with responsibility for the inner guidance of mankind, the refinement of their souls, the maturing of their spiritual capacities, and, in general, the preservation of the truth.

Second, Ibrāhīm was addressed by God in this manner when he was approaching the final part of his life and at a time when he was fully established in the rank of prophet and already had responsibility for the guidance of his *ummah* in matters of belief and conduct. God nonetheless promised him an additional station, which proves that the office of Imāmate, with the ability to exercise inner influence on the *ummah* in order to advance on the inner path, was a higher and more exalted office than his prophethood.

Third, immunity from the pollution of sin *('iṣmah)* is one of the conditions of Imāmate. For the verse proclaims that wrongdoers who transgress the bounds of piety and inerrancy, whether they wrong others or their own selves, will be denied the rank of Imāmate.

Fourth, the Imāmate is a divine covenant, bestowed only on the just, the pious, and the utterly pure; it is only they who aid and guide the *ummah*. The Imāmate is not, then, a station which is at the disposal of men to be awarded to whomever they see fit.

Fifth, prophethood and Imāmate can be combined in a single person, as was the case with Ibrāhīm. For he had already received revelation in his capacity of prophet, correcting men's erroneous beliefs by means of decisive arguments and proofs, and in the very process of doing this, he had acquired the strength and capacity needed for inner guidance, so that the gate of Imāmate was opened before him.

Finally, the verse indicates that members of Ibrāhīm's progeny who are not wrongdoers *(ẓālīmīn)* will be granted the station of Imāmate. There can be no doubt that the most righteous of God's servants from among that progeny were the Prophet, peace and blessings be upon him and his family, and the Inerrant Imāms, so they must count as Imāms from Ibrāhīm's line who were entrusted with inner guidance and the knowledge of the unseen.

Imām Ja'far al-Ṣādiq, peace be upon him, is reported in *al-Kāfī* to have said:

"Before appointing Ibrāhīm as prophet, God Almighty appointed him His servant. Before ennobling him with His friendship, He bestowed on him the rank of messengerhood. Before granting him the rank of Imāmate, He made him His sincere and devoted friend. It was therefore after Ibrāhīm had attained a whole series of high ranks that he was given the station of Imāmate."[203]

Numerous traditions exist affirming and emphasizing the need for an Imām to be present among the people in order to guide them. These traditions indicate that as long as the human species exist in this world, a proof of God and the truth must also exist to provide and protect the intellectual, social and credal framework for the *ummah*. This proof is none other than the Imām, the Friend of God, who in his very person is a living exponent and exemplar of true Islam.

The Commander of the Faithful, 'Alī, peace be upon him, said: "The Family of Muḥammad, peace and blessings be upon him and his family, are like the stars; as soon as one of them sets, another rises."[204]

Imām Ja'far al-Ṣādiq, peace be upon him, said in the course of a sermon:

"God has illumined His religion with the Imāms from the Household of the Prophet and made them the abundant spring from which knowledge of religion gushes forth. Whoever recognizes the claims of the Imāms, based on sound knowledge and insight, will taste the sweetness of faith and come to know the luminous and beautiful visage of Islam. For God has appointed the Imāms to be His proof among men and their guide; has placed on their heads the crown of sublimity and leadership; caused the light of His own splendor to shine on their beings; and sustained and supported them with inexhaustible heavenly power. It is only by means of causes that God's grace reaches His servants, and God does not accept men's knowledge of Himself except by means of their recognition of the Imām.

"The Imām is versed in all the complexities, problems and metaphoric aspects of revelation, and he is chosen by God from among the descendants of Ḥusayn, peace be upon him. Whenever an Imām departs for the realm of eternity to meet God, he appoints another Imām from among his own offspring in order to illumine the path men should travel. God has chosen all of them to lead the *ummah* in order that they should guide the people and judge justly among them.

"They are among the choice descendants of Ādam, Nūḥ, Ibrāhīm, and Ismā'īl. The jewel of their being shone in the world even before their bodies were fashioned of clay. God made their existence the substance of life for all men and the firm pillars of Islam."[205]

He said in another tradition:

"Even if there were only two people left on earth, one of them would be an Imām. The last person to close his eyes on the world will be the Imām, so that no one will be to argue before God that he was left without an Imām."[206]

al-A'mash asked Imām Ja'far al-Ṣādiq: "How will people benefit from the existence of an absent *(ghā'ib)* Imām?" He answered: "In the same way that they benefit from the sun when it is hidden behind a cloud."[207]

Isḥāq b. Ghālib relates the Imām to have said:

"The Imām is designated by God and the Messenger to be God's proof before men. Through the blessed existence of the Imām a link is established between God's servants and the suprasensible realm and God's grace flows down upon them. God will not accept the deeds of His servants unless they are loyal to the Imām. God does not abandon His servants to their own devices after creating them; instead, by means of the Imām, he lays out the path of piety before them and thus establishes His proof."[208]

Imām al-Bāqir, peace be upon him, said:

"I swear by God that from the time God took Ādam's spirit and conveyed him to the realm of eternity, He has never left the earth empty of an Imām. Hereafter, too, the world will never be without the existence of an Imām, so that God's proof will always be present among His servants."[209]

Abū Khālid al-Kābulī says that he once asked the fifth Imām to interpret the verse "*So believe in God and His Messenger and the light He has sent you.*" (64:8) The Imām replied: "I swear by God that that light *(al-nūr)* is the Imām. The brilliance of the light of the Imām in the heart of the believer is greater than that of the sun. It is the Imām who illumines the hearts of the believers. God prevents the brilliance of that light from reaching the hearts of whomsoever He wills, this being the explanation for the darkness of their hearts."[210]

al-Ṣadūq writes in his *'Ilal al-Sharā'i'*:

"Jābir once asked Imām al-Bāqir, peace be upon him, why men need prophets and Imāms. He replied that the existence of prophets and Imāms is indispensable for the continuance and welfare of the world. For it is by means of them that God wards off His punishment from men. God says in the Qur'ān: '*(O Muḥammad) as long as you are among them, punishment shall not descend on them.*'" (8:33)

The Most Noble Prophet himself, peace and blessings be upon him and his family, said:

"Just as the stars bestow safety on the inhabitants of the heavens, the People of my House grant security to the inhabitants of the earth. If the stars in the heaven are destroyed, it will be a catastrophe for the inhabitants of the heavens, and if the People of my House are no longer to be found among men, the whole earth will be overtaken by disaster.

"What is meant by the People of the House are those leaders obedience to whom God has conjoined with obedience to Himself in the verse, '*O you who believe, obey God, the Messenger, and the Holders of Authority*' (4:59). The Holders of Authority from the People of the Prophet's House are adorned with inerrancy and utter purity; they never disobey any of God's commands and are always guided and supported by Him. Their deeds are beyond the reach of crookedness and deviation, and their feet are firmly planted on His straight path. It is through the blessed existence of these great ones that

God's servants receive their sustenance, cities become prosperous, and the rainfall descends. The Holy Spirit always accompanies them, and there is never any separation between them and the Qur'ān."[211]

Muḥammad b. Fuḍayl asked Imām al-Riḍā, peace be upon him, whether the earth could subsist without an Imām. He answered that it could not. Muḥammad b. Fuḍayl continued: "It has been related to us from Imām Ja'far al-Ṣādiq that the world will never remain without a proof *(ḥujjah)* and an Imām, for were it to do so, the people of the world would instantly be caught up in God's wrath." The Imām then said: "The earth will never be without an Imām. Were there to be no Imām, destruction and collapse would be the ineluctable fate of the world."[212]

Lesson Eighteen
The Inerrancy of the Imāms and the Necessity of Belief in it

Throughout the history of Islam, different sects have debated among themselves the question of whether inerrancy is necessary in prophets and Imāms or not.

The Shī'ah are unanimously agreed on the inerrancy *('iṣmah)* of the Imāms, and they regard only the one who possesses this fundamental quality as fit for the office of Imāmate, given the sensitive and portentous nature of the office. There is always the danger that a leader burdened with responsibility for the manifold concerns of the *ummah* may knowingly or unknowingly veer in the direction of error, in which case the honor and values of the *ummah* will be at risk, with undesirable consequences for Islamic society as a whole.

Insistence upon inerrancy as a condition for leadership is a hallmark of the Shī'ah and a proof of the maturity of their religious thinking and comprehensive grasp of Islam, for with great care and alertness they have identified who the leader should be and designated inerrancy and extensive knowledge as two of his inseparable qualities. His inerrancy and immunity from sin are the result of his piety and self-discipline, and his knowledge is the result of divine grace and generosity, bestowed upon him from God's limitless ocean of wisdom. These two qualities are to be found in combination only in the Imāms of the Prophet's Household, peace and blessings be upon him and his family. The Sunnīs accept anyone as caliph or Imām, without any precondition, and they do not insist on inerrancy and immunity from sin.

Inerrancy is an inner faculty of self-restraint, springing up from the great source of faith, piety, and insight; it insures man against all kinds of sin and moral corruption. This powerful inner attribute, derived as it is from vision of the suprasensible world and the very essence of all creation, is so effective that it prevents man from embarking on any kind of sin or rebellion, whether small of great, open or hidden.

When we say that the factors leading to rebellion and sin have no effect on such a person, we do not mean that in accordance with divine will and decree an overwhelming force prevents him from being attracted to sin, so that the capacity to sin and disobey is removed from him. It is rather that the possessor of inerrancy, while having freedom to choose and to act, is prevented by his awareness of the majesty and constant presence of God from approaching the sphere of sin. He has had such success in establishing the dominion of piety over his soul that he cannot even conceive of sin in the purified sanctuary of his mind, so that the possibility of his actually committing a sin is reduced to zero.

Generally speaking, the commission of any undesirable act is the result of not knowing how ugly the act is and how harmful its consequences are. Even if one is aware to a certain extent of the ugliness of the act and his faith seeks to warn him and alert him to the danger, he is overpowered by his desires and loses all self-control, and is drawn to impurity and sin. It is only attention to the damaging consequences of one's deeds, the restraining force of piety, and a powerful sense of obedience toward divine law, that create a certain immunity in man; there will then be no need for any other means of restraint and control. Muḥammad b. Abī 'Umayr says: "I asked Hishām, the celebrated pupil of Imām Ja'far al-Ṣādiq, peace be upon him, whether the Imām possessed the quality of inerrancy. He answered that he did, and I then asked him to explain inerrancy to me.

"He said: 'Several things lie at the origin of rebellion and sin — greed, envy, lust, anger, and so forth — and not one of these can penetrate the being of the Imām. How might he be greedy, considering that he has everything at his disposal, including even the treasury of the Muslims? How might he be envious, for only he who is aware of a station higher than his own can be envious, and no station higher than the Imāmate can be conceived? As for anger, it is impossible that the Imām be angered by any worldly concern, for God has entrusted to him the implementation of His laws. But in connection with anything touching on the hereafter, anger in not at all undesirable. The Imām will never fall prey to lust, for he is well aware that the pleasures and desirable things of this world are transitory and valueless when compared to the reward that God shall bestow on His worshippers on the Day of Resurrection."[213]

People will submit fully to the requirements of religious duty in response to the summons of their leader and unquestioningly accept his commands and instructions when they regard all his orders as being the command of God, without having doubt on the matter. If someone not be thoroughly immune to sin and error, can complete trust be placed in his words or his orders be obeyed with devotion?

The effect of inerrancy is such that it protects man from deception by the allurements of this world — power and position, wealth and possessions — and enables him to remáin steadfast in the face of all types of distraction.

If it is not possible to trust the leader fully, the mission of religion, which is to enable man to attain perfection, will necessarily remain unfulfilled, for the credal structure of the religion will be distorted by inevitable suspicions that the commands and edicts of the leader are not based on revelation and the authentic principles of Islam.

In addition, possession of the attribute of inerrancy cannot be restricted to the period in which the leader of the Muslims actually exercises the office of Imām. Throughout his life, including the period before assuming the Imāmate, his heart must have been free of all darkness and his person of all sin. In addition to the fact that sinning entails a loss of human dignity, people will always suspect of continuing sinfulness and pollution one whom they know to have erred in the past, however slightly. This suspicion will in turn rob the leadership of such a person of all legitimacy. He will no longer be regarded as an exemplar of piety and purity, as one endowed with unique virtues.

The bitter memory of a life spent partially in sin and corruption can never be erased, and it will always serve as a pretext for his opponents. They will have a powerful and credible tool for attacking him and destroying his reputation and base of popular support. He will be unable to defend his honor or answer his critics convincingly.

If we examine the life of the Immaculate Imāms, peace be upon them, we will see that the groups opposed to them, for all their impudence and shamelessness, never resorted to accusations of corruption in order to destroy their reputation. If there had been the slightest grounds for making such an accusation, the enemies of the Imāms would never have remained silent, and the people in general would have entertained doubt concerning the Imams' pronouncements on matters relating to revelation and God's law. We read in the story of Mūsā, peace be upon him, that the Fir'awn (Pharaoh), that cruel tyrant, unhesitatingly pointed the finger of accusation at Mūsā when he confronted him, saying:

"*Are you not that child that grew up under our tutelage and spent many years with us? Who then committed murder and rebelled against our divinity?*"

Mūsā answered: "*Yes, indeed I killed someone, but not deliberately; my intention was to save an oppressed person, and the result was and accidental killing. I then fled out of fear of you until my Lord taught me knowledge and wisdom and appointed me as one of His prophets.*" (26:16-19)

The first and most essential condition for the office of Imāmate is, then, inward purity and profound piety, divinely accorded protection from sin, the possession of a lustrous heart both before and after appointment to the rank of leader and Imām.

It is true that everyone is exposed to the possibility of error, for the simple reason that whatever knowledge and information he has consists of a series of concepts and images acquired by means of the senses and other ontological faculties, none of which are infallible.

However, the Imām observes the innermost nature of the world, including its suprasensible aspect, by means of the eye of the heart, and this grants him access to a whole treasure house of true and certain knowledge. His perception of reality is not dependent on his senses and is for this reason immune against error. Fallibility arises only when a person wishes to apply his mental concepts to the world of external reality; it does not exist in the case of the Imām who has a direct and unmediated perception of reality and is inwardly connected with the essence of all being.

The comprehensive infallibility and inerrancy of the Imām, manifested in his speech, his acts, and his thoughts, results from his privileged knowledge of the realm of the unseen. No one can comprehend the totality of reality by recourse to external and conventional means, and perceive the true nature of things as they are; it is only divinely bestowed knowledge, a mode of comprehension derived from the world of the unseen, that can guide man infallibly to a knowledge of the reality of all things.

Piety expressing itself in deeds is far more effective than verbal exhortation in bringing about the moral education of men and advancing them on the path of spiritual growth. If the one who assumes the task of the spiritual guidance of the people is lacking himself in spiritual virtue and no sign of moral purity or practical piety can be discerned in him, he will be totally unable to fashion upright and exalted human beings, to exercise any positive role in their development, or to guide them toward the general goals inculcated by religion.

It may appear that the Qur'ān has attributed sins to some of the prophets. However, the sin must be carefully examined in each case to gain a proper understanding of the matter. The essence of true sin is to rebel against God, to disobey His commands, to plunge into the whirlpool of vice, all of these being acts for which a specific punishment has been decreed; in this sense, the prophets are completely free of all sin.

Another kind of sin might be called relative, for its commission does not entail any specific punishment. Even this kind of sin is not to be expected from those true travellers on the path of God who are in direct communication with the source of all being and directly perceive all hidden truths. Given the vision with which they are endowed, it is not to be thought that they would be unaware of God for even an instant, for even such temporary inattention would diminish their closeness to God.

Considering the fact that these favored friends of God possess vast treasuries of faith and knowledge and have direct and precise awareness of reality, it will be considered a sin on their part if their orientation to God is interrupted for even a moment, even though such brief inattention would not occasion so much as a reproach in the case of lesser persons.

Something similar can be observed in the case of socially prominent people who carry certain titles and ranks; people have higher expectations of them than they do of others. Everyone is obliged to try to fulfil the expectations that others have of him, based on his rank and position in society. Sobriety and dignity of speech are expected of a learned scholar, but not of an illiterate and unlearned man.

It is true that awareness of the undesirable consequences of sin does not in itself create immunity against sin and that its restraining influence is neither reliable nor constant. However, a knowledge that is deeply rooted and shows clearly all the grievous results of sin, a perception and an awareness that permits the reality of all things to be seen directly, in such a fashion that limitations of time and space are transcended, and a lively fear of severe punishment by God — all these taken together constitute a mechanism which makes the commission of a sin by a possessor of inerrancy impossible.

No intelligent pilot will consent to take off in a plane which he knows to be carrying a time bomb and is therefore destined to blow up in midair. It is not, however, that he has some immunity to this suicidal course of action built into him, involuntarily; he can freely decide whether to take off or not. The fact that he refrains from taking off is because he is fully aware of the disastrous consequences that would inevitably follow if he did; it is his intelligence and awareness that guide him and reduce to zero the possibility that he would do so.

This may serve as an illustration for the way in which profound and immediate knowledge of the fatal consequences of an act can provide immunity against committing that act, in the most powerful and practical way imaginable.

The leader of religion is not subject to compulsion or determination in his obeying divine command or adorning his soul with purity and virtue, nor does inerrancy negate his possession of free will and choice, in the sense of making it impossible for him to sin, without any involvement of his ability to decide.

It is rather that the Imāms' constant orientation to the pure essence of God, their selfless struggles for His sake, their devotion, self-sacrifice, and exertions in seeking His satisfaction, powerfully insure these exalted personages against the commission of sin. Although they retain the capacity for committing evil deeds, they never pollute themselves by committing them, and their minds never even incline in that direction.

Their comprehensive knowledge of the corruption caused by sin, joined to their thorough awareness of the sublimity of the divine essence, suffices fully to rein in any instinctual tendencies that might exist in their beings and to render them steadfast on the path of purity, piety, and virtue.

Quite apart from the Inerrant Imāms, peace be upon them, who are of course situated at exalted levels of knowledge and insight, there are those who are not inerrant but are nonetheless sincere and ardent lovers of God who sacrifice their whole beings for His sake, and effectively acquire a degree of immunity from sin in their exertions to attain God's pleasure, so that the mere thought of disobeying divine command has no attraction for them.

It is of course possible that in their case the desired result is attained not by breadth of understanding or completeness of awareness, but by a strong sense of obedience to God, an innate purity of mind which quells any tendency to sin that may exist within them and leads them to a categorical rejection of evil.

The commission of a sin arises either from incomplete knowledge of the ugliness of the sin, unawareness of its evil consequences, deficiency of intelligence, or feebleness of the will when confronted with the onslaught of passionate desire. None of these factors can obtain in the case of one who possesses abundant spiritual knowledge, who perceives in detailed form all the corruption sin causes, and who has subordinated his ego to the demands of piety.

In addition, freedom from error and sin is ensured by the protection God extends for the sake of the correct conveyance of the message. In just the same way that God watches over the first receipt of revelation by the Prophet, peace and blessings be upon him and his family, in order to exclude all error, divinely guaranteed inerrancy is also called for at this stage in the process. For it is necessary that God's message and commands should be conveyed to mankind without the least error or mistake, whether intentional or accidental.

Thus the Qur'ān says:

"Were it not for God's grace and mercy toward you, a group of God's enemies would have conspired to make you deviate from the right path. Thanks to God's kindness, it was only themselves that they caused to wander from the truth, and they are completely unable to harm you. God has bestowed on you this Book, wisdom and prophethood, and taught you what you knew not, for God's kindness to you is great and His favor unbounded." (4:111)

The propagation and implementation of God's revealed commands is similar, in that it is a prolongation of messengerhood and the leader and Imām to whom these tasks fall must like the Prophet be unassailably immune to error in his words, actions, and deeds. To commit any error in the exposition of God's commands would negate the whole purpose of the Imāmate, in just the same way that corrupt and unworthy rulers are a threat to the authenticity of religion.

There can be absolutely no doubt that if the responsibility for preserving and implementing the laws of religion is not entrusted to a trustwortny and inerrant individual who heads the executive power and applies them faithfully and integrally, the aims and purposes of religion will suffer decay and distortion, for there is a possibility that an unreliable and errant individual who heads the executive power may implement the laws incorrectly or on the basis of incorrect knowledge, or deliberately distort in conformity with his personal desires and interests.

Furthermore, there are numerous verses of the Qur'ān which call for elucidation and interpretation by the Imām; it is he who must supply the necessary clarifications.

One in whom all human perfections have been actualized is a complete human exemplar of the religion. He embodies the state that is the ultimate aim of man's evolution and is always situated on the straight path which leads in that direction. He is inherently bound to act in accordance with the *sharī'ah* in every period of his life and is never polluted by sin or impurity at any point in his life. If even a brief portion of his life were to be spent in sin, resulting in a temporary deviation from the straight path, he could no longer be regarded as an exemplary individual, a perfect model of religion, and the divine aim of providing men with the means of ascent toward Him could not be realized.

It is impossible therefore to renounce the principle that the one who expounds and implements divine law must possess comprehensive inerrancy and freedom from sin, even before his actual assumption of the Imamāte. Were it to be otherwise, society cold never submit to the guidance and instructions of the Imām with full confidence.

Lesson Nineteen
Confirmation from the Qur'ān and the *Sunnah*

One of the scriptural proofs for the inerrancy of the People of the Prophet's House is the "purification verse" *(āyah al-taṭhīr)*, a verse which depicts their utter purity and their unique character as follow:

"*God wishes to remove all filth and impurity from you, O People of House of the Prophet, and to render you utterly free of all pollution.*" (33:33)

Rijs, translated by us as "filth", has the meaning in Arabic of dirt and impurity, whether it be outer or inner, the latter being essentially synoymous with sin. The word has been used in both senses in the Qur'ān. Outer impurity is what is at issue in the following verse: "*Carrion, blood that has been shed, and the flesh of the pig — all these are filth.*" (6:145) By contrast, inner impurity is what is meant in this verse: "*Those whose hearts are afflicted with sickness will find their filth increased by God so that they ultimately die in a state of unbelief.*" (9:125)

In the verse which speaks of the removal of filth and impurity from the Prophet's House, the word *rijs* cannot be interpreted as referring to outer impurity, insofar as all Muslims are required to shun outer impurity as a matter of religious obligation; this is not something that pertains exclusively to the Prophet's House, whereas the verse clearly implies the grant of a particular distinction. Moreover, the avoidance of filth and impurity does not count as a virtue that in the view of the Qur'ān characterizes a particular group of people. Given all of this, in order for the verse to be comprehensible. the word *rijs* must be taken in the sense of inward pollution of the spirit.

God's will and desire to remove all impurity from the People of the Prophet's House is a desire related to the whole scheme of creation, in that God wished that within His created order the members of that house be free of all impurity and adorned with all purity. If we related God's wish to matters of law and legislation, the meaning would simply be that in the sphere of law they should not sin or pollute themselves. This meaning would be clearly unacceptable, for the avoidance of sin and the shunning of impurity is a universal religious duty, the imposition of which does not confer honor or special status on anyone. It would certainly not cause the Prophet, peace and blessings be upon him and his family, to engage in the unprecedented act of gathering together the members of his House behind closed doors and casting a piece of cloth or a cloak *(kisā')* over them.

The revelation of the "purification verse" aroused a great deal of attention in the time of the Prophet among his Companions, and the select group to whom the verse was addressed and whose sanctity and purity now became a matter of common acceptance were known as the Companions of the Cloak *(ahl al-kisā')*. Whenever the People of the Prophet's House found it necessary to draw attention to their unique spiritual rank, they would proudly refer to this verse.

At the gathering that was convened after the death of 'Umar to select a caliph, the Commander of the Faithful, 'Alī, peace be upon him, made the following argument:

"Is there any among us apart from myself concerning whom the 'purification verse' was revealed?"

When they answered "no," he proceeded: "The People of the House are overflowing with abundant virtue, for the Qur'ān says, *'God wishes to remove all filth and impurity from you, O House of the Prophet, and to render you utterly free of pollution.'* (33:33) God has therefore removed from us all evil, outer and inner, and placed us firmly on the path of truth and righteousness."[214]

Ibn 'Abbas reports the following important tradition from the Prophet:

"God Almighty has divided all men into two groups, and placed me among the best of all men. For He said. *'The Companions of the Right Hand — how pleasant will be their state!'* (56:27), and *'The Companions of the Left Hand, how evil will be their state!'* (56:41)

"I am among the Companions of the Right Hand, and I am in fact the best of them.

"Then God divided men into three groups, and again placed me in the purest of them. For He said, *'The Companions of the Right Hand — how pleasant will be their state! The Companions of the Left Hand, the wretched, how miserable will be their state! The third group are those foremost in faith, those who are in truth nigh unto Me.'* (56:8-11). And I am the best of the foremost.

"Then He divided men into peoples and tribes, and placed me among the best of them. For He said, *'O mankind, We have created you from a single man and woman, and made of you different peoples and tribes in order that you might recognize one another, and the greatest of you in the sight of God is the most pious.'* (49:13). And I am the most pious and the greatest of mankind, and yet I take no pride in this.

"Then God divided people into families and households, and placed me in the most virtuous of all households. For He said, *'God wishes to remove all filth and impurity from you, O House of the Prophet, and to render you utterly free of pollution.'*(33:33) I and my House are, then, utterly free of all impurity and immune to sin."[215]

In this tradition we see that the Prophet, peace and blessings be upon him and his family, has unambiguously interpreted the "purification verse" as referring to inerrancy.

The events that constituted the occasion for the revelation of the verse were the following, as related by Umm Salamah, a wife of the Prophet renowned for her piety and nobility, in whose the events took place:

"One day, Fāṭimah, peace be upon her, the daughter of the

Prophet, brought a dish of food to her father. He told her to summon her husband 'Alī, peace be upon him, and their children, Ḥasan and Ḥusayn, peace be upon them, which she did. When they were all gathered and engaged in eating, the 'purification verse' was revealed. Thereupon the Prophet took a piece of cloth that he had on his shoulders and cast it over their heads, saying three times, 'O Lord, these are the People of my House; remove filth and impurity from them and render them utterly pure.'"[216]

Many Sunnī scholars remark that the "purification verse" was revealed concerning five people: The Prophet, 'Alī, Fāṭimah, Ḥasan, and Ḥusayn.[217]

'Umar b. Abī Salamah who was a witness to the incident described it as follows:

"The 'purification verse' was revealed in the house of Umm Salamah. Then the Prophet, peace and blessings be upon him and his family, told 'Alī, Fāṭimah, Ḥasan, and Ḥusayn to approach him and threw over their heads a piece of cloth that was covering his shoulders, and said, 'These are the People of my House; remove from them all filth, and render them utterly pure.' Umm Salamah then asked, 'O Messenger of God, am I also one of them?' He replied, 'Be content with your own place, for you are one of the virtuous.'"[218]

'Ā'ishah relates: "One day the Prophet left the house, with a piece of cloth slung over his shoulders. Ḥasan, Ḥusayn, Fāṭimah, and 'Alī came to see him, and he threw the cloth over their heads, reciting the 'purification verse.'[219]

Abu 'l-Ḥamrā', one of the Companions, relates: "I stayed in Madīnah for eight months, watching the Prophet constantly. He would never leave his house to perform the prayers without first passing by 'Alī's house. He would place his hands on each side of the door and cry out, 'Prayer! Prayer! God wishes to remove all filth from you, People of the House, and to make you utterly pure!'"[220]

Only a few people witnessed the Prophet, peace and blessings be upon him and his family, casting his cloak over the People of the House, so in order to disseminate news of it as broadly as possible among the people and convey make them aware of the standing of his progeny, for them in turn to convey it others, he repeated this procedure for an extended period. Ibn 'Abbās relates that for a period of nine months, whenever the Prophet passed by the house of 'Alī, peace be upon him, he would call out: "Peace be upon you, O People of the House!" and then he would recite the: "purification verse."[221]

Anas b. Mālik similarly relates: "For a period of six months, whenever the Messenger of God, peace and blessings be upon him and his family, passed by the house of Fāṭimah, peace be upon her, at the time of the dawn prayer, he would say, 'Rise for prayer, O People of my House!' Then he would recite the 'purification verse'."[222]

The Commander of the Faithful, 'Alī, peace be upon him, relates: "Every morning when the Most Noble Messenger passed in front of our house, he would say, 'God's mercy be upon you, rise for prayer!' Then he would recite the 'purification verse'."[223]

Some people maintain that the "purification verse" cannot refer to the inerrancy of the Imāms because the context in which it occurs relates to the wives of the Prophet and necessitates that it, too, should refer to them, or that at the very least they cannot be excluded from the category it addresses; if it were to imply inerrancy, then the wives of the Prophet would also have to be inerrant, a belief that no one holds. We must therefore interpret the verse as referring to the wives of the Prophet, not to their putative inerrancy or that of the other members of the Prophet's house.

This objection is groundless, and incompatible with the wording of the verse. For if it had been intended to address the wives of the Prophet, the second person feminine plural would have been used, not the second person masculine plural (*'ankunna* instead of *'ankum, yuṭahhirakunna* instead of *yuṭahhirakum*).

In addition, the traditions that we have cited clearly demonstrate that only four people are meant by the expression People of the House, for the Messenger of God says: "O God, these are the People of my House." In the lifetime of the Prophet, membership in his house was restricted to the four named individuals. As for his wives and other relatives, including even Ja'far b. Abī Ṭālib and his uncle al-'Abbās, none of them belong to the category of his house.

Furthermore, many other traditions mention clearly the occasion for the revelation of the verse.

When Umm Salamah, Zaynab, and 'Ā'ishah asked the Most Noble Messenger, peace and blessings be upon him and his family, whether they too were part of the People of the House *(Ahl al-Bayt)*, he told them to be content with their station and not to attempt to draw close.

There is no problem in regarding the "purification verse" as a parenthetic statement inserted in the verses dealing with the wives of the Prophet, for such recourse to parenthesis is by no means contrary to good usage and is also found elsewhere in the Qur'ān.

Finally, purification *(taṭhīr)* is synoymous here with inerrancy *('iṣmah)*, and according to the unanimous opinion of all traditionists and historians the wives of the Prophet did not possess the lofty attribute of inerrancy. They frequently vexed the Prophet, peace and blessings be upon him and his family, during his lifetime, and matters once reached such a pitch that the Prophet shunned some of them for a whole month and threatened them with divorce. Worse than all of this, the Messenger of God, peace and blessings be upon him and his family, was standing one day with a group of his Companions near the door to the house of one of his wives, and pointing in its direction he said: "This is where trouble starts."[224]

Taking all this into consideration, how can the wives of the Prophet be regarded as covered by the "purification verse"?

In addition, there are numerous traditions specifically proclaiming the inerrancy of the Imāms.

Thus Ibn 'Abbās reports the Prophet to have said:

"I, 'Alī, Ḥasan, Ḥusayn, and nine descendants of Ḥusayn, are inerrant and pure."[225]

Salīm b. Qays records the Commander of the Faithful,

'Alī, peace be upon him, to have said:

"Obedience is incumbent only to God, the Messenger and the Holders of Authority *(ulu'l-amr)*. It is obligatory to follow the Holders of Authority because they are inerrant, far removed from all sin, and they issue no command contravening God's law."[226]

He also said: "Why are you bewildered and confused in your attempts to find the right path? The Prophet's progeny is among you; they are guides to the truth, the banners of religion, and the tongues of honesty and veracity. Place them on the same level as the Qur'ān, and hasten to them as the thirsty rush toward water."[227]

Imām al-Riḍā, peace be upon him, said: "The Imām is a personage who is free of all sin, major and minor, devoid of all faults, and replete with knowledge."[228]

Imām al-Ṣādiq, peace be upon him, said: "The prophets and their successors are sinless and pure, for they all possess inerrancy."[229]

He expressed the same matter in the following more detailed form: "The Imām is a unique figure, elected by God. He is men's guide to God Almighty; the one who arises in order to plant hope in men's hearts; the one chosen by God who nurtured by Him arises first in the world of the particle and then in the created universe. He was situated to the right of the divine throne in phantasmal form before the creation of all animate life, and learned knowledge and wisdom from the world of the unseen, on account of which he was appointed Imām and selected as one of the pure.

"The Imām is the choice offspring of Ādam and Nūḥ, the select descendant of Ibrāhīm, the quintessence of the progeny of Ismā'īl, the foremost of the line of Muḥammad. God Almighty shows him particular concern, for He guards and protects him with His most sacred essence. The wiles of Satan are warded off from him; the tenebrous temptations of the evildoers have no effect on him. He is immune to all reprehensible conduct, devoid of all faults and defects, and protected against the commission of error. He is never polluted by evil, and is celebrated for his steadfastness, virtue, knowledge and chastity from the very beginning of his maturity".[230]

Abū Sa'īd al-Khudrī reports the Prophet, peace and blessings be upon him and his family, as saying:

"O people, I am leaving among you two great and precious trusts; if you hold fast to them, you will never go astray. One of the two is greater than the other, and that is the Book of God, for that is the link between the earth and the heavens. The second is my progeny the People of my House; know that my progeny and the Qur'ān shall never be separated from each other until the Day of Resurrection."[231]

This is the well-known *ḥadīth* of the two precious trusts *(thaqalayn)*, which has been cited by both Shī'ī and Sunnī scholars in their books of tradition, with numerous chains of transmission. A number of points can be deduced from this tradition of indubitable authenticity.

First, the deeds and conduct of the Inerrant Imāms must be regarded as exemplary and demanding of imitation; failure to do so will lead to misguidance. This can be true only if their steps never deviate in the direction of error or sin and they are in an unvarying state of inerrancy. Were it to be otherwise, the *ummah* would fall into the whirlpool of perdition by following them, whereas the Prophet categorically declares that whoever follows his progeny will not go astray. They are Islam personified, and their conduct is the example the whole *ummah* must follow and implement in their everyday lives.

Second, the Prophet, peace and blessings be upon him and his family, declares that the Qur'ān and his progeny *('itrah)* shall never be separated until the Day of Resurrection, so that just as the survival of the Qur'ān is guaranteed until the Day of Resurrection, the earth will never be without an Imām.

Third, the People of the House constitute, from the point of view of the Prophet, an authority and a source of learning for all Muslims, irrespective of the historical circumstances under which they live; reference should therefore be made to them in order to learn the ordinances of God's religion.

The eighth Imām, al-Riḍā, peace be upon him, says:

"Whenever God chooses someone to administer the affairs of His servants, He expands his breast for him and makes of his heart a repository of wisdom. Incessantly He inspires him with knowledge, and there is no question he is unable to answer. He is never uncertain of the correct path, and through his inerrancy he is pure of all sin and rebellion. He is sustained always by God, and succeeds always in traversing His path. Error and sin cannot touch him. God it is Who has bestowed this exalted station on him, so that he might be a proof to His servants and a witness to His creation. This is generosity that God bestows on whomsoever He wills from among His servants, and God's generosity is great."[232]

Finally, let us draw attention to a possibility that 'Allāmah Sharaf al-Dīn has raised:

"Although we are convinced that no distortion has taken place in the verses of the Noble Qur'ān and that our heavenly Book has not been tampered with in any way, it is by no means clear that the arrangement and recension of the verses is precisely that in which they were revealed. For it is quite possible that the 'purification verse' concerning the People of the House was revealed separately and then, when the verses of the Qur'ān were being assembled, was placed in the middle of the verses relating to the wives of the Prophet, either in error or deliberately."[233]

Lesson Twenty
The Imām's Comprehensive Knowledge of the Islamic Sciences

It is, then, the Imām, that being replete with virtue and overflowing with blessedness, who is aware of all the needs of the *ummah* and of whatever is conducive to a happy and dignified life, in this world and the hereafter, and plays a determining role in securing their spiritual and material well-being. He knows, too, whatever is needful for guiding men and administering their affairs and is fully aware of all matters, great and small, that arise as they traverse the ocean of life.

All these various types of knowledge and awareness derive from the comprehensiveness of the Imām and his functions, for his person represents a continuation or extension of the personality of Muḥammad, the Seal of the Prophets, peace and blessings be upon him and his family. In his knowledge, characteristics and attributes, the Imām is like a representation of the Prophet in miniature, this being a particular favor granted him by God.

Once a leader comes to perceive the inner truth of the ordinances of religion and to possess a religious knowledge that is based on immediacy and certainty, not fallible mental exertion, it is inconceivable that he should be ignorant of any aspect of the Islamic sciences. How can one attribute ignorance of divine law to one who serves as a channel for divine grace and the guide of humanity?

It is the Inerrant Imām who as the guardian and treasurer

of God's law creates the environment in which men may grow to perfection and advance on the straight path.

It is also one of his duties to preserve the doctrinal integrity of the *ummah* and its collective interests, for God's limitless mercy necessitates that humanity should never be left wandering and distraught, abandoned to its own devices. The leader must therefore be in a position to act as the spiritual and intellectual authority of the community by the gate of knowledge of God's commands being always opened to him so that by means of his instruction he can guide men to fulfil the purposes of religion. He constantly provides men with the means of solving their problems so that there is no excuse or pretext left for them to make. Answers to all kinds of conceptual and practical problems are contained in the thousands of traditions that have been transmitted from the Imāms.

The firm and categorical responses they gave to all kinds of religious queries and doubts, their clear and rational refutation of various kinds of unbelief, their logical mode of dispute and argumentation — all bear witness to the breadth of their Islamic knowledge and vision.

The one whose soul is more illumined than others, whose knowledge more elevated, whose vision more expansive, whose intelligence loftier, whose concentration more profound, and — most important of all — who is equipped with the quality of inerrancy, such a one is better qualified to lead men than anyone else.

One whose knowledge is limited and the scope of whose religious perception is restricted is always in danger of acting in a sense contrary to the Qur'ān, whether knowingly or not. There is no guarantee that his words and deeds will always accord with divine law, and if he were to contravene the Qur'ān, so too would those who follow him. The source of the danger lies in the fact that his knowledge in many cases is suppositional, not definite, and there can be no doubt that someone who generally chooses the best among a series of possibilities may sometimes deviate from the path of the

Qur'ān without there being any evil intention on his part.

Imām al-Ṣādiq, peace be upon him, says in a certain tradition:

"God illumines His religion with the brilliant light of the People of the House and by means of them displays His sources of knowledge. The one who recognizes the Imām's claim to his obedience will taste the sweetness of faith and understand the superiority of Islam and its perfect and flawless nature, for God has made the Imām the banner of guidance and His proof to men, and placed on his head the crown of splendor and magnificence. The Imām is one whose whole being is submerged in divine light. He is aided with heavenly truths and the scope of his knowledge is unending. God's bounties cannot be known except by means, and the Imām is the means. Knowledge of God is not possible except by means of knowledge of the Imām. The Imām is versed in all the complexities of the revelation and the *Sunnah*, and is one whom God will always appoint from among the progeny of Ḥusayn, peace be upon him."[234]

There are authoritative texts to the effect that whatever was taught to the previous prophets was also known to the Prophet, peace and blessings be upon him and his family, and to the Imāms, peace be upon them. Thus Imām al-Bāqir, peace be upon him, said: "God has two kinds of knowledge, particular and general. The prophets have no access to the former, nor can the cherubim become aware of it. It is the latter to which the prophets and the cherubim have access, and God's Messenger has transmitted it to us."[235]

Imām Mūsā b. Ja'far, peace be upon him, is reported to have said: "I swear by God that truths have been bestowed on us that were not given to Sulaymān (Solomon) or anyone else. And recall God's address to Sulaymān: *'This is Our gift to you; either teach it to others or keep it to yourself; you will not be called to account for it.'*" (38:39)[236]

Imām al-Ṣādiq, peace be upon him, said:

"The one who has knowledge of the Book is 'Alī, peace be upon him, for he himself said, 'Be aware that the knowledge that came to earth with Ādam, and all the knowledge with which the prophets were ennobled down to the Seal of the Prophets, exists in his progeny."[237]

He also said the following:

"The sacred divine essence has two forms of knowledge: one peculiar to God Himself, inaccessible to all men; and the other knowledge which is bestowed on angels and prophets. This second category of knowledge is accessible to us Imāms too."[238]

Imām al-Bāqir, peace be upon him, said:

"The knowledge that came down with Ādam, the father of mankind, did not vanish, for it was handed down from one generation to the next. 'Alī had complete knowledge of religion and the *sharī'ah*, and none of us (Imāms) dies without designating a successor who will inherit his knowledge or whatever God wishes him to know."[239]

Again, he said: "We are treasurers not of gold and silver but of divine knowledge."[240]

The Commander of the Faithful, 'Alī, peace be upon him, says:

"God will never leave the earth devoid of His proof, the one who will rise up for truth, whether he be manifest among men or hidden from their view. The reason for this is that God's proof can never be disproved or disputed.

"How many are the proofs and where are they to be found? I swear by God that they are few in number, but their rank in God's presence is most exalted. God preserves His clear verses by means of them, for them in turn to entrust to those like unto them, and their accumulated treasure of knowledge is all marked by clear vision and certainty. What appears difficult to others is easy for them; they are at ease with intimidating problems from which the ignorant shrink back in fear, and they converse with those whose spirits are at the apex of loftiness and attached to the divine throne. They are God's viceregents on earth, guiding men to His religion."[241]

On many occasions during the lifetime of 'Alī, when problems arose that were beyond the capacity of the caliph to solve, 'Alī was the only authority to whom recourse might be had to find a solution. Conversely, not a single occasion can be found on which 'Alī turned to anyone else in order to learn something of Islamic law or find the solution to some problem or other.

Sa'īd b. al-Musayyib is recorded to have said: "No one other than 'Alī b. Abī Ṭālib ever said, 'Ask me my opinion, before you lose me.'"[242]

The one who assumes responsibility for the administration of the Islamic state must then be a person whose opinion will be a decisive criterion for the *ummah* in all that touches on the law of Islam. The Qur'ān says: "*Is the one who guides to God more fitting to be followed, or the one who himself needs guidance? How judge you this matter?*"(10:35)

This verse constitutes an address to men's consciences, for the decision is left to them. Clearly man's conscience will dictate that he deserves to be followed who has discerned the true path, identified the truth, and summoned society to advance in its direction. One who himself needs someone else to aid him in the problems he encounters has no claim to being obeyed. Only a ruler who has no need of instruction by others in all the concerns of Islam may legitimately be followed and obeyed.

A Christian scholar by the name of Burayd once went to see Imām al-Ṣādiq, peace be upon him, in the company of Hishām b. Ḥakam. In the way they encountered Imām Mūsā b. Ja'far, peace be upon him, who asked Burayd how thoroughly he was acquainted with his own scripture. Burayd answered that there was none who could equal him in his knowledge of the Gospels. The Imām then asked him whether he relied on himself for the interpretation of the scriptures, and he replied that he had full confidence in his own understanding and knowledge.

Thereupon Imām Mūsā al-Kāẓim, peace be upon him, began reciting the Gospels. Burayd was astonished and profoundly affected. He said: "For fifty years I have been searching for one such as you." Then he embraced Islam, as did the woman who was accompanying him.

Hishām, Burayd and the woman then came into the presence of Imām al-Ṣādiq, peace be upon him, and Hishām related to him what had happened on the way. Imām Ja'far al-Ṣādiq, peace be upon him, then recited this verse of the Qur'ān as a description of Imām Mūsā al-Kāẓim: "*Offspring, one of the other, generation after generation, and God hears and knows all that they say and all of their states.*" (3:34)

Burayd asked Imām Ja'far al-Ṣādiq, peace be upon him, how he knew the Torah, the Gospels, and the other books revealed to the prophets. He answered: "This is knowledge we have inherited. We recite and pronounce each of those books just as its followers and believers do. God would not place on earth a proof who would have to say in answer to any question, 'I do not know.'"[243]

al-Nawfalī says: "After Imām al-Riḍā, peace be upon him, arrived, al-Ma'mūn, the 'Abbāsid caliph, gave that invitations to go out to various religious leaders to attend a meeting: the head of the Christian bishops, the leading Jewish rabbi, the leading starworshippers, people that followed no religious law whatsoever, the Zoroastrian judge, a Greek physician, and Muslim theologians all well versed in dogmatics. al-Ma'mūn then sent a message to the Imām inviting him to participate in discussions with these religious leaders if he felt inclined. The Imām agreed to attend, and asked me what might be al-Ma'mūn's purpose in convening such a gathering."

al-Nawfalī answered that al-Ma'mūn wished to test him and learn the extent of his knowledge. He next enquired of al-Nawfalī if he feared that any of those luminaries might defeat him in debate, and he answered that far from entertaining any such fear, he was confident that God would permit him to triumph over them all. Then the Imām said: "Would you like to know when the caliph will repent of his initiative?" — "Yes."

"When I argue against the followers of the Torah by citing the Torah, against the followers of the Gospels by citing the Gospels, against the followers of the Psalms by citing the

Psalms, against the Sabeans in their own Hebraic tongue, against the Zoroastrian priests in their own Persian tongue, against the Greeks in their own Greek tongue, and against the theologians in their own Arabic tongue; when I defeat all of them with my proofs and arguments so that they abandon their religions and accept the truth of what I say — then al-Ma'mūn will understand that the seat of authority on which he resides is not rightfully his."

The next day, the meeting was convened at the appointed time, in the presence of the Imām. The leading Jewish rabbi said: "We will accept from you no argument that is not derived from the Torah, the Gospels, the Psalms of Dāwūd (David), or the pages revealed to Ibrāhīm." The Imām accepted this stipulation, and proceeded to prove with the utmost clarity that the Prophet of Islam, peace and blessings be upon him and his family, was the Seal of the Prophets. The arguments he advanced were so firm and unassailable that no doubt remained for anyone. The rabbi immediately conceded the truth of the Imām's words and embraced the truth.

Then the Imām engaged in similar debate with the scholars of other religions, and when they had all fallen silent, he said: "If any among you have further questions, do not hesitate to ask."

'Imrān the Sabean, and unparalleled expert in theology, said: "I have been to Baṣrah, Kūfah, Damascus and the Jazīrah, and talked to all the theologians of those regions, but none among them was able to convince me of the oneness of God."

The Imām thereupon expounded in detail the proofs of God's unity, in the manner recorded in al-Ṣadūq's *Kitāb al-Tawḥīd*. The Imām's powerful arguments thoroughly convinced 'Imrān, and he declared: "I bear witness that God is one as you have demonstrated and that Muḥammad is His servant, sent by Him to guide mankind." Then he turned in the direction of the *qiblah*, prostrated himself, and embraced Islam.

At the end of the meeting, al-Ma'mūn rose from the assembly, went inside with the Imām, and the people dispersed.[244]

The Commander of the Faithful, 'Alī, peace be upon him, said: "Make piety your rule and follow your Imām, for a righteous and just society will attain salvation by following a just Imām, and a corrupt and sinful society will be perished through following an impious and sinful leader."[245]

This tradition makes plain the direct connection between the moral characteristics of an Imām on the one hand and the ultimate fate of the society he leads on the other hand: the just Imām is the guarantor of a people's salvation and the evil leader condemns his following to perdition.

Lesson Twenty-One
The Sources of the Imām's Knowledge

The exceedingly precise and profound knowledge possessed by the Imāms is derived from their communication with the world of the unseen and from inspiration *(ilhām)*.

The Noble Qur'ān was also a rich source on which the Immaculate Imāms drew for their knowledge. Given the breadth of their religious vision and perception, they were able to derive various ordinances from revelation and to extract all manner of truths from its innermost layers of meaning.

The third source on which they drew consisted of the books and pages which they inherited from the Most Noble Messenger, peace and blessings be upon him and his family, these permitted them to advance still further their level of knowledge and to broaden its scope.

There are numerous traditions relating to these three sources, some of which we will now cite.

Imām Ja'far al-Ṣādiq, peace be upon him, said:

"The Prophet Dāwūd inherited the knowledge of the preceding prophets, and he then bequeathed it to Sulaymān. From Sulaymān it was transmitted to the Prophet Muḥammad, peace and blessings be upon him and his family, and we in turn have inherited it from him."

Abū Baṣīr who was present then saw fit to remark: "There are all kinds of knowledge!" The Imām responded: "The knowledge you have in mind is not particularly valuable. The knowledge of which I speak is truly precious; it is inspired in us night and day, from one hour to the next."[246]

Imām 'Alī b. Mūsā al-Riḍā, peace be upon him, said:

"When someone is chosen by God to administer the affairs of men, God expands his breast for him, places the wellsprings of wisdom in his heart, and inspires him with knowledge, so that he will be able to solve any problem that arises. He will know well the straight path of the truth. Such a one is none other than the Inerrant Imām, who enjoys the aid and support of his Lord and who lies beyond the reach of all error and sin."[247]

Ḥasan b. 'Abbās once asked Imām al-Riḍā, peace be upon him, in a letter: "What is the difference between a messenger, a prophet, and an Imām?"

The Imām answered as follows:

"The messenger *(rasūl)* is a person to whom Jibrīl descends and who both sees him and hears the words that he speaks. He is thus in communication with divine revelation *(waḥy)*, which he sometimes receives in the form of a dream, as was the case with Ibrāhīm, peace be upon him. The prophet *(nabiyy)* sometimes hears the words spoken by Jibrīl and at other times sees him without hearing anything from him. The Imām hears the words that Jibrīl utters without seeing him."[248]

The seventh Imām, Mūsā b. Ja'far, peace be upon him, said:

"Our knowledge is of three kinds: relating to the past; relating to the future; and relating to newly emergent situations. Knowledge relating to the past is interpreted for us; knowledge relating to the future is written down for us; and knowledge relating to newly emergent situations is infused in our hearts and our ears. This last category is the most noble part of our knowledge. However, no prophet will come after the Most Noble Messenger, peace and blessings be upon him and his family."[249]

God's effusions of grace thus continue throughout time by means of the Inerrant Imām, in such a way that the link between man and the Creator is not severed with the passing of the Prophet.

As for the inexhaustible source that the Qur'ān

represented for the Immaculate Imāms, let us hear what they themselves have to say on the subject:

Imām al-Bāqir, peace be upon him, says:

"One of the forms of knowledge we possess pertains to the interpretation of the Qur'ān and its ordinances, while another form relates to the developments and occurrences that take place in time. Whenever God desires a certain group of men to attain virtue and purity, He bestows on them the capacity to hear. However, one whose ear is incapable of hearing will encounter God's word in a way that suggests he has no awareness of it."

He then fell silent for a moment before continuing: "If we were to find anyone with the requisite spiritual capacity, we would transmit our knowledge to him. God is our protector and refuge."[250]

Imām Ja'far al-Ṣādiq, peace be upon him, says:

"The Noble Qur'ān contains knowledge of the past and the future, as well as the precepts for judging; we have all of that knowledge."[251]

The Commander of the Faithful, 'Alī, peace be upon him, says:

"Try to make the Qur'ān speak; it will not speak to you. I declare to you that the Qur'ān contains knowledge of the past and the future, as well as all the ordinances of which you stand in need and the interpretation of matters concerning which you disagree among yourselves. If you but ask me, I will instruct you in all of this."[252]

One of the companions of Imām Mūsā b. Ja'far, peace be upon him, asked him:

"Is all that you say to be found in the Qur'ān and the *Sunnah* of the Prophet, or do you also speak on your own authority?"

He replied: "It is impossible that we should say anything on our authority. Whatever we say is to be found in the Qur'ān and the *Sunnah* of the Prophet."[253]

The interpretation of the inner meaning of the Qur'ān is a science that derives from the world of the unseen; in other words, it is not a science that can be acquired by conventional means. Such interpretation, which is the uncovering of the true nature of things, words, and needs, can be attained only through bestowal by God.

The Qur'ān says: "*He it is who brought the Book down to you. Part of it consists of verses firm and categorical in meaning, these being the foundation of the Book, and part of others allegorical in meaning. Those in whose hearts is perversion and deviance follow only the metaphorical verses in order to create confusion and disorder while claiming to be interpreting those verses. Their interpretation is known, however, only to God and those firmly rooted in knowledge.*" (3:7)

"Those firmly rooted in knowledge" *(al-rāsikhūna fī 'l-'ilm)* are then those who like God know the interpretation of the metaphorical verses, and there are numerous traditions testifying to the Imāms' command of Qur'ānic interpretation.

One of the companions of Imām al-Bāqir, peace be upon him, asked him to explain the tradition that, "There is no part of the Qur'ān that does not have an outer and an inner aspect, and there is no letter contained in it that does not have a defining limit, and that limit is knowable."

He replied: "The outer aspect of the Qur'ān is the totality of that which has been revealed. Its inner aspect is the interpretation thereof. Part of this has already been accomplished, and part remains to be accomplished in the future. For the interpretation of the Qur'ān traverses its course, like the sun and the moon, and whenever the time is apposite, a further portion of it is accomplished. God said: '*Its interpretation is known only to God and those firmly rooted in knowledge.*' We it is who are throughly acquainted with the interpretation of the Qur'ān."[254]

Imām al-Ṣādiq, peace be upon him, is reported to have said: "The most exalted of those firmly rooted in knowledge was the Messenger of God. Whatever God Almighty sent to him, He taught him also its interpretation. Indeed God has revealed nothing in the interpretation of which He has not instructed the Prophet and his successors. When one of those who has no share in the science of interpretation expresses an opinion on the subject, God responds to him, 'All they can say is, "We believe it all to be from God."' The Qur'ān contains verses that are specific in their application and others that are general; verses that are categorical and others that are metaphorical; and verses that are abrogating and others that are abrogated. It is those firmly rooted in knowledge who have the knowledge of all this."[255]

Another source on which the Imāms, the successors to the Prophet, drew, consists of the books and scrolls that they inherited from him.

Imām al-Ṣādiq, peace be upon him, said:

"We have at our disposal a book which frees us of the need to rely on anyone else; it is, on the contrary, others that need us. This book was dictated by the Prophet to 'Alī and it deals with everything relating to the forbidden and the permitted. Whenever you ask us concerning a given course of action, we know what consequences will result if you follow it, and what will happen if you do not."[256]

One of the close companions of Imām Ja'far al-Ṣādiq, peace be upon him, says:

"I asked the Imām whether the legacy of knowledge he had at his disposal related simply to the general principles of knowledge or contained detailed instructions on matters such as divorce and bequests."

He replied:

"'Alī, peace be upon him, wrote down all of the sciences of judgeship and bequests. Were our cause to triumph, no problem would arise that we could not solve by means of the knowledge we have."[257]

The Commander of the Faithful, 'Alī, peace be upon him, relates: "The Most Noble Messenger, peace and blessings be upon him and his family, told me to write down and record what he was about to tell me. I replied that I was afraid of forgetting it. He then told me: 'This will not happen, for I have beseeched God to make you a memorizer of the Qur'ān. However, you should record what I am about to tell you for the sake of your partners, that is the Imāms from your progeny. It is because of those blessed beings that the rain falls on my *ummah*, that their prayers are answered, that divine punishment is withheld, and God's mercy descends.' Then he pointed to Imām Ḥasan and said, 'This is the first of them,' and to Imām Ḥusayn said, 'This is the second of them, and all the other Imāms will be from among his descendants!'"[258]

Imām Ja'far al-Ṣādiq, peace be upon him, said:

"The books were kept by 'Alī. When he decided to make a journey to Iraq, he entrusted them to Umm Salamah. When he died, they were passed on to Imām Ḥasan, and from him to Imām Ḥusayn. When he was martyred, they came into the possession of 'Alī b. Ḥusayn, after which they were passed on to my father."[259]

Imām al-Bāqir, peace be upon him, told Jābir:

"If we were to narrate traditions based on our own views, we would surely perish. Know that we narrate only traditions that we have stored up from the Messenger of God just as people store up silver and gold."[260]

The Commander of the Faithful, 'Alī, peace be upon him, said:

" There is not a single verse in the Qur'ān the time and place of the revelation of which are unknown to me. Abundant knowledge is stored in my breast, so ask me whatever you will before you lose me. Whenever a verse was revealed to the Prophet, peace and blessings be upon him and his family, and I happened not to be in his presence, he would wait until I arrived and then tell me, ''Alī, some verses were revealed while you were gone,' and explain their interpretation to me."[261]

He also said:

"There are numerous sciences hidden in my breast, taught to me by the Messenger of God. If people were to be found with the capacity to learn and retain them, to transmit them accurately and faithfully, I would entrust some of those sciences to them, and open for them a door leading to one thousand other doors."[262]

Mālik b. Anas says: "The Messenger of God told 'Alī,

'After I am gone, clarify whatever causes disagreement among people!'"[263]

There can be no doubt that this process of instruction did not take place by conventional or usual means, through the Messenger of God, peace and blessings be upon him and his family, opening up myriad gates of knowledge before 'Alī on the limited occasions that were available to him, thus making the treasury of his heart overflow with knowledge. The instruction was accomplished in a special way deriving from the power of prophethood and inner guidance inherent in prophethood; it was in this way that the heart of 'Alī, peace be upon him, became replete with the profound truths that his deep faith, wide-ranging intellect, and exalted vision fitted him to receive.

Sālim b. Qays reports the Commander of the Faithful,'Alī, peace be upon him, to have said:

"Not all the Companions of the Prophet, peace and blessings be upon him and his family, had the intellectual capacity to ask him concerning certain things, or to understand the answer he might give. Those who found it difficult to put their questions before the Prophet often preferred that someone else should do it on their behalf and obtain the necessary answers.

"I, however, was constantly in the company of the Prophet, day and night, and often I was alone with him. Whenever he went, I would accompany him. The Companions knew that no one had this relation with him except me. Sometimes he would come to our house, and sometimes I would meet him in one of his residences. Whenever I entered his presence, he would dismiss everyone else, even ordering his wives to leave the room. But when he came to our house, Fāṭimah, peace be upon her, and our children would remain in the room. I would pose my questions to him, and he would answer, and sometimes when I was silent, he would begin speaking. He recited for me all the verses of the Qur'ān that were revealed to him, and I would write them down and record them in my own hand. He expounded for me the interpretation of the Qur'ān, its abrogating and abrogated verses, its categorical and metaphorical verses, its specific and general verses. He would beseech God to grant me the power to retain and understand whatever he told me, and indeed I have not forgotten any part of the knowledge he conveyed to me. He instructed me in the permitted and the forbidden, God's commands and prohibitions, and the scriptures that had been revealed to preceding prophets, and I committed all of it to memory, not forgetting so much as a letter. Then he placed his blessed hand on my breast and besought God to fill my heart with knowledge, wisdom, understanding, and light.

"I then said to him, 'O Messenger of God, ever since you prayed for me, nothing has been effaced from my memory; do you fear that forgetfulness might overtake me?' He answered, 'I have no fear of ignorance or forgetfulness on your part, and my confidence in you is complete.'"[264]

It was the presence of such qualities in 'Alī, who attained the same loftiness of thought as the Prophet, that caused the Prophet to declare of him: "I am the city of knowledge, and 'Alī is its gate; whoever is desirous of knowledge must enter by that gate."[265]

In this utterance the Prophet is informing the *ummah* that whoever wishes to attain any part of his knowledge must seek the aid of 'Alī.

The Prophet also said in this connection: "O 'Alī, I am the city of knowledge, and you are the gate to that city. Anyone who imagines he can enter by other than that gate is in error."[266]

And again: "I am the house of wisdom and 'Alī is its door."[267]

Insofar as correct action depends on knowledge, it is incumbent on all Muslims to seek the knowledge and guidance of 'Alī in order for their deeds to be in conformity with the teachings of the Prophet.

The Messenger of God, peace and blessings be upon him and his family, being fully aware of the future needs of the Muslims, decided to entrust his knowledge to one who would be able to satisfy the religious needs of society after his death, and present God's commands and ordinances in uncorrupted form to all those who had recently become Muslim. He was therefore commanded by God to exert himself in the training and education of 'Alī, that enlightened one whose being concealed precious treasure of learning, who had the necessary qualities for guarding and preserving God's laws, and who had all the attributes requisite in a leader.

Ibn 'Abbās reports: "The Messenger of God used to say, 'When I readied myself to engage in intimate discourse with God, He would speak to me in turn. Whatever I learned from God Almighty, I taught to 'Alī, so 'Alī is the gate to my learning and knowledge.'"[268]

Imām Ḥusayn b. 'Alī, peace be upon him, said: "When the verse, *'And We have everything plain for you in a clear book (imām)'* (10:12) was revealed, the Companions asked the Prophet whether the book in question was the Torah or the Gospels. He answered, 'Neither.' And then, looking in the direction of my father he declared, 'This is an Imām the treasury of whose being God has caused to overflow with knowledge and learning.'"[269]

The Commander of the Faithful, 'Alī, peace be upon him, said:

"The Most Noble Messenger used to spend part of his time every year in the cave on Mount al-Ḥirā', and no one would see him go there except me. At that time the only household that had accepted Islam was that of the Prophet himself, peace and blessings be upon him and his family, and Khadījah, with myself counting as the third member of their family. I could see in him the light of revelation and messengerhood and smell the scent of prophethood. When revelation came to the Prophet, I would hear the sound of Satan in my ear, and I would ask him, 'O Messenger of God, what is this sound?' He said, 'It is Satan, despairing of ever being worshipped. 'Alī, whatever I hear, you hear, and whatever I witness, you witness, the difference between us being that you are not a prophet but my support and a virtuous man.'"[270]

al-Tirmidhī reports the Messenger of God to have said regarding 'Alī:

"May God extend His favor to 'Alī and make him the pivot around which truth turns."[271]

Lesson Twenty-Two
A Word Concerning the Unseen and the Manifest

The world of the unseen is the counterpart of the manifest realm, consisting of whatever lies beyond the scope of the senses and cannot be externally perceived. We have, for example, no direct knowledge of the circumstances of resurrection or the nature of reward and punishment, nor do we know anything of the composition of the angels or the attributes and essence of God, not because all of these are minute or subtle entities, but because they transcend our limited horizons of thought and lie outside time and space.

The unseen may be divided into two parts, absolute and relative. There are certain entities that are unseen in an absolute sense, for they will always be unseen by everyone and at all times, being intrinsically beyond the external senses of man, God's essence being an example of this. As for the relative unseen, this comprises entities that are manifest to some but unseen by others.

Everything that can be perceived by one of the five senses and thereby falls within the scope of man's sense perception counts as part of the manifest realm. This applies to matter and all of its effects, even if it be a question of items such as atoms, microbes and viruses which are invisible to the naked eye because of their minuteness. Our senses cannot perceive them unassisted, but once they are magnified several million times by means of special instruments they come within range of our perception.

Similarly, scientific discoveries of certain facts relating to this world full of secrets and mysteries, such as laser beams, x-rays, and gravity, do not relate to the world of the unseen, even though they appear to be imperceptible, for they are attained through the observation of natural causes.

This serves to demonstrate the limitations of our senses; even within the natural world they do not suffice for the perception of everything.

It sometimes happens that the sensory power of certain animals is much greater than our own. They can see things that are hidden from us or perceive them by non-visual means, whereas we can infer their existence only from the effects they produce.

As for the world of the unseen and what it contains, it stands in contrast to all the phenomena that are perceptible to our senses in one way or other and to some degree or other. Unable to perceive it with our senses, we can conceive of it only by means of rational proofs or the reports of those persons who do have awareness of it and the hidden matters it contains. Such persons guide us with their pronouncements to truths of which we would otherwise be unaware. This is a part of our creed and our faith.

Our deficient and limited beings are, then, imprisoned within the four walls of matter and we are deprived of perceiving many mysteries. In fact even our ability to perceive the phenomena of the sensory world is limited and conditional. Thus it is that for us being is divided into the two categories of the manifest and the unseen.

However, the hidden, non-sensory phenomena that are concealed from our perception are utterly clear and manifest to the Lord of the Worlds, the Creator Whose dominion and power embrace every atom in the universe and Who comprehends the totality of time and space. No obstacle hinders His infinite knowledge and unbounded power.

Past events that have been effaced from our memories and not even recorded in history, are present to God's view and observable by Him.

Paradise, hellfire, and resurrection, all of which are, from our vantage point, due to occur at some distant and unknown point in the future and the nature of which is utterly inconceivable, are present realities for God, the Creator Whose essence escapes all limitation and Whose sacred presence informs every part of the universe; He is aware of everything without exception.

Phenomena that occurred billions of years ago or will occur billions of years from now are fully known to God. For us, however, the ability to conceive of past and future events is strictly limited by the fact that we exist within the confines of time and space, for we are material beings, and according to the law of relativity matter needs time and space for the process of constant change in which it is engaged.

God's knowledge is unmediated, immediate in the fullest sense of the word, although somewhat comparable to our own awareness of our selves. While His essence is utterly other than the phenomena He creates, neither is it separate from them; all things, past and present, are immediately present before Him.

Thus the Commander of the Faithful, 'Alī, peace be upon him, said: " Every mystery is manifest to You and every hidden thing present before You."[272]

He is aware of the totality of the atoms that make up the earth and the oceans, of the movements of all creatures, great and small, throughout the universe, and of the manifest and hidden aspects of all things. His knowledge is not restricted to that which has already occurred nor to creatures and phenomena presently existing; it also embraces the future.

If we were present everywhere instead of occupying a particular point in time and space, we too would be aware of all the truths and details of existence; nothing, great or small, would escape our expansive vision.

God's knowledge bears no similarity to human knowledge and is utterly incomparable with it; we cannot understand His knowledge by drawing an analogy with our own. Man's knowledge is dependent on the thing known having an external existence; the thing known must first exist, appear in the manifest realm, for man's knowledge to attach itself to it. Such is not the case with God's knowledge; there is nothing that is unseen for Him, and everything is manifest for Him.

Whenever we attain knowledge of something by means of our outer senses, it does not count as knowledge of the unseen. Conversely, knowledge the attainment of which does not depend on the five senses is the knowledge of the unseen.

All the phenomena of the material world can be said to have descended from a more perfect, non-sensory world, where they exist in a more elevated form. Now if we perceive the external aspects of things by means of our senses, thereby obtaining some portion of the truth, such perceptions do not count as knowledge of the unseen. If, on the other hand, we observe the hidden essences of things by means of our inner eye, discern their existential evolution, and thereby find the inner aspects of things divulged to us, without any involvement by our senses, the resulting knowledge will count as knowledge of the unseen.

The Qur'ān says the following concerning God's knowledge:

"*He knows the hidden and the manifest, and He is the Compassionate and Merciful.*" (59:22)

"*He it is Who knows the unseen and the manifest, the Great, the Sublime.*" (13:9)

"*O Knower of the manifest and the hidden, judge among Your servants in that concerning which they dispute.*" (39:46)

"*I know the hidden aspects of the heavens and the earth and that which you make manifest and that which you conceal.*" (2:33)

"*Return, then to God, Who knows the manifest and the hidden; He shall make apparent to you all you have done.*" (62:8)

"*He it is that knows the hidden and manifest dimensions of His creation; He is wise and well acquainted with all things.*" (6:73)

The Commander of the Faithful, 'Alī, peace be upon him, says: "He knows all things, but not by means of instruments and faculties the absence of which would negate His knowledge. His knowledge is not something superadded to

His existence, interposed between Him and the objects of His knowledge; it is identical with His essence." [273]

A crucial issue arises at this point: is knowledge of the unseen exclusively God's and confined to His essence? Is it only for the Creator, Whose absolute being embraces the whole of the universe, that the unseen and the manifest are as one? Or can a human being also possess the ability to communicate with the world of the unseen?

Certain thinkers insist that knowledge of the unseen and awareness of hidden truths is restricted to God's essence. They maintain that even the prophets had no access to these matters, and they cite in support of their view a number of verses in which God, the principle of absolute perfection, mentions knowledge of the unseen as one of His distinguishing attributes, or the prophets reject categorically the possession of such knowledge.

For example:

"*God holds the keys to the treasuries of the unseen; none is aware of the unseen except Him.*" (6:59)

"*Say: 'I have no control over that which benefits me and that which harms me; it all results from God's will. Were I to be aware of the unseen, I would constantly augment that which benefits me and I would never suffer pain or loss. I am naught but a bearer of warnings and glad tidings to a people that believe.'*" (7:188)

"*I do not say that I have the treasuries of God, nor do I lay claim to His knowledge of the unseen, or that I am an angel.*" (11:31)

"*Say: 'There is none in the heavens and earth but God Who knows the unseen, and they know not when they shall be brought back to life.'*" (27:9)

"*Say: 'I am a prophet, newly appeared, not different from the prophets who preceded me; I do not know what will befall me and you.'*" (46:9)

"*Among the people of Madīnah are those who make a habit of hypocrisy, and you do not know who they are.*" (9:101)

From these verses it is concluded, then, that not even the prophets had access to knowledge of the unseen.

It is of course true that no one has absolute and complete

knowledge of the unseen apart from God, Whose infinite existence embraces the whole scheme of creation; such knowledge is indeed confined to Him. Even though the prophets are in other respects superior to the rest of mankind, they too are limited in their beings and are inherently unable to have comprehensive knowledge of the world of the unseen. However, this limitation does not mean that the gates of the unseen are always closed to them and that God through the exercise of His will may not make it accessible to them, for He is, after all, the Owner of both the unseen and the manifest. Access to that realm is a gift that God may bestow on whomsoever He wills from among His messengers and other appropriate individuals. The knowledge that then results is a ray of God's own knowledge, pertaining to His essence; it is not autonomously acquired knowledge, distinct from His.

The verses cited above show that the people of the *Jāhiliyyah* used to imagine that a prophet must have total control over the world and all it contains, and have the power of attracting to himself whatever is beneficial and repelling whatever is harmful.

God therefore instructs the Prophet, peace and blessings be upon him and his family, to refute these notions by categorically proclaiming that he had no such powers; that whatever powers he did have came from God; that whatever knowledge he had was derived from revelation and divine instruction; and that were it to be otherwise he would be able to uncover vast subterranean wealth for himself and, equipped with suitable foreknowledge, to ward off any evil.

Quite apart from these instructions, we find the Prophet himself denying the possession of such far reaching knowledge and power and attempting to convince men of the fact. However, at the very same time, we also find the Prophet being made aware by revelation of the evil plans of those conspiring against him and saved thereby from certain danger. The verses in question cannot therefore be taken to exclude totally the possession of any form of knowledge of the unseen on the part of other than God, nor can one overlook the existence of other verses which deal explicitly with the conveyance of knowledge of the unseen to the prophets.

The verse, "*Say: 'I am not a newly appeared (prophet) among the prophets (who preceded me)'*" (46:9), is intended to establish the principle that knowledge in all of its various forms does not spring up automatically from the Prophet, without his being dependent on the infinite source that is God's knowledge, any more than the knowledge of the preceding prophets was intrinsic to their own persons; for they, too, denied knowing what the future might hold in store for them without divine instruction and revelation.

As for the verse concerning the Hypocrites, it is obvious that their habitual practise of hypocrisy could bar the way to their identification by conventional means, but it does not exclude the possibility of being uncovered by other means; what the verse negates is the possibility of gaining knowledge of the unseen by the normal channels of cognition.

History in fact teaches us that the Prophet, peace and blessings be upon him and his family, not only knew who the Hypocrites were, but revealed their identity at the appropriate times to his confidants among the Companions.

Thus it is written that the Prophet, peace and blessings be upon him and his family, identified the Hypocrites to Ḥudhayfah, one of his close Companions and confidants. One day, the second caliph asked him: "Is there any Hypocrite among those I have appointed to various offices?" He answered that there was, but refused to name the person in question until the caliph insisted that he did, with the result that the Hypocrite was dismissed.

It was also the habit of 'Umar never to participate in the funeral prayers for anyone unless Ḥudhayfah was present.[274]

Apart from this, it is obvious that no duty can be imposed on anyone unless he has the knowledge requisite for performing that duty, and we know that God entrusted the Prophet with the duty of doing battle with the Unbelievers and the Hypocrites and shunning their views, in the verse: "*O Messenger, do battle with the Unbelievers and the Hypocrites, and be harsh with them.*" (9:73) Or again: "*Do not obey the Unbelievers and the Hypocrites; assign their punishment to Us and place your trust in God.*" (33:48)

Is it possible that God should order the Prophet, peace and blessings be upon him and his family, to fight the Hypocrites and be harsh with them, and not to obey their wishes, while making it impossible for him to recognize them throughout the entirety of his life? Clearly we must conclude that the verse concerning their unknowability must have been temporary in its force, not permanent.[275]

In the following verses, the Qur'ān establishes the principle that by God's command the prophets may gain access to the knowledge of the unseen:

"*God does not make you aware of the mysteries of the unseen, but selects for this station whomsoever He wills from among His prophets; believe, then, in God and His prophets.*" (3:179)

"*This is knowledge of the unseen which We reveal to you.*" (3:44)

"*He knows the unseen dimensions of the world and informs none thereof unless it be one with whom He is well pleased, such as one of the prophets, whom He sends angels to protect from in front and behind.*" (72:26)

This verse stresses that God alone is in His essence the true possessor of all knowledge concerning the unseen, and He will impart this knowledge only to those with whom He is pleased. To this category belongs the prophets for whom He appoints angelic guardians.

Elsewhere in the Qur'ān God says:

"*This Qur'ān is the word of God conveyed by His (angelic) messenger (=Jibrīl), an angel most powerful who enjoys high rank in the sight of the Lord of the Throne. He is the commander of the angels and the trustee of revelation. The messenger sent unto you (=Muḥammad) whom you call possessed is not possessed, for he did indeed witness Jibrīl, the trustee of revelation, at the highest point on the eastern horizon, and he does not begrudge you that which he has learned of the unseen (and if he were to judge fit, he would convey to you what he has learned of the unseen).*" (81:19-23)

Here the Prophet, peace and blessings be upon him and

his family, is declared innocent of begrudging others his knowledge of the unseen, and he is therefore implicity declared to possess such knowledge.

"*God does not inform you of the unseen, but He chooses whomsoever He wills from among His messengers.*" (3:179)

What is at issue in this verse is God's choosing certain of His messengers for the bestowal upon them of knowledge of the unseen.

When we correlate and compare the two groups of verses, the indications contained in the verses themselves show that there is no contradiction. The first group of verses declare the impossibility of independent knowledge of the unseen on the part of any but God, while the second group points to God's conveyance of such knowledge to certain select and qualified people.

Revelation is in itself an unknowable mode of communication between God's messengers and the world of the unseen; it may be described as a ray of divine knowledge that He causes to shine on the hearts of His chosen servants.

It should also be pointed out that the prophets' knowledge of the unseen is limited and proportional to their capacity and degree of spiritual growth. Those who assert that the prophets, not to mention the Imāms, have knowledge of the unseen do not claim that their knowledge is intrinsic to them or autonomous.

The sense of the two groups of verses is thus entirely clear: the first group negates the possibility of any but God having independent and total knowledge of the unseen, and the second group establishes that God may by an exercise of His will bestow a portion of that knowledge on some of His servants.

Apart from all this, any claim to messengerhood and prophethood is necessarily accompanied by a claim to communication with the world of the unseen by way of revelation. It would be utterly meaningless for someone to claim prophethood for himself but to renounce all claim to knowledge of the unseen. If the Qur'ān stresses that the prophets have no independent access to that knowledge, it is in order to refute erroneous notions held in the *Jāhiliyyah* concerning the extraordinary powers and attributes of prophets; it was thought that they utterly transcended all the characteristics of ordinary men and had superhuman knowledge of the whole of creation, enabling them to do whatever they wanted.

There can be no doubt that this *Jāhilī* view of the prophets would have prepared the way for them to be worshipped as superhuman beings. In order to prepare those infected by this mentality to accept the truth, the Qur'ān therefore declares that like other men, the prophets engage in such activities as eating, walking and resting, and that their most important distinguishing feature is their receipt of revelation for conveying it to others.

The aim of the Qur'ān is, on the one hand, to vindicate to men the truth of the messengerhood of the prophets in the communities from which they have arisen and, on the other hand, to refute erroneous notions concerning them and prevent them becoming the objects of idolatrous worship. Thus the Qur'ān says:

"*They say: 'We will never believe in you unless you cause a spring of water to gush forth, or produce a garden full of dates and grapes, with streams flowing through it; or cause the heavens to fall on our heads; or present us with God and His angels in visible form; or have a house built of gold; or ascend to the heavens. Nor will we believe that you went up to the heavens unless you bring back a book for us to read.' Say: 'God is exalted beyond my being able to bring Him or His angels before you in visible form; I am but a man whom God has appointed as a messenger.'*" (17:90-94)

"*Again they said: 'Why does this messenger eat food and walk in the markets? Why does no angel come to him in visible and sensory form, as witness to his veracity? Why does no treasure descend upon him, and why does he have no garden to eat of its fruits?'*" (25:7-8)

This was the mentality of the *Jāhiliyyah* the Qur'ān had to combat.

Lesson Twenty-Three
The Imām's Communication with the World of the Unseen

There are those to whom a gate is opened onto the treasuries of the unseen and who become aware thereby of certain hidden truths. This takes place by means of inspiration and illumination, for entry into that sphere by means of mental activity and ratiocination is completely impossible.

Such non-sensory and non-rational perception, made possible by flashes of illumination and inspiration, is a valid way of knowing reality, for although it might appear difficult to justify from the point of view of a monodimensional and materialist worldview, there is no scientific reason to deny it.

Dr. Alexis Carrel is one of the well known scientists who assign a particular value to inspiration and gnostic perception, regarding it in fact as a divine gift. This is what he says:

"Scientific geniuses, in addition to their great capacities for research and perceptive insight, also possess qualities such as illumination, by means of which they discern things that are hidden from others. They see connections between phenomena that are apparently unconnected and instinctively perceive the existence of unknown things. Thanks to their clear vision, they are able to read the thoughts of others, without recourse to their sensory faculties; to observe phenomena that are more or less distant, in terms of time and space; and to provide more definite information concerning certain things than that which is yielded by the senses.

"For one illumined in this sense, it is as easy to read

someone's thoughts as to describe his face, and in fact it is misleading to use the words 'see' or 'feel' in connection with what passes through his consciousness, for he neither sees anything nor seeks it in a given place — he simply knows it.

"Numerous are those people who under normal circumstances do not have this kind of illumined vision but have experienced it once or twice during their lives. It sometimes becomes possible for us to perceive the outer world by means other than our outer senses. There is no doubt that the mind can sometimes establish communication between two individuals over great distances, and instances of this type, the study of which is known to present day science as metapsychics, have to be accepted just as they are. For they contain truths within them and present us with a dimension of human existence that is not yet properly known. It may be that one day the cause for the extraordinary perceptive powers of some people will become clear."[276]

The human spirit thus has means of communicating with the external world that lie beyond sensory and rational perception, and through the appropriate researches scholars have come to accept that communication with the world of the unseen is not only possible for man, but a reality.

In just the same way that experience shows it to be possible to make contact with the external world in a dream and even to gain information concerning it, there is nothing to prevent our inner, spiritual faculties providing us with similar experiences while we are awake. This is an aperture that God has opened for His servants, permitting them to glimpse certain hidden mysteries and truths.

Given the fact that such a gift is bestowed on ordinary people, what is to prevent perfect human beings, such as the prophets and the friends of God who possess exalted qualities and attributes, from communicating with the world of the unseen and learning hidden truths, on a higher level and in a more extensive fashion than others, thanks to the depth of their devotion and inward purity?

One of the sources of the knowledge of the Imāms is the

inspiration that is bestowed on them by God's order; through communication with the world of the unseen, truths and realities become disclosed to them. There are numerous traditions bearing on this, confirming that persons chosen by God can indeed establish communication with the unseen and come to perceive a whole series of complex mysteries.

The inspiration that comes to the Imāms initiating them into certain hidden concerns, is different from revelation, because the one who receives inspiration does not see the angel of revelation. However, the truths that are bestowed on the Imāms help them greatly in expanding the scope of their vision and augmenting their cognitive abilities.

It needs to be added, of course, that the communication of the Imāms with the world of the unseen is not unbounded, resulting in a complete awareness of all things unseen, or independent of God's infinite power; their relationship is with a specific zone or region of the unseen within boundaries set by God Himself. Given the inherent limitation of their knowledge and their dependence for it on divine power, they cannot attain that which is absolutely unknowable to all except God. However, since each of the Imāms is the most perfect man of his age, thanks to his rank and luminosity, and a complete manifestation of the divine names and attributes, the Creator of the World, the Knower of the Unseen and the Manifest, discloses to them certain matters relating to the unseen, thereby broadening and deepening their vision and opening an aperture onto what otherwise remains hidden.

It is not possible for them to enter into contact with the world of the unseen independently, as is apparent from the traditions in which the Imāms deny they have knowledge of the unseen; what is meant is that they have no complete or absolute access to the unseen and cannot gain any knowledge of it without God's will and permission.

In addition, the Imāms received certain knowledge concerning the unseen that had been vouchsafed to the Most Noble Messenger — peace and blessings be upon him and his family.

One of the companions of Imām al-Bāqir, peace be upon him, asked him about the meaning of the verse: "*None knows God's unseen realm except those whom He chooses from among His messengers.*" (72:26)

He replied: "I swear by God that Muḥammad, peace and blessings be upon him and his family, was one of those whom God desired to acquaint with the knowledge of the unseen. If God designated Himself as 'Knower of the Unseen,' this is because knowledge of certain matters is restricted to Him and hidden from His servants: things He predetermines in His knowledge before creating them and informing the angels of them, and which He then exercises His will to create or not to create. As for the knowledge of that which He both predetermines and wills to create, this is the knowledge that was conveyed to the Messenger of God, peace and blessings be upon him and his family, and then to us."[277]

The Noble Qur'ān declares with the utmost clarity that God Almighty gives knowledge of the unseen to chosen servants such as the prophets in various ages. The Immaculate Imāms can also make contact with the world of the unseen whenever necessary by seeking God's aid and support and thereby gain access to knowledge they need.

This does not mean that the Imāms made regular use of some inner force in order to make contact with the world of the unseen in the course of their daily lives to obtain supernatural support. For it is a fundamental principle that the Prophet and the Imāms should not exhibit any fundamental difference from other human beings in their mode of life; in taking decisions, they relied on their own judgement of matters as they appeared to be, and often consulted their companions. Their acts took place in accordance with their own will and choice and were based on knowledge acquired by conventional means. Like other humans, they were subject to all the duties and obligations of religious observance. The way in which they exercised their teaching and guiding function in society was not visibly different from that of others, as a result of which some people came to imagine that they were on the same level as ordinary scholars of religion.

Attention must also be drawn to the fact that awareness of the unseen world, in the sense of the foreknowledge of events that are bound to occur, neither has any effect on the actual course of events, nor enables the Imāms to exert any control over the actions of others, nor implies any obligation on their part to attempt to do so.

The Imām's knowledge that a certain individual is about to embark on a certain course of action, in accordance with his own choice and free will, has not the slightest effect on that individual's decision, nor does it in any way serve to restrain him, thereby negating his free will. Knowledge of that which God has definitively decreed is simply a form of awareness of events that will come to pass; it does not create for the Imām any additional duty of either enjoining a given course of action or forbidding it.

One of the companions of Imām al-Bāqir, peace be upon him, relates that someone from Fars once asked the Imām whether he had knowledge of the unseen. He answered: "Sometimes knowledge of the unseen is granted to us, and sometimes it is not. God entrused some of His mysteries to Jibrīl, and he conveyed them to Muḥammad, peace and blessings be upon him and his family, who in turn informed of them whomsoever he wished."[278]

Someone once asked Imām Ja'far al-Ṣādiq, peace be upon him, whether the Prophet witnessed the hidden dimensions of the heavens and the earth, as Ibrāhīm did. He answered: "Yes, the Prophet saw those dimensions, and so does your Imām."[279]

On another occasion Imām Ja'far al-Ṣādiq also said: "Whenever the Imām wishes to be informed of something, God informs him of it."[280]

"We are the administrators of God's affair, the treasures of His knowledge, and the repository of His revealed mysteries."[281]

"God's greatness requires that when He appoints a person as His proof to mankind He discloses to him the knowledge of the heavens and the earth."[282]

"If I were to meet with Mūsā and Khiḍr, I would tell them

that I am more knowledgeable than both of them, and I would expound to them matters unknown to them. For they knew only what had been and what was, and they knew nothing of what would happen down to the Day of Resurrection, whereas we have inherited knowledge of all that from the Prophet."[283]

"I swear by God that knowledge of the first things and the last things has been bestowed on us." On hearing this utterance of the Imām, one of his companions asked him whether he had knowledge of the unseen. He answered: "Woe upon you that you find it necessary to ask such a question. We are fully informed of each drop of sperm in the loins of men and the wombs of women. Woe upon you; open your eyes, and let your hearts perceive the truth! We are God's proof, dwelling among His creation, but only the believer whose faith is as firm as the mountains of Tihāmah has the ability to perceive this truth. I swear by God that if I wished I could inform you how many pebbles exist in the world, even though their number is constantly growing, by night and by day. I swear by God that after me you will rise up in enmity against each other until one group among you destroys the other."[284]

Imām al-Bāqir, peace be upon him, said: "Once the Commander of the Faithful, 'Alī, peace be upon him, was asked about the extent of the Prophet's knowledge. He replied: 'He had the knowledge of all the preceding prophets; he knew all of the past and all of the future. I swear by God Who holds my soul in His hand that I know all that the Prophet knew, and that I know all of the past and all of the future, up until the Day of Resurrection.'"[285]

Imām al-Bāqir, peace be upon him, also said: "I am astonished at those who believe in following us and accept that obedience to us is equivalent to obeying God and the Messenger, but then contradict themselves and oppose us because of a sickness in their hearts. They underestimate us and object to those who fully appreciate our worth. Do you imagine that God would make it obligatory for His servants to obey us unless we had been given complete knowledge of the heavens and the earth and provided us with all we need to know for solving the problems people encounter?"[286]

Imām Ja'far al-Ṣādiq, peace be upon him, reported the Commander of the Faithful, 'Alī, peace be upon him, to have said: "God bestowed upon me nine distinguishing qualities that He gave to none other save the Prophet: He opened up for me channels of knowledge permitting me to know when every death occurs, when disasters descend, what are men's genealogies, and the decisive speech (that separates truth from falsehood); He permitted me to look upon the world of the unseen, so that past and future events were unfolded before me; He perfected religion for mankind, completed His blessing for them, and accepted Islam for them as religion for them by appointing me as the holder of divine authority; and He instructed Muḥammad, peace and blessings be upon him and his family, to inform the people of all that. These are God's gifts to me, so may praise be given to Him alone."[287]

This is a selection from the very copious traditions on the subject that have been transmitted from the Immaculate Imāms. Whenever the Imāms deemed it a necessary part of their duty to proclaim truths from the world of the unseen, they made manifest matters that would otherwise have remained hidden.

The Sunnī scholar Ibn Abi 'l-Ḥadīd writes:

"When 'Alī, peace be upon him, invited people to ask him about the future, he was claiming neither divinity nor prophethood. What he meant thereby was that he had learned knowledge of the unseen from the Messenger of God. As for the predictions that he made we have tested and examined them all, and found them to correspond to reality, which is a proof of the accuracy of his words and the unique knowledge of the unseen that he possessed. For he said, 'I swear by God Who holds my soul in His hand that I have knowledge of the future and can tell you whatever you want to know.'"[288]

There is a celebrated story about a certain Maytham al-Tammār, one of the close companions of 'Alī. One day, in the presence of a number of other people, 'Alī foretold the sad fate that was to overtake him in the following words:

"O Maytham, know that after my death you will be arrested and hung from the gibbet. On the second day your beard will be reddened with the blood of your nose and your mouth, and on the third day, you will be pierced with a spear, and you will go to the presence of your Lord. The place where this will occur is near the house of 'Amr b. Ḥurayth, and you will be the tenth person to die in that way, the only difference being that the gibbet from which you are hung will be shorter than the others. I will show you the tree from which it will be fashioned." Two days later, he showed Maytham the datepalm in question.

For days Maytham stayed close to that datepalm, which was situated in a quiet open space, immersed in worship and supplication. Every now and then he would look at the tree, murmuring to it: 'May God bless you, for I have been created for you, and you have been created for me."

Whenever he ran into 'Amr b. Ḥurayth he would say: "I am to be your neighbor, so take good care of me." 'Amr did not understand what he meant, so he asked him in surprise: "Have you decided to buy the house of Ibn Mas'ūd or Ibn Ḥakam?"

Time passed, 'Alī was martyred, and Maytham's ordeal began. He was arrested and turned over to 'Ubaydullāh b. Ziyād, who had been informed of Maytham's zealous devotion to 'Alī. Drunk with power, and intent on extinguishing the fire of belief in 'Alī's family, 'Ubaydullāh asked Maytham: "What happened to your God?"

Unintimidated by 'Ubaydullāh, Maytham replied: "He is setting a trap for the oppressors."

'Ubaydullāh said: "I hear he foretold your fate." "Yes," Maytham answered, and when 'Ubaydullāh insisted on hearing the details, he continued: "My master 'Alī, peace be upon him, told me that you will hang me from the gibbet, and that I will be the tenth person you martyr in that fashion, and that my gibbet will be shorter than the others."

Full of anger, 'Ubaydullāh told Maytham that he would deal with him in a manner other than that which 'Alī had foretold.

To which Maytham responded: "How can you oppose what he said? It was the Messenger of God, peace and blessings be upon him and his family, who informed 'Alī what my fate would be, and he had been informed of it by Jibrīl, the trustworthy spirit and angel, who learned of it from God Almighty Himself. I know the exact place where I will be hung from the gibbet, and I know, too, that I will be the first Muslim in whose mouth a muzzle is placed."

'Ubaydullāh gave orders for Maytham to be imprisoned. While in prison, he came into contact with al-Mukhtār and told him that he would be set free and rise up one to day to avenge the death of Ḥusayn b. 'Alī by killing 'Ubaydullāh.

Not long passed before al-Mukhtār was indeed set free, while Maytham was brought once again before 'Ubaydullāh. He ordered him to be hung from a gibbet fashioned from a datepalm near the house of 'Amr b. Ḥurayth, who immediately remembered what Maytham had told him and accordingly instructed his servant every night to sweep the area in front of the datepalm and to light a lamp there.

For as long as Maytham hung from the gibbet, the people would gather to hear him discoursing on the virtues of the Prophet's House, for love for the family of 'Alī had become intermingled with Maytham's faith. 'Ubaydullāh was informed of the situation, and told that Maytham was humiliating and mocking him by his behavior. Accordingly, in a fit of rage, he ordered that a muzzle be placed in Maytham's mouth.

Maytham's fate proceeded to unfold just as 'Alī had predicted. On the second day that he hung from the gibbet, blood poured down from his nose and his mouth, and after all kinds of torture had been inflicted on that pious man, he was martyred with a thrust from a spear. Such was the painful end of that man of God."[289]

'Alī, peace be upon him, once said in a sermon after the Battle of the Camel was over and his army had entered Baṣrah:

"I swear by God that this city of yours will be flooded so that your mosque will look like a ship floating on the waters;

God will punish this city from above and below."

Commenting on these words, Ibn Abi 'l-Ḥadīd writes:

"Baṣrah has been flooded twice up to now. One of the two occasions was during the caliphate of al-Qādir Bi'llāh when the waters of the Persian Gulf rose and flooded the town, and from all of its buildings only a part of the congregational mosque could be seen, in just the same way that 'Alī described it. The whole city was destroyed, and many people perished."[290]

Imām Ḥasan b. 'Alī, peace be upon him, predicted that his wife Ju'dah would poison him, and he also told Imām Ḥusayn, peace be upon him, that thirty people claiming to belong to the *ummah* of Islam would conspire to kill him and enslave his household and children.[291]

The Banī Hāshim once decided to make Muḥammad b. 'Abdullāh the caliph and they convened a meeting for the purpose. Imām Ja'far al-Ṣādiq, peace be upon him, accepted their invitation to participate, but when 'Abdullāh asked him to swear allegiance to Muḥammad b. 'Abdullāh, he answered as follows:

"You and your sons Muḥammad and Ibrāhīm will never be able to win the caliphate. The first person to seize it will be this person," — pointing to al-Saffāḥ — "followed by that person" - pointing to al-Manṣūr - "and then the caliphate will fall into the hands of the descendants of al-'Abbās. Matters will reach the point that even children will hold the office of caliph, and the counsel of women will be sought. As for your children, Muḥammad and Ibrāhīm, they will both be killed."[292]

Imām, al-Bāqir, peace be upon him, told his brother Zayd b. 'Alī, who was later hung from the gibbet in the Kannāsah quarter of Kufāh:

"Do not allow suspicious people to incite you, for they will be unable to ward off God's punishment from you. Be not hasty, for God does not conform Himself to the haste of His servants. Do not seek to outpace God (by acting prematurely), for difficulties and disasters will defeat and destroy you. I entrust you to God, O my brother, for you will be hanged at Kannāsah."[293]

Shaykh Ḥurr al-'Āmilī writes: "The prediction made by Imām al-Bāqir, peace be upon him, in this *ḥadīth* is well-known and of indubitable authenticity."

According to Ḥusayn b. Bashshār, Imām al-Riḍā, peace be upon him, said: "'Abdullāh al-Ma'mūn (the 'Abbāsīd caliph) will kill his brother, Muḥammad al-Amīn." Ḥusayn asked for clarification, and the Imām said: "'Abdullāh who is now in Khurāsān will have Muḥammad the son of Zubaydah put to death in Baghdād."[294]

Ḥudhaytah reports Imām Ḥusayn b. 'Alı, peace be upon him, to have said the following:

"I swear by God that the Umayyads will decide to shed my blood, and 'Umar b. Sa'd will be the commander of their army."

Since the Prophet, peace and blessings be upon him and his family, was alive at the time, Ḥudhayfah asked Ḥusayn: "O grandson of the Messenger, has the Prophet informed you of this?" And Ḥusayn responded that he had not. Then Ḥudhayfah went to the Prophet and informed him of what Ḥusayn had said. The Prophet said thereupon: "What I know, Ḥusayn knows, and what Ḥusayn knows, I know."[295]

Abū Hāshim, one of the companions of Imām al-'Askarī, peace be upon him, says: "I wrote a letter to the Imām complaining about the hardships of prison, and in his reply he wrote that very same day I would perform the noonday prayer in my own home. When noontime arrived, I was indeed set free, and I performed the prayer in my own home."[296]

Khayrān reports: "One day I went to see Imām al-Hādī, peace be upon him, in Madīnah. He asked me what news I had of al-Wāthiq. I told him that I had been al-Wāthiq ten days earlier and that he had seemed to be in good health. The Imām remarked that according to the people of Madīnah al-Wāthiq had died, and he then asked about Ja'far. I told him that Ja'far had been imprisoned, under very harsh conditions. The Imām responded that Ja'far had been released and made caliph. Next he asked concerning Ibn Zayyāt, and I informed him that Ibn Zayyāt was busy taking care of people's affairs. He told me that such activity had proved harmful for Ibn Zayyāt. After pausing a minute, the Imām continued: 'What God has foreordained must necessarily come to pass. al-Wāthiq has died, and Ja'far has become caliph and put Ibn Zayyāt to death.' I asked when all this had happened, and he told me, 'Six days after you left Baghdād.'"[297]

Suwayd b. Ghaflah says: "One day when 'Alī, the Commander of the Faithful, peace be upon him, was delivering a sermon in the mosque at Kūfah, a man got up and said: 'O Commander of the Faithful, when passing through the Wādi 'l-Qurā I heard that Khālid b. 'Urfaṭah had died; beseech God that his sins may be forgiven.' 'Alī, peace be upon him, said: 'I swear by God that he is still alive, and will remain so until he leads an army of the misguided of which the flagbearer will be Ḥabīb b. Ḥammār.' Then somebody else got up and said, 'I am Ḥabīb b. Ḥammār; why do you say this of me even though I am one of your devoted conpanions and followers?' 'Alī asked him, 'Are you truly Ḥabīb b. Ḥammār?' 'Yes,' he answered. Then 'Alī said, 'I swear by God that you will indeed be the flagbearer of that army, and that you will enter the mosque of Kūfah by this gate.' As he said this, he pointed to the Bāb al-Fīl (Elephant Gate)."

Thābit al-Thumālī says: "I swear by God that I witnessed the whole event. Later I came to see that 'Ubaydullāh b. Ziyād sent 'Amr b. Sa'd against Ḥusayn b. 'Alī, peace be upon him, at the head of a vast army, which was commanded by Khālid b. 'Urfaṭah and had Ḥabīb b. Ḥammār as its flagbearer. They entered the mosque of Kūfah through the Bāb al-Fīl."[298]

One of the remarkable events foreseen by the Commander of the Faithful was what happened to Rashīd al-Hujriyy. When he was captured and taken before 'Ubaydullāh b. Ziyād, he was asked: "What did 'Alī tell you I would do to you?" He replied: "That you would cut off my hands and feet and hang me from the gibbet."

'Ubaydullāh exclaimed: "I swear by God that I will do the opposite of what 'Alī predicted to make it obvious that he was lying." So he commanded that Rashīd be set free. But just as Rashīd was about to leave the hall, 'Ubaydullāh gave orders for him to be brought back, saying the harshest punishment I can conceive for him is to cut off his hands and feet and to hang him from the gibbet." For he thought that this would help him to efface all trace of justice from society. 'Ubaydullāh's orders were carried out, but Rashīd continued courageously to voice his convictions.

Fury overcame 'Ubaydullāh, and losing all self-control he gave orders for Rashīd's tongue to be plucked out. When Rashīd heard of this, he said, "This, too, is part of what 'Alī foretold for me." Then his tongue was cut out, and he was hung from the scaffold.[299]

These are a few examples of the stories that are to be found in books of history and tradition drawn up by compilers who lived at different places and in different periods. They compel any fair minded person to conclude that the Immaculate Imāms were in communication with the world of the unseen and had the ability, with the permission of God, to gain knowledge of hidden truths whenever they wished.

Lesson Twenty-Four
The Method of Choosing the Imām or Leader

One of the topics which have been constantly under discussion among Muslims since the very rise of Islam is the question of selecting the Imām or the leader; it is in fact this question that brought about the division of the *ummah* into Shī'ah and Sunnī.

The Shī'ah are committed to the principle that the right to designate the Imām belongs exclusively to God, and that the people have no role to play in this respect. It is the Creator alone Who selects the Imām and identifies him to the people by means of the Prophet.

The attachment of the Shī'ah to this understanding of the Imāmate, and the attention they have lavished on the belief that God and the Prophet alone may choose the Imām who serves as God's proof in each age, spring, however, from a profound respect for the rights and dignity of man.

In just the same way that prophethood implies a whole series of attributes and conditions, so too the office of the Imām, coming after the Prophet, must similarly be accompanied by certain qualities. This necessity arises from the fact that the Shī'ah refuse to accept as leader of the community anyone lacking in the key qualities of justice, inerrancy, and perspicacity. A proper command of the religious sciences, an ability to proclaim God's laws and ordinances and to implement them in society in the appropriate way, and, in general, to guard and protect God's religion — none of this is possible in the absence of those qualities.

God is aware of the spiritual capacities, religious rank, and piety of the Imām, and in accordance with this awareness He knows, too, to whom the custodianship of religious knowledge should be entrusted: who it is that can carry this burden and not neglect for a minute the duties of summoning men to God and implementing divine justice. But quite apart from this aspect of the matter, the Shī'ī understanding of the Imāmate also reflects a lofty human ideal.

If we say that people have no right to interfere in the matter of choosing the Imām, it is because they cannot be adequately informed of the inner purity and piety of individuals, of the degree to which they adhere to the values of Islam and the Qur'ān; above all, they cannot perceive the presence or absence of the divine principle of inerrancy.

It was therefore the prerogative of the Prophet to designate his successor, and of the Imām in each age to select and appoint leaders.

If, however, a claimant to the Imāmate was able to demonstrate ability to communicate with the unseen and to display inerrancy in his exercise of leadership, in a fashion akin to the miraculous powers of the prophets, then his claim might legitimately be accepted.

There are the methods proposed by the Shī'ah for recognizing and gaining access to the Imām; they form a set of criteria that prevented the true leader of the Muslims in each age from remaining unrecognized.

The other approach to the matter is in stark contrast to that of the Shī'ah. Because there was a certain vagueness and ambiguity surrounding the consultative principle in its application to the question of leadership from the very beginning, the Sunnī community resorted to a variety of methods for selecting and designating the caliph, so that in practice the following elements came to play an important role.

1: Consensus *(ijmā')*. The Sunnīs say that the choice of caliph rests first and foremost on selection by the community, so that if the *ummah* elects a given individual as its leader, he must be accepted as such and his commands must be obeyed.

As proof of this they cite the method followed by the Companions of the Prophet, peace and blessings be upon him and his family, after his death. Gathered together at the Saqīfah to select a caliph, a majority decided upon Abū Bakr and swore allegiance to him, so that thereby he was recognized by consensus as successor to the Prophet without any objection being raised. This constitutes one method for designating a caliph.

2: The second method consists of consultation and the exchange of views among the prominent members of the Muslim community. Once they agree among themselves on the choice of a leader for the community, his caliphate becomes legitimate and it is incumbent on everyone to obey him.

This is the method that was adopted by the second caliph. When 'Umar was about to die, he nominated six people as candidates for the caliphate and told them to select one of their own number as leader of the Muslim community by discussing the matter among themselves for not more than six days; if four or five people were able to reach an agreement, the opponent were to be disregarded. A six-man assembly was accordingly convened, and after the necessary deliberations the caliphate was awarded to 'Uthmān. This, too, is said to constitute a legitimate means of selecting the caliph.

3: The third method consists of the caliph nominating his own successor. This happened in the case of 'Umar, who was appointed caliph by Abū Bakr without any objection being raised by the Muslims.

Such, in essence, is the position of the Sunnīs on this matter.

Let us now review the objections to which each of these proceedings is subject.

The necessity of the inerrancy of the Imām, of his possessing a firm grasp and a comprehensive command of all religious matters, in both principle and detail, is rooted in the Qur'ān and the *Sunnah*, as well as being vindicated by historical experience. All the oppression, wrongdoing, corruption and error that we see in Islamic history arose from the fact that the leaders did not have the necessary qualities of an Imām. Even if all the members of the Islamic *ummah* choose a given individual as Imām and successor to the Prophet, peace and blessings be upon him and his family, this cannot in and of itself bestow legitimacy and validity on his caliphate.

As for the caliphate of Abū Bakr, all the Muslims, in any event, did not swear allegiance to him, so there was no question of any true consensus being formed. It is also an undeniable historical fact that no real election took place, in the sense of all the Muslims who were scattered in various places converging on Madīnah to take part in an electoral process. Indeed, not all the people of Madīnah participated in the meeting where the decision was made, and some of the Prophet's Family and Companions, as well as some of those present at the Saqīfah, refused to proclaim their loyalty to Abū Bakr.

'Alī b. Abī Ṭālib, peace be upon him, al-Miqdād, Salmān, al-Zubayr, 'Ammār b. Yāsir, 'Abdullāh b. Mas'ūd, Sa'd b. 'Ubādah, 'Abbās b. 'Abd al-Muṭṭalib, Usāmah b. Zayd, Ibn Abī Ka'b, 'Uthmān b. Ḥunayf, as well as a number of other leading Companions, objected vocally to the caliphate of Abū Bakr and by no means concealed their opposition. How then can the caliphate of Abū Bakr be regarded as having rested on consensus?

It might be said that the participation of everyone in the selection of the successor to the Prophet is not necessary, and that if a number of leading and well-informed people reach a certain decision this is enough and entitles the caliph to acceptance and obedience.

However, why should their decision be binding on everyone else? Why should other reputable and outstanding figures, whose commitment and devotion were beyond all doubt, have been excluded from making a decision that was to have such far-reaching consequences for the fate of the Islamic *ummah*? Why should they submit unconditionally to a decision reached by others?

What proof is there for the legitimacy of such a procedure? Why should a historical event of this type constitute a legitimate or binding precedent?

A procedure of this type can be regarded as legitimate only if it is explicitly designated as such in the Qur'ān or the *Sunnah,* in the sense of the verse in which God declares: "*Take and accept that which the Messenger ordains, and abandon that which he forbids.*" (59:7)

As for the Companions, there is no proof that they necessarily acted correctly, apart from which some of them disagreed with others, and there is no reason in principle to prefer the views of one group of the Companions over those of another.

It is true that a majority of the people of Madīnah gave their allegiance to Abū Bakr and thus ratified his selection as caliph, but those who refused to do so did not commit any sin, for freedom to choose is the natural right of every Muslim, and the minority is not obliged to follow the views of the majority. No one can be compelled to swear allegiance to someone whom he does not wish to see at the helm of Muslim affairs or to join a compact he rejects.

When a majority does force a minority to conform to its own views, it violates the rights of the minority.

Now those Companions who were gathererd around 'Alī, peace be upon him, were compelled to follow the majority that had given allegiance to Abū Bakr, even though neither God nor the Prophet, peace and blessings be upon him and his family, had ordained any such act; it was therefore a clear violation of their rights and their freedom. Worse than this was the fact that 'Alī b. Abī Ṭālib was forced to participate in the swearing of allegiance and to change his position, even though he was the one whom the Messenger of God had named an authority for every believing man and woman. No one with a sense of justice can approve such a denial of freedom.

It must also be said that Muslims of later generations who adopt a negative attitude to a granting of allegiance made by their ancestors cannot be condemned for this or regarded as sinners.

During the caliphate of 'Alī, people such as Sa'd b. Abī Waqqās and 'Abdullāh b. 'Umar refused him their allegiance, but in his magnanimity the Imām left them free to do so and did not compel them to pledge him their obedience.

In addition to all this, if the caliph is not designated by the Prophet, no one can be forced to follow the mode of conduct prescribed by a caliph whose only claim to legitimacy is popular election. Such election does not bestow on him immunity from error and sin, nor does it enhance his religious knowledge and awareness. The ordinary believer retains the right of following someone other than the caliph, and this applies still more forcefully to the one whose level of religious learning is higher than of the caliph.

However, when allegiance is sworn in obedience to a command of the Prophet, peace and blessings be upon him and his family, this indeed counts as a swearing of allegiance to the Messenger of God himself; then no disobedience may be countenanced, and obedience to the one to whom allegiance is given is incumbent not only on the Muslims of that time but on those of all succeeding generations. In addition, the Qur'ān regards allegiance given to the Prophet as equivalent to allegiance given to God. Thus the Qur'ān says:

"*O Messenger, the believers who swear allegiance to you have in reality pledged their allegiance to God; God's hand is placed on their hands. Whoever thereafter violates his oath of allegiance works towards his own perdition, and whoever remains faithful to the covenant he has concluded with God will soon receive from Him an abundant reward.*" (48:10)

It is self-evident that the successor chosen by the Prophet will be the most perceptive of men and the most knowledgeable concerning the ordinances of the Qur'ān and the religion of God; in fact he will possess all the qualities of the Prophet with the exception of receiving revelation, and whatever command he gives will be based on justice and the implementation of God's laws.

The Prophet, peace and blessings be upon him and his

family, is related to have said: "My community will never agree upon an error." However, this tradition cannot be adduced with respect to the question of successorship for it would then contradict the commands of the Prophet and effectively cause people to disregard his words; it would permit them to prefer their own views to his. Whatever applicability it may have must be confined to cases where there is no clear or authoritative ruling from the Qur'ān or the *Sunnah*.

What was intended by the Prophet, peace and blessings be upon him and his family, was that the community would not agree upon an error in cases where the *ummah* is permitted by God to solve its affairs by mutual consultation, where such consultation takes place in an atmosphere free from intimidation, and where a given choice of action is unanimously approved. If, however, a certain group of people incline in a certain direction and then try to impose their views on others and compel their agreement, there is no reason to regard the outcome as respresenting a valid consensus.

As for the swearing of allegiance *(bay'ah)* that took place at the Saqīfah even if God and the Messenger had given permission for the matter to be decided on the basis of consultation, no true consultation took place. A certain group of individuals set the agenda in advance and then expended great effort to attain the result they themselves wanted. This is the reality of the matter, as was even the second caliph himself came to acknowledge:

"The selection of Abū Bakr as leader came about by accident; it did not happen through consultation and the exchange of views. If someone invites you to follow the same procedure again, kill him."[300]

In the course of a sermon he delivered at the beginning of his caliphate, the first caliph apologized to the people in these words:

"The swearing of allegiance to me was a mistake; may God protect us from its evil consequences. I myself am fearful of the harm it may cause."[301]

During his event-filled life, the Prophet of Islam, peace

and blessings be upon him and his family, showed great concern for the welfare of the Muslims and paid great attention to the preservation of religion and the unity and security of the Muslim community. He feared greatly the emergence of division and disunity, and wherever the Muslims went and established their control, the first thing he did was to appoint a governor or commander for the region. Similarly, commanders were always appointed in advance whenever a battle was being planned, and even deputy commanders were appointed to take over the leadership of the army if necessary.

Whenever he set out on a journey, he appointed someone as governor to administer the affairs of Madīnah.

Given all this, how is it possible that he should not have given any thought to the fate of the community after his death, to its need for a guide and a leader, a need on which the destiny of the community in this world and the hereafter depended?

Is it possible that God should send a messenger to guide men and to found a religion; that the messenger should endure all kinds of hardship and difficulty in order to convey God's commands to mankind, and that he should then quit this world without making any further provision? Would this at all be a wise or logical course of action?

Would any leader be content to entrust the fruit of his efforts and struggles to blind chance?

Messengerhood was a divine trust given to the Prophet, peace and blessings be upon him and his family, and he was far too exalted a personality to neglect that trust in any way, particularly by leaving its preservation to chance. Making the designation of his successor dependent on election would have been tantamount to precisely that, for the outcome of any election is always a matter of chance.

If the purpose of religion is to educate humans in their humanity and if the laws of religion are to promote the development and refinement of humanity, a leader must always exist together with the religion in order to secure the material and spiritual needs of the individual and the community and guide men in their upward progress. There can be no doubt that governmental power is needed in order to obtain the implementation of God's laws and the preservation of His commands, and this need implies in turn the necessity for a leader and guide who will assist men in their strivings and counteract their lack of full awareness and their vulnerability to satanic suggestion. In the absence of such a leader, religion will become muddied and distorted by superstition and arbitrary opinion, and the divine trust that is religion and revelation will be betrayed.

Furthermore, if the Prophet, peace and blessings be upon him and his family, had left it to the Muslims to select the caliph, he would have done so with the utmost clarity and in the most categorical way possible, also specifying the procedures they were to follow in choosing and appointing him.

Are the affairs of the *ummah* after the death of the Prophet of no concern to God and His Messenger? Are the people more farsighted than God and His Messenger, or better able to discern who the leader should be?

If the Prophet did not appoint a successor *(khalīfah)* to himself, why did Abū Bakr do so? And if the Prophet did do so, why was the one he selected pushed aside?

Another problem that arises with respect to the choice of caliph on the basis of mutual consultation is that the Imām must be the guide of the *ummah* in all matters of religious knowledge. No one can doubt that he must have in addition to faith and commitment comprehensive knowledge of God's laws, because in confronting the numerous and complex problems that arise the Muslims need a suitable authority to whom to turn for sure and reliable guidance. The successor to the Prophet must therefore be the heir to his knowledge, which makes the identification and recognition of the successor a matter of particular importance.

We have already explained the fundamental role of inerrancy *('ismah)* in both the Prophet and in the leader *(imām)* designated by the Prophet. Now how can the

Companions, who themselves lack inerrancy, take it on themselves to recognize one who is inerrant?

Furthermore, if it is the right of the Muslims that they should choose the successor to the Prophet, how can this right be restricted by 'Umar to a mere six people? All six were from among the Migrants, and not even a single one of the Helpers was assigned to advise them.

The verse: "*The Muslims are to organize their affairs on the basis of mutual consultation*" (42:38) serves only to indicate that one of the characteristics of the believers is to consult each other in their undertakings; it does not indicate in any way that leadership of the Muslims is to be based on majority vote, nor does it make incumbent obedience to the decisions taken by a caliph so elected. The verse does not even say anything about the way in which consultation is to be organized and whether or not the presence of all the Muslims is required.

Even if the consultative *(shūrā)* principle were to be applicable to the question of leadership, the decision would have to be made by means of a general exchange of views, not one restricted to a mere six people, in the selection of whom 'Umar did not see fit himself to consult with any of the Companions. He even awarded a veto to 'Abd al-Raḥmān b. 'Awf, who was well known for his wealth, something that cannot be justified by reference to Islamic principles. The deliberations of those six were, moreover, overshadowed by threats and intimidation, in that orders had been given for those who failed to agree with the majority to be put to death.

When appointing 'Umar to be caliph, Abū Bakr did not consult with anyone, nor — obviously enough — did he leave the question of his successor to the people for them to decide; it was entirely a personal decision on his part.

In any event, the consultative principle becomes operative only when the leader himself convenes a consultative assembly for an exchange of views on various questions, notably current topics touching on social relations and policies adopted by the leader in response to social need. Consultation with relevant specialists takes place, but after their opinions have been heard, it is the leader himself who takes the final decision. For his religious knowledge is superior to that of everyone else, and it is his pronouncements that enjoying public support are worthy of being put into effect. Unity of direction and leadership must at all times be preserved, because a divergence of opinion, in the absence of a leader making the final decision, will paralyze the government.

Thus the Qur'ān says: "*Obey God and the Messenger, and never be drawn into dispute and disagreement, lest you be defeated and your power be scattered to the winds.*" (8:49)

It should also be borne in mind that Sūrah al-Shūrā was revealed in Makkah, at a time when the Islamic system of government had not yet taken shape, and that at no time was the government of the Prophet, peace and blessings be upon him and his family, based upon consultation.

The verse concerning consultation is, then, a general encouragement of the believers to consult with each other, and it has nothing to do with matters of governance and leadership. It relates to practical concerns of the Muslims, to the various problems that confront the Muslims. There is absolutely no justification for interpreting the verse as sanctioning the designation of the caliph by means of mutual consultation, for during the age of revelation government was exclusively in the hands of the Prophet, peace and blessings be upon him and his family.

Furthermore, the part of the verse recommending consultation treats of the desirability of spending one's property in God's path, which is also something desirable but not mandatory.

Yet another consideration is that the verse occurs in a context dealing with the wars of the Prophet, peace and blessings be upon him and his family. Some of the verses are addressed to the Muslims in general and the warriors among them in particular, and others to the Prophet individually. It is plain that in this context the encouragement to consult is inspired by compassion for the believers, by concern for their morale; it is not that the Prophet is obliged to act in accordance with the opinions of those he consults. For the Qur'ān clearly proclaims:

"*Whenever you take a decision, place your trust in God and act in accordance with your own opinion and wish.*" (3:159)

This context also suggests that consultation applies to military matters, particularly to the concerns that arose during the Battle of Badr, for the Prophet, peace and blessings be upon him and his family, consulted his Companions about the advisability of attacking the Quraysh trade caravan led by Abū Sufyān that was returning from Syria. First Abū Bakr expressed his opinion, which was rejected by the Prophet; then 'Umar expressed his, which was likewise rejected; and finally al-Miqdād gave his opinion, and the Prophet accepted it.[302]

If the Prophet consulted with others, it was not in order to learn from them an opinion superior to his own as a prelude to acting in accordance with it. His aim was rather to train them in the methods of consultation and the discovery of correct views. In contrast to worldly rulers who refused ever to consult ordinary people, because of their pride and arrogance, the Prophet was instructed by God to show the believers his concern and compassion for them by consulting with them, at the same time increasing their self-esteem and learning what they thought. However, the final decision was always his, and in the case of the Battle of Badr, God informed him in advance of what the result would be, and he in turn conveyed this to his Companions after consulting with them.

The command to consult and to exchange views is also for the sake of finding the best way of fulfilling a given duty, not for identifying what is a duty and what is not; this is an important difference.

Once a clear and authoritative prescription exists in the Qur'ān or the *Sunnah*, there is no ground for consultation to take place. Society has no right to discuss commands that are grounded in revelation, for in principle such discussion might result in the annulment of God's laws. In just the same way, consultation is meaningless in any human society once the legal duties of its members have been determined.

The successorship of 'Alī, peace be upon him, was clearly established by the Prophet in accordance with divine command at Ghadīr Khumm, at the beginning of the Prophet's mission, and again when he was on his deathbed. There was therefore no issue needing to be settled by consultation.

The Qur'ān does not permit individuals to entertain their own views on any subject where divine legislation exists, for it says: "*When God and His Messenger determine a matter, no choice remains therein for any believing woman or man. Whoever turns away from the command of God and His Messenger has openly chosen misguidance.*" (33:36)

Or again: "*God creates and chooses whatever He wishes, and men have no right to choose in opposition to His choice.*" (28:67)

Since the choice and selection of a leader is exclusively God's prerogative, and since in fact He designated a leader, it is meaningless to seek out others as possible leaders.

The task of the Imām is guiding men and demonstrating to them the path that will lead them to happiness. That being the case, the correct method for the selection of an Imām is the same as that which the Qur'ān spells out for the prophets: "*It is indeed incumbent on Us to guide mankind, for the kingdom of this world and the hereafter is Ours.*" (92:11-12)

It is then the responsibility of God alone to provide for the guidance of mankind and to make available to it whatever it needs at the various stages of existence. Part of what it needs is assuredly guidance, and only the one whom God has appointed may present himself as a guide. Numerous verses of the Qur'ān bear witness that God bestowed the status of guide on the Prophet.

The appointment of an Imām as successor to the Messenger of God takes place for exactly the same purpose as the mission of the Prophet, peace and blessings be upon him and his family, which is serving mankind as a guide and exemplar to whom obedience is due. This being the case, no one has the right to lay claim to this function or to demand obedience without a proof of having been appointed by God. If someone nonetheless does do so, he will be usurping God's right.

The Sunnī theory that sees in Abū Bakr's designation of his successor a justification for such a procedure is open to another objection. If the designation is made by an inerrant Imām, it is valid and authoritative, for one possessor of inerrancy can recognize another and safely entrust the affairs of the *ummah* to him. If this not be the case, one lacking the quality of inerrancy has no right to designate a caliph whom people are obliged to obey. If it be said that this is what Abū Bakr did and no one objected, it must be answered that severe objections were indeed raised, but no attention was paid to them.

Such are the views of the Sunnī scholars concerning the legitimacy of three different methods of choosing the caliph, and the objections that need to be made to those views.

Lesson Twenty-Five
The Imāmate of the Most Excellent

One of the questions that has been the subject of much discussion between Shīʿī and Sunnī scholars is the Imāmate of the Most Excellent. The Sunnī position is that if someone can be found to exist in the ranks of the *ummah* who is unequalled with respect to virtue, knowledge, and piety, someone less excellent than he may still legitimately become leader of the community and exercise the functions of successor to the Prophet, peace and blessings be upon him and his family.

In order to prove their point, they cite the caliphate of Abū Bakr and ʿUmar, and they maintain that although ʿAlī b. Abī Ṭālib, peace be upon him, was present at the time and his worthiness and perfection were far more apparent than those of anyone else, the Companions nonetheless selected Abū Bakr as successor to the Prophet.

The Shīʿah believe that the Imāmate constitutes an extension of prophethood in its spiritual dimension. The one who after the death of the Prophet is to serve as an authority for the Muslims in their learning the ordinances and principles of religion, who is to settle newly occurring problems for which no precedent can be found in the Qurʾān and the *Sunnah*, whose words are to be a decisive criterion — such a one must indubitably be more excellent than all others in his virtues and perfections. When God selects someone as the teacher of humanity and the guide of the *ummah*, to expound His laws, to interpret the complexities of the Qurʾān, and to defend the truth and develop the personality of the *ummah*, He entrusts this position to an exceptional and inerrant person who is utterly unique in his spiritual qualities, his outer and inner attributes, his communication with the world of the unseen. Such a person perceives the inner truth of things with his inner eye and is always oriented to the truth in such a way that his faith is never corrupted and his deeds never deviate from the right path.

The Imām is therefore the most excellent being of his time, the foremost of all his contemporaries. Imām al-Riḍā, peace be upon him, says the following concerning the distinctive qualities of the Imām:

"The Imām is utterly free of sin and pure of all fault. He is celebrated for his knowledge and his forebearance. His existence is a source of pride to the Muslims, of anger to the hypocrites, of perdition to the unbelievers. The Imām is unique in his age, in the sense that no one can attain his rank. No scholar can come within range of his knowledge, and he is unequalled in all his qualities. He possesses all virtues and worthy attributes without any striving on his part, and he is adorned with all lofty characteristics. This is a great gift bestowed on him by God in His generosity."[303]

Footnotes

(For full names of the books and authors, see Bibliographical Index)

1. al-Bāqillānī, *al-Tamhīd*, p. 186.
2. al-Dūrī, *al-Nuẓum al-Islāmiyyah*, Vol. I, pp. 72-84.
3. al-Majlisī, *Biḥār al-Anwār*, Vol, XVII, p. 129.
4. Aḥmad b. Ḥanbal, *al-Musnad*, p. 96.
5. Ibn Mājah, *al-Sunan*, "Bāb al-Fitan."
6. al-Ya'qūbī, *al-Tārīkh*, Vol. II, pp. 126-7.
7. Aḥmad b. Ḥanbal, *al-Musnad*, Vol. I, p. 344; Ibn Sa'd, *al-Ṭabaqāt*, Vol. II, p. 242; al-Bukhārī, *al-Ṣaḥīḥ*, Vol. I, p. 22; al-Ṭabarī, *Tārīkh*, Vol. II, p. 436.
8. al-Mas'ūdī, *Ithbāt al-Waṣiyyah*; al-Ya'qūbī, *al-Tārīkh*.
9. Ibn 'Asākir, *al-Tārīkh*, Vol. III, p. 5; *Riyāḍ al-Naḍirah*, Vol. II, p. 178.
10. Ibh Kathīr, *al-Bidāyah*, Vol. V, pp. 209-13; al-Haythamī, *Majma' al-Zawā'id*, Vol. IX, pp. 163-5.
11. al-Wāhidī, *Asbāb al-Nuzūl*, p. 150; al-Suyūṭī, *al-Durr al-Manthūr*, Vol. III, p. 298; al-Qundūzī, *Yanābī' al-Mawaddah*, p. 130; al-Ālūsī, *al-Tafsīr*, Vol. II, p. 172; al-Shawkānī, *Fatḥ al-Qadīr*, Vol. III, p. 57; Fakhr al-Dīn al-Rāzī, *al-Tafsīr al-Kabīr*, Vol. III, p. 636; Badr al-Dīn al-Ḥanafī, *'Umdah al-Qārī*, Vol. VIII, p. 584; 'Abduh, *Tafsīr al-Manār*.
12. Aḥmad b. Ḥanbal, *al-Musnad*, Vol. IV, p. 281; Ibn Kathīr, *al-Bidāyah*, Vol. V, p. 212.
13. Aḥmad b. Ḥanbal, *al-Musnad*, Vol. V, p. 181.
14. al-Tirmidhī, *Jāmi' al-Ṣaḥīḥ*, Vol. V, p. 328.

15. al-Muttaqī al-Hindī, *Kanz al-'Ummāl*, Vol. XV, p. 123.
16. Aḥmad b. Ḥanbal, *al-Musnad*, Vol. I, p. 118-19; al-Ḥākim, *al-Mustadrak*, Vol. III, p. 109; Ibn Kathīr, *al-Bidāyah*, V, pp. 209, 213.
17. al-Haythamī, *Majma' al-Zawā'id*, Vol. IX, pp. 104-5; al-Ḥasakānī, *Shawāhid al-Tanzīl*, Vol. I, p. 193; Aḥmad b. Ḥanbal, *al-Musnad*, Vol. I, p. 119; Ibn Kathīr, *al-Bidāyah*, Vol. V, p. 212.
18. The *ḥadīth* concerning Ghadīr Khumm is to be found with various chains of transmission in the Sunnī sources. See *al-Ghadīr*, Vol. I, pp. 14-72, where the *ḥadīth* is reported from 110 Companions of the Prophet, including Abū Bakr, 'Umar b. al-Khaṭṭāb, Ubayy b. Ka'b, Usāmah b. Zayd, Anas b. Mālik, Jābir b. 'Abdullāh, Zayd b. Arqam, Ṭalḥah, al-Zubayr, and Ibn Mas'ūd. See too al-Tirmidhī, *Jami' al-Ṣaḥīh*, Vol. II, p. 297; al-Ḥākim, *al-Mustadrak*, Vol. III, p. 109; Fakhr al-Dīn al-Rāzī, *al-Tafsīr al-Kabīr*, Vol. XII, p. 50; al-Wāḥidī, *Asbāb al-Nuzūl*, p. 150; al-Suyūṭī, *al-Durr al-Manthūr*, Vol. II, p. 298; al-Ya'qūbī, *al-Tārīkh*, Vol. II, p. 95; Ibn Kathīr, *al-Bidāyah*, Vol. V; al-Khaṭīb al-Baghdādī, *Tārīkh Baghdād*, Vol. VII, p. 377; al-Tha'labī, *al-Tafsīr*, p. 120; Ibn Ḥajar, *Ṣawā'iq*, Chapter 5.
19. al-Suyūṭī, *al-Durr al-Manthūr*, Vol. II, p. 256; Ibn Kathīr, *al-Bidāyah*, Vol. II, p. 14; al-Ḥamawīnī, *Farā'id al-Simṭayn*, Chapter 12; al-Khatīb al-Baghdādī, *Tārīkh Baghdād*, Vol. VIII, p. 290; al-Suyūṭī, *al-Itqān*, Vol. II, p. 31; al-Khwārazmī, *al-Tārīkh*.
20. al-Ya'qūbī, *al-Tārīkh*, Vol. II, p. 36.
21. Ibn Khallikān, *Wafayāt al-A'yān*, Vol. I, p. 60.
22. al-Mas'ūdī, *al-Tanbīh wa al-Ishrāf*, p. 32.
23. al-Bīrūnī, *al-Athar al-Bāqiyah*, (Persian translation), p. 334.
24. Cited in *al-Ghadīr*, Vol. I, p. 267.
25. For example, Qur'an, 57:15 and 22:13.
26. Aḥmad b. Ḥanbal, *al-Musnad*, Vol. IV, p. 281; Ibn Ḥajar, *al-Ṣawā'iq*, p. 26; al-Ṭabarī, *al-Tafsīr*, Vol. III, p. 428; al-Ghazālī, *Sirr al-'Ālamīn*, p. 9; Fakhr al-Dīn al-Rāzī, *al-Tafsīr al-Kabīr*, Vol. III, p. 636; al-Ḥamawīnī, *Farā'id*

al-Simṭayn, Chapter XIII; Ibn Kathīr, *al-Bidāyah*, Vol. V, p. 209; Ibn Ṣabbāgh, *Fuṣūl al-Muhimmah*, p. 25; al-Muḥibb al-Ṭabarī, *Riyaḍ al-Naḍirah*, Vol. II, p. 169.

27. Sunnī and Shī'ī commentators alike are agreed that this verse alludes to 'Alī.
28. al-Tirmidhī, *Jāmi' al-Ṣaḥīḥ*, Vol. V, p. 300. See also Ibn Mājah, *al-Sunan*, Vol. I, p. 44, and Aḥmad b. Ḥanbal, *al-Musnad*, Vol. IV, pp. 164-5.
29. al-Ḥākim, *al-Mustadrak*, Vol. III, p. 131.
30. *Amīr al-Mu'minīn*.
31. Ibn Qutaybah, *al-Imāmah wa al-Siyāsah*, Vol. I, pp. 12-13; Ibn Abī al-Ḥadīd, *Sharḥ*, Vol. II, p. 5.
32. al-Khwārazmī, *al-Manāqib*, p. 217.
33. al-Muḥibb al-Ṭabarī, *Riyāḍ al-Naḍirah*, Vol. II, p. 162; Ibn Kathīr, *al-Bidāyah*, Vol. V, p. 212; Aḥmad b. Ḥanbal, *al-Musnad*, Vol. I, pp. 118-19.
34. Aḥmad b. Ḥanbal, *al-Musnad*, Vol. IV, p. 370; Ibn Kathīr, *al-Bidāyah*, Vol. V, p. 212.
35. Ahmad b. Ḥanbal, *al-Musnad*, Vol. IV, p. 370. See also Ibn Qutaybah, *Kitāb al-Ma'ārif*, p. 194.
36. Ibn Mājah, *al-Sunan*, Vol. IV, p. 370.
37. al-Ḥamawīnī, *Farā'id al-Simṭayn*, Chapter 58.
38. See the "Khuṭbah Shaqshaqiyyah" in al-Raḍī's *Nahj al-Balāghah*.
39. Sharaf al-Dīn, *al-Murāja'āt*, (Persian translation), p. 429.
40. See Qur'ān, 26:214.
41. Aḥmad b. Ḥanbal, *al-Musnad*, Vol. I, pp. 111, 159; Ibn al-Athīr, *al-Kāmil*, Vol. II, p. 22; al-Ṭabarī, *al-Tafsīr*, Vol. II, p. 216; Abū al-Fidā', *al-Tārīkh*, Vol. I, p. 119; al-Ganjī, *Kifāyat al-Ṭālib*, p. 89; al-Nasā'ī, *al-Khaṣā'is*, p. 18; al-Ḥalabī, *al-Sīrah*, Vol. I, p. 304; Ibn Abi 'l-Ḥadīd, *Sharḥ*, Vol. III, p. 255; al-Suyūṭī, *Jam' al-Jawāmi'*, Vol. VI, p. 408; al-Khifājī, *Sharḥ al-Shifā'*, Vol. III, p. 37.
42. Ibn Hishām, *al-Sīrah*, Vol. I, p. 245.
43. al-Ḥākim, *al-Mustadrak*, Vol. III, p. 312.
44. Ibn Mājah, *al-Sunan*, Vol. I, p. 44; al-Ḥākim, *al-Mustadrak*, Vol. III, p. 112.

45. al-Ṭabarī, *Tārīkh*, Vol. II, p. 172.
46. al-Bukhārī, *al-Ṣaḥīḥ*, Vol. III, p. 58; Muslim, *al-Ṣaḥīḥ*, Vol. II, p. 323; Ibn Mājah, *al-Sunan*, Vol. I, p. 28; al-Ḥākim, *al-Mustadrak*, Vol. III, p. 190; Ibn Ḥajar, *Ṣawā'iq*, p. 30; al-Muttaqī al-Hindī, *Kanz al-'Ummāl*, Vol. VI, p. 152; al-Qundūzī, *Yanābī' al-Mawaddah*, p. 240; al-Nasā'ī, *al-Khaṣā'iṣ*, p. 7; Ibn Sa'd, *al-Ṭabaqāt*, Vol. III, p. 24.
47. al-Ḥākim, *al-Mustadrak*, Vol. III, p. 63; al-Nasā'ī, *al-Khaṣā'iṣ*, p. 63; al-Ḥamawīnī, *Farā'id al-Simṭayn*, Vol. I, p. 328; al-Dhahabī, *Talkhīṣ al-Mustadrak*, Vol. III, p. 132; Aḥmad b. Ḥanbal, *al-Musnad*, Vol. I, p. 331; al-Khwārazmī, *al-Manāqib*, p. 72; al-Ganjī, *Kifāyat al-Ṭālib*, p. 116; Ibn 'Asākir, *al-Tārīkh al-Kabīr*, Vol. I, p. 203; al-Bilādhurī, *Ansāb al-Ashrāf*, Vol. II, p. 106; Ibn Kathīr, *al-Bidāyah*, Vol. VII, p. 338; al-'Asqalānī, *al-Iṣābah*, Vol. II, p. 509.
48. Muslim, *al-Ṣaḥīḥ*, Vol. VII, p. 120; Ibn 'Asākir, *al-Tārīkh al-Kabīr*, Vol. I, p. 334; Ibn Kathīr, *al-Bidāyah*, Vol. VII, p. 341; al-Muttaqī al-Hindī, *Kanz al-'Ummāl*, Vol. XIII, p. 163; Ibn Mājah, *al-Sunan*, Vol. I, p. 58; al-Nasā'ī, *al-Khaṣā'iṣ*, p. 50; al-Qundūzī, *Yanābī' al-Mawaddah*, p. 51.
49. See Qur'ān, 20:29-32.
50. al-Muttaqī al-Hindī, *Kanz al-'Ummāl*, Vol. V, p. 31.
51. al-Ḥalabī, *al-Ṣīrah*, Vol. II, p. 97; Ibn Hishām, *al-Sīrah*, Vol. I, p. 505.
52. Ibn Sa'd, *al-Ṭabāqat*, Vol. VIII, p. 114.
53. Ibn 'Abd al-Barr, *al-Isti'āb*, Vol. II, p. 460; al-Khaṭīb al-Baghdādī, *Tārīkh*, Baghdādī, Vol. XII, p. 268; al-Fīrūzābādī, *Faḍā'il al-Khamsah*, Vol. I, p. 114.
54. al-Ḥākim, *al-Mustadrak*, Vol. III, p. 414; al-Tirmidhī, *Jāmi' al-Ṣaḥīḥ*, Vol. V.
55. al-Muttaqī al-Hindī, *Kanz al-'Ummāl*, Vol. VI, p. 395.
56. Ibn 'Asākir, *al-Tārīkh al-Kabīr*, Vol. I, pp. 360-61; al-Khaṭīb al-Baghdādī, *Tārīkh Baghdād*, Vol. VII, p. 453.
57. al-Muttaqī al-Hindī, *Kanz al-'Ummāl*, Vol. I, p. 250; Ibn Ḥajar, *al-Sawā'iq*, p. 75; al-Ḥākim, *al-Mustadrak*, Vol. III, p. 343; al-Qundūzī, *Yanābī' al-Mawaddah*, p. 257; Ibn al-Ṣabbāgh, *al-Fuṣūl al-Muhimmah*, p. 10; al-Ṣabbān, *Is'āf*

al-Rāghibīn, p. 111; al-Shiblanjī, *Nūr al-Abṣār*, p. 114.
58. Ibn Ḥajar, *al-Sawā'iq*, p. 140; al-Ḥākim, *al-Mustadrak*, Vol. III, p. 149.
59. Ibn Ḥajar, *al-Sawā'iq*, p. 140; al-Ḥākim, *al-Mustadrak*, Vol. III, p. 149.
60. Aḥmad b. Ḥanbal, *al-Musnad*, Vol. V, p. 181.
61. Shaykh Muḥammad Abū Zahrah, *al-Imām al-Ṣādiq*, p. 66.
62. Ibn Ḥajar, *al-Sawā'iq*, p. 108. See too al-Fīrūzābādī, *Faḍā'il al-Khamsah*, Vol. II, p. 81.
63. al-Shiblanjī, *Nūr al-Abṣār*, p. 104.
64. Muslim, *al-Ṣaḥīḥ*, Vol. VII, p. 122; al-Tirmidhī, *Jāmi' al-Ṣaḥīḥ*, Vol. II, p. 308; al-Ḥākim, *al-Mustadrak*, Vol. III, p. 109; Aḥmad b. Ḥanbal, *al-Musnad*, Vol. III, pp. 14-17; Ibn al-Ṣabbāgh, *Fuṣūl al-Muhimmah*, p. 24; al-Ganjī *Kifāyat al-Ṭālib*, p. 130; al-Qundūzī, *Yanābī' al-Mawaddah*, pp. 17-18; al-Ya'qūbī, *al-Tārīkh*, Vol. II, p. 92; Fakhr al-Dīn al-Rāzī, *al-Tafsīr al-Kabīr*, Vol. III, p. 18; al-Naysābūrī, *Gharā'ib al-Qur'ān*, Vol. I, p. 349.
65. al-Qundūzī, *Yanābī' al-Mawaddah*, pp. 32-40; Ibn Ḥajar, *al-Sawā'iq*, p. 57; al-Irbidī, *Kashf al-Ghummah*, p. 43.
66. al-Ḥalabī, *al-Sīrah*, Vol. III, p. 308.
67. Ibn Ḥajar, *al-Sawā'iq*, p. 89.
68. Ibn Qutaybah, *al-Imāmah wa al-Siyāsah*, Vol. I, p. 68; al-Ḥamawīnī, *Farā'id al-Simṭayn*, Chapter 37; al-Khaṭīb al-Baghdādī, *Tārīkh Baghdād*, Vol. IV, p. 21; Fakhr al-Dīn al-Rāzī, *Fuṣūl al-Muhimmah*.
69. Ibn Ḥajar, *al-Sawā'iq*, p. 153.
70. al-Raḍī, *Nahj al-Balāghah*, Sermon 145.
71. Muslim, *al-Ṣaḥīḥ*, Vol. XIII, p. 202.
72. Muslim, *al-Ṣaḥīḥ*, Vol. VI, p. 2; al-Bukhārī, *al-Ṣaḥīḥ*, Chapter XV of "Kitāb al-Aḥkām"; Aḥmad b. Ḥanbal, *al-Musnad*, Vol. I, p. 397, Vol. V, p. 86; Ibn Kathīr, *al-Bidāyah*, Vol. VI, p. 245; al-Qundūzī, *Yanābī' al-Mawaddah*, p. 373.
73. Muslim, *al-Ṣaḥīḥ*, Vol. XIII, p. 202.
74. Qur'ān, 42:23.
75. al-Qundūzī, *Yanābī' al-Mawaddah*, p. 446.
76. Ibn Hishām, *al-Sīrah*, Vol. IV p. 338; al-Ya'qūbī, *al-Tārīkh*,

Vol. II, p. 92; Ibn al-Athīr, *al-Kāmil*, Vol. II, pp. 120-21.
77. Ibn Sa'd, *al-Ṭabaqāt*, Vol. II, p. 249.
78. al-Ḥalabī, *al-Sīrah*, Vol. III, p. 336.
79. Ibn Sa'd, *al-Ṭabaqāt*, Vol. III, p. 25; al-Ḥākim, *al-Mustadrak*, Vol. III, p. 1.
80. Aḥmad b. Ḥanbal, *al-Musnad*, Vol. I, p. 346; Muslim, *al-Ṣaḥīḥ*, Vol. V, p. 76; al-Ṭabarī, *Tārīkh*, Vol. II, p. 436; Ibn Sa'd, *al-Ṭabaqāt*, Vol. II, p. 242.
81. al-Bukhārī, *al-Ṣaḥīḥ*, Vol. I, p. 22; al-Ṭabarī, *al-Tārīkh*, Vol. II, p. 436; Muslim, *al-Ṣaḥīḥ*, Vol. V, p. 76; Aḥmad b. Ḥanbal, *al-Musnad*, Vol. III, p. 346.
82. Ibn Sa'd, *al-Ṭabaqāt*, Vol. II, p. 243.
83. Ibn Sa'd, *al-Ṭabaqāt*, Vol. II, p. 242; Muslim, *al-Ṣaḥīḥ*, Vol. XI, p. 95; Aḥmad b. Ḥanbal, *al-Musnad*, Vol. I, p. 336.
84. Ibn Kathīr, *al-Bidāyah*, Vol. V, pp. 227-28; al-Dhahabī, *Tārīkh al-Islām*, Vol. I, p. 311; al-Diyār Bakrī, *Tārīkh al-Khamīs*, Vol. I, p. 182; *al-Bid' wa al-Tārīkh*, Vol. V, p. 95; *Taysīr al-Wuṣūl*, Vol. IV, p. 194.
85. Ibn Abi 'l-Ḥadīd, *Sharḥ*, Vol. III, p. 97.
86. Muslim, *al-Ṣaḥīḥ*, Vol. III, p. 1259; al-Bukhārī, *al-Ṣaḥīḥ*, Vol. IV, p. 5; Aḥmad b. Ḥanbal, *al-Musnad*, *ḥadīth* no. 2992.
87. al-Ṭabarī, *Tārīkh*, Vol. IV, p. 51.
88. Ibn Hishām, *al-Sīrah*, Vol. IV, p. 237; Muslim, *al-Ṣaḥīḥ*, Vol. IV, pp. 37-8, 46; al-Ṭabarī, *Tārīkh*, Vol. II, p. 401; Aḥmad b. Ḥanbal, *al-Musnad*, Vol. III, pp. 304, 380.
89. Muslim, *al-Ṣaḥīḥ*, Vol. VIII, p. 169.
90. al-Amīnī, *al-Ghadīr*, Vol. VI, p. 23.
91. Aḥmad b. Ḥanbal, *al-Musnad*, Vol. III, p. 408; Muslim, *al-Ṣaḥīḥ*, Vol. III, p. 183; al-Ḥalabī, *al-Sīrah*, Vol. II, p. 105; Ibn Kathīr, Vol. III, p. 23.
92. al-Tirmidhī, *Jāmi' al-Ṣaḥīḥ*, Vol. IV, p. 38.
93. Ibn Kathīr, *al-Bidāyah*, Vol. V, p. 141.
94. Muslim, *al-Ṣaḥīḥ*, Vol. IV, pp. 183-4.
95. *Risālat al-Islām*, Vol. XI, no, 1.
96. al-Ya'qūbī, *al-Tārīkh*, Vol. II, p. 107.
97. Ibn Abi 'l-Ḥadīd, *Sharḥ*, Vol. VIII, p. 11; Ibn Sa'd, *al-Ṭabaqāt*, Vol. III, pp. 296-7.

98. Ṭāhā Ḥusayn, *al-Fitnat al-Kubrā*, Vol. I, p. 108.
99. al-Sayyid Sharaf al-Dīn, *Fuṣūl al-Muhimmah*, pp. 177-92.
100. al-Ya'qūbī, *al-Tārīkh*, Vol. II, p. 103.
101. Ibn Abi 'l-Ḥadīd, *Sharḥ*, Vol. II, p. 18.
102. al-Bukhārī, *al-Ṣaḥīḥ*, "Kitāb al-Fitan".
103. Muslim, *al-Ṣaḥīḥ*, Vol. XV, p. 64.
104. al-Taftāzānī, *Sharḥ al-Maqāṣid*, p. 46.
105. al-Mas'ūdī, *Murūj al-Dhahab*.
106. Ibn Kathīr, *al-Bidāyah*, Vol. V, p. 260; al-Ya'qūbī, *al-Tārīkh*, Vol. II, p. 94; Aḥmad b. Ḥanbal, *al-Musnad*, Vol. IV, p. 104; al-Ṭabarī, *Tārīkh*, Vol. II, p. 451; Ibn al-Athīr, *Usd al-Ghābah*, Vol. I, p. 34; Ibn 'Abd Rabbih, al-*'Iqd al-Farīd*, Vol. III, p. 61.
107. al-Ṭabarī, *Tārīkh*, Vol. II, p. 456.
108. *Yawm al-Islām*, quoted in al-Amīn's *A'yān al-Shī'ah*, (Persian translation), Vol. I, p. 262.
109. al-Ṭabarī, *Tārīkh*, Vol. V, p. 31; Ibn al-Athīr, *al-Kāmil*, Vol. III, p. 3.
110. Ibn Abi 'l-Ḥadīd, *Sharḥ*, Vol. VI, p. 391.
111. al-Ya'qūbī, *al-Tārīkh*, Vol. II, p. 103; al-Ṭabarī, *Tārīkh*, Vol. III, p. 108.
112. Ibn Hishām, *al-Sīrah*, Vol. IV, p. 336; Ibn Kathīr, *al-Bidāyah*, Vol. V, p. 246.
113. Ibn Qutaybah, *al-Imāmah wa al-Siyāsah*, Vol. II, p. 9.
114. al-Ṭabarī, *Tārīkh*, Vol. II, pp. 455-59.
115. Ibn Abi 'l-Ḥadīd, *Sharḥ*, Vol. I, p. 133; Ibn 'Abd Rabbih, *al-'Iqd al-Farīd*, Vol. III, p. 63.
116. Ibn Hishām, *al-Sīrah*, Vol. IV, p. 343; al-Muḥibb al-Ṭabarī, *Riyāḍ al-Naḍirah*, Vol. I, P. 164.
117. al-Muttaqī al-Hindī, *Kanz al-'Ummāl*, Vol. III, p. 140.
118. Ibn Bakkār, *al-Muwaffaqiyāt*, p. 583.
119. al-Mas'ūdī, *Murūj al-Dhahab*, Vol. I, p. 441; Ibn Qutaybah, *al-Imāmah wa al-Siyāsah*, Vol. I, pp. 12-14.
120. al-Ya'qūbī, *al-Tārīkh*, Vol. II, p. 124; al-Ṭabarī, *Tārīkh*, Vol. IV, p. 843.
121. Abū al-Fidā', *al-Tārīkh*, Vol. I, p. 156; al-Diyār Bakrī, *Tārīkh al-Khamīs*, Vol. I, p. 188; Ibn 'Abd Rabbih, *al-'Iqd*

al-Farīd, Vol. III, p. 63; al-Muḥibb al-Ṭabarī, *Riyāḍ al-Naḍirah*, Vol. I, p. 167; Ibn Abi 'l-Ḥadīd, *Sharḥ*, Vol. I, pp. 130-34;

122. al-Ya'qūbī, *al-Tārīkh*, Vol. II, p. 105; al-Ṭabarī, *Tārīkh*, Vol. II, pp. 443-46; al-Muḥibb al-Ṭabarī, *Riyāḍ al-Naḍirah*, p. 167; al-Diyār Bakrī *Tārīkh, al-Khamīs*, Vol. I, p. 188; al-Muttaqī al-Hindī, *Kanz al-'Ummāl*, Vol. III, p. 128; Ibn Abi 'l-Ḥadīd, *Sharḥ*, Vol. I, pp. 122, 132-34.
123. Ibn Hishām, *al-Sīrah*, Vol. IV, p. 308.
124. Ibn Qutaybah, *al-Imāmah wa al-Siyāsah*, p. 19.
125. al-Ṭabarī, *Tārīkh*; Ibn al-Athīr, *al-Kāmil*.
126. Ibn Qutaybah, *al-Imāmah wa al-Siyāsah*, Vol. I, p. 5.
127. Ibn Hishām, *al-Sīrah*, Vol. IV, p. 34; Ibn Kathīr, *al-Bidāyah*, Vol. VI, p. 303; Ibn al-Athīr, *al-Kāmil*, Vol. II, p. 129; al-Ṭabarī, *Tārīkh*, Vol. II, p. 460.
128. Ibn Abi 'l-Ḥadīd, *Sharḥ*, Vol. III, p. 107.
129. Ibn Qutaybah, *al-Imāmah wa al-Siyāsah*, Vol. I, p. 16.
130. al-Ṭabarsī, *al-Iḥtijāj*, Vol. I, p. 96.
131. al-Ṭabarī, *Tārīkh*, Vol. I, p. 159.
132. Ibn Abi 'l-Ḥadīd, *Sharḥ*, Vol. VI, p. 5.
133. al-Ya'qūbī, *al-Tārīkh*, Vol. II, p. 114.
134. Ibn Abi 'l-Ḥadīd, *Sharḥ*, Vol. II, p. 131, Vol. VI, p. 17.
135. *Ibid.*
136. al-Ṭabarsī, *al-Iḥtijāj*, Vol. I, p. 253.
137. Ibn Abi 'l-Ḥadīd, *Sharḥ*, Vol. IV, p. 520.
138. al-Qundūzī, *Yanābī' al-Mawaddah*, p. 253.
139. *Ibid.*, pp. 156-57, 222.
140. *Ibid.*, p. 373; Ibn Abi 'l-Ḥadīd, *Sharḥ*, Vol. III, p. 283.
141. *Tārīkh*, Vol. II, p. 137.
142. Ibn al-Athīr, *al-Kāmil*, Vol. III, pp. 24-25.
143. al-Qundūzī, *Yanābī' al-Mawaddah*, p. 111.
144. al-Muttaqī al-Hindī, *Kanz al-'Ummāl*, Vol. VI, p. 408.
145. al-Qundūzī, *Yanābī' al-Mawaddah*, pp. 226-53.
146. al-Ya'qūbī, *al-Tārīkh*, Vol. II, p. 137.
147. Ibn Abi 'l-Ḥadīd, *Sharḥ*, Vol. II, pp. 411-12.
148. al-Tirmidhī, *Jāmi' al-Ṣaḥīḥ*, Vol. V, p. 329.
149. Ibn Abi 'l-Ḥadīd, *Sharḥ*, Vol. II, p. 411.

150. 'Abd al-Fattāḥ 'Abd al-Maqṣūd, *al-Imām 'Alī*, Vol. I, p. 287.
151. al-Raḍī, *Nahj al-Balāghah*, Sermon 64.
152. Ibn Abi 'l-Ḥadīd, *Sharḥ*, Vol. III, p. 224.
153. al-Ṭabarī, *Tārīkh*, Vol. II, p. 84.
154. Frank Cont (?) *Sīmā-ye Shujā'ān*, p. 35.
155. al-Ya'qūbī, *al-Tārīkh*, Vol. II, p. 114.
156. al-Mas'ūdī, *Murūj al-Dhahab*.
157. For more details concerning this mythical personality, see Murtadā al-'Askarī, *'Abdullāh bin Sabā'*.
158. Ṭāhā Ḥusayn, *al-Fitnat al-Kubrā*, Vol. II, p. 90.
159. Cited in Dr. Haykal, *Ḥayāt Muḥammad*, p. 136.
160. Kurd 'Alī, *Khiṭaṭ al-Shām*, Vol. VI, p. 246.
161. al-Nawbakhtı, *al-Maqālāt wa al-Firāq*, p. 15.
162. Ibn Ḥajar, *al-Sawā'iq*, Chapter 1; al-Khwārazmī, *al-Manāqib* p. 66; al-Ḥamawīnī, *Farā'id al-Simṭayn*, Vol. I, Chapter 13; al-Qundūzī, *Yanābī' al-Mawaddah*, Chapter 56; Ibn al-Sabbāgh, *Fuṣūl al-Muhimmah*, p. 105; al-Ganjī, *Kifāyat al-Ṭālib*, p. 118.
163. Cited in *al-Murāja'āt*, p. 10.
164. al-Raḍawī, *Ma'a Rijāl al-Fikr fī al-Qāhirah*, pp. 40-41.
165. al-Ṭabarī, *Tārīkh*, Vol. II, p. 446.
166. al-Ḥākim, *al-Mustadrak*, Vol. III, p. 383.
167. al-Tirmidhī, *Jāmi' al-Ṣaḥīḥ*, Vol. V, p. 233.
168. Ibn Mājah, *al-Sunan*, Vol. I, p. 53.
169. al-Tirmidhī, *Jāmi' al-Ṣaḥīḥ*, Vol. V, p. 334.
170. al-Tirmidhī, *Jāmi' al-Ṣaḥīḥ*, Vol. V, p. 332.
171. al-Ḥākim, *al-Mustadrak*, Vol. III, p. 536.
172. Ibn Nadīm, *al-Fihrist*, p. 263.
173. Ibn Qutaybah, *al-Imāmah wa al-Siyāsah*, Vol. I, p. 12.
174. al-Ṭabarī, *Tārīkh*, Vol. II, p. 67.
175. Ibn Qutaybah, *al-Imāmah wa al-Siyāsah*, Vol. I, p. 12.
176. al-Qundūzī, *Yanābī' al-Mawaddah*, p. 211.
177. al-Amīnī, *al-Ghadīr*, Vol. VI, pp. 110-11.
178. Ibn Sa'd, *al-Ṭabaqāt*, Vol. II, p. 103.
179. For further cases of this type, see *al-Ghadīr*, Vol. VI-VIII.
180. al-Majlisī, *Biḥār al-Anwār*, Vol. XXV, p. 200.
181. Ḥurr al-'Amilī, *Ithbāt al-Hudāt*, Vol. III, p. 131.

182. al-'Ayyāshī, *al-Tafsīr*, Vol. I, p. 252.
183. Ḥurr al-'Amilī, *Ithbāt al-Hudāt*, Vol. III, p. 123.
184. al-Qundūzī, *Yanābī' al-Mawaddah*, p. 137.
185. See the creed of Abū Bakr al-Mu'min as cited in al-Mar'ashī, *Ihqāq al-Ḥaqq*, Vol. III, p. 425; Abū Ḥayyān al-Andalūsī, *al-Baḥr al-Muḥīṭ*, Vol. III, p. 276; al-Qundūzī, *Yanābī' al-Mawaddah*, pp. 114-16.
186. al-Suyūṭī, *al-Durr al-Manthūr*, Vol. II, p. 293; Ibn Ḥajar, *al-Kāfī al-Shāfī*, p. 53; 'Abduh, *Tafsīr al-Manār*, Vol. VI, p. 442; al-Zamakhsharī, *Tafsir al-Kashshāf* under the said verse; *Jāmi' al-Usūl*, Vol. IX, p. 487; al-Ṭabarī, *al-Tafsīr*, p. 165; al-Muttaqī al-Hindī, *Kanz al-'Ummāl*, Vol. VI, p. 391; Fakhr al-Dīn al-Rāzī, *al-Tafsīr al-Kabīr*, Vol. III, p. 431; al-Wāḥidī, *Asbāb al-Nuzūl*, p. 148.
187. al-Ṭabarī, *al-Tafsīr*, Vol. XXVIII, p. 270; al-Suyūṭī, *al-Durr al-Manthūr*, Vol. VI, p. 223.
188. al-'Ayyāshī, *al-Tafsīr*, Vol. I, p. 247.
189. Asad Ḥaydar, *al-Imām al-Ṣādiq wa al-Madhāhib al-Arba'ah*.
190. Ibn Shahrāshūb, *al-Manāqib*, Vol. IV, p. 247.
191. Asad Ḥaydar, *Imām Ṣādiq wa Madhāhib-i Chahārgāneh*, (Persian translation), Vol. III, 27-28, 46.
192. Ibn Abi 'l-Ḥadīd, *Sharḥ*, Vol. I, p. 6.
193. al-Kulaynī, *al-Kāfī*, Vol. I, p. 170.
194. Aḥmad b. Ḥanbal, *al-Musnad*, Vol. I, pp. 2, 14.
195. Cited in al-Nawawī, *Aḍwā' 'alā al-Sunnat al-Muḥammadiyyah*, p. 224.
196. Mālik, *al-Muwaṭṭā'*, p. 335.
197. Ibn Sa'd, *al-Ṭabaqāt*, Vol. III, p. 151.
198. al-Nawawī, *Aḍwā'* p. 204.
199. Ibn Mājah, *al-Sunan*, Vol. I, p. 200.
200. al-Nawawī, *Aḍwā'*, p. 204.
201. al-Amīnī, *al-Ghadīr*, Vol. VI, p. 87.
202. al-Bayhaqī, *al-Sunan (al-Kubrā)*, Vol. VIII, p. 33.
203. al-Kulaynī, *al-Kāfī*, Vol. I, p. 175.
204. al-Raḍī, *Nahj al-Balāghah*, p. 146.
205. al-Qundūzī, *Yanābī' al-Mawaddah*, pp. 23, 524.
206. al-Kulaynī, *al-Kāfī*, Vol. I, p. 180.

207. al-Qundūzī, *Yanābī' al-Mawaddah*, p. 21.
208. Ḥurr al-'Amilī, *Ithbāt al-Hudāt*, Vol. I, p. 247.
209. al-Kulaynī, *al-Kāfī*, Vol. I, p. 179.
210. Ibid, Vol. I, p. 195.
211. al-Majlisī, *Biḥār al-Anwār*, Vol. XXIII, p. 19.
212. al-Kulaynī, *al-Kāfī*, Vol. II, p. 179.
213. al-Ṣadūq, *al-Amālī*, p. 376.
214. al-Baḥrānī, *Ghāyat al-Marām*, p. 295.
215. al-Suyūṭī, *al-Durr al-Manthūr*, Vol. V, p. 199.
216. al-Qundūzī, *Yanābī' al-Mawaddah*, p. 125.
217. *Ibid.*, p. 126; al-Suyūṭī, *al-Durr al-Manthūr*, Vol. V, p. 199; Aḥmad b. Ḥanbal, *al-Musnad*, Vol. I, p. 331; Fakhr al-Dīn al-Rāzi, *al-Tafsīr al-Kabīr*, Vol. I, p. 783; al-Suyūṭī, *al-Khaṣā'is al-Kubrā*, Vol. II, p. 264; Ibn Ḥajar, *al-Sawā'iq*, p. 85.
218. Ibn al-Athīr, *Jāmi' al-Usūl*, Vol. I, p. 101; al-Muḥibb al-Ṭabarī, *Riyāḍ al-Naḍirah*, Vol. II, p. 269; al-Haythamī, *Majma' al-Zawā'id*, Vol. IX, pp. 119, 207.
219. al-Qundūzī, *Yanābī' al-Mawaddah*, p. 124.
220. al-Suyūṭī, *al-Durr al-Manthūr*, Vol. V, p. 198; Ibn al-Athīr, *Usd al-Ghābah*, Vol. V, p. 174; al-Haythamī, *Majma' al-Zawā'id*, Vol. IX, p. 168.
221. al-Ganjī, *Kifāyat al-Ṭālib*, p. 232; Asad Ḥaydar, *al-Imām al-Ṣādiq wa al-Madhāhib al-Arba'ah*, Vol. I, p. 89; Ahmad b. Ḥanbal, *al-Musnad*, Vol. I, p. 330; al-Nasā'ī, *al-Khaṣā'iṣ*, p. 11; al-Muḥibb al-Ṭabarī, *Riyāḍ al-Naḍirah*, Vol. II, p. 269; al-Haythamī, *Majma' al-Zawā'id*, Vol. IX, pp. 119, 207.
222. al-Tirmidhī, *Jāmi' al-Ṣaḥīḥ*, Vol. II, p. 308; al-Ḥākim, *al-Mustadrak*, Vol. III, p. 158; Ibn Kathīr, *al-Bidāyah*, Vol. III, p. 438; Ibn al-Ṣabbāgh, *Fuṣūl al-Muhimmah*, p. 8; al-Ṭabarī, *al-Tafsīr*, Vol. XXII, p. 5; al-Suyūṭī, *al-Durr al-Manthūr*, Vol. V, p. 199; al-Muttaqī al-Hindī, *Kanz al-'Ummāl*, Vol. VII, p. 102; Aḥmad b. Ḥanbal, *al-Musnad*, Vol. III, p. 286.
223. al-Baḥrānī, *Ghāyat al-Marām*, p. 295.
224. al-Bukhārī, *al-Ṣaḥīḥ*, Vol. II, p. 189.
225. al-Qundūzī, *Yanābī' al-Mawaddah*, p. 534.

226. Ḥurr al-'Amilī, *Ithbāt al-Hudāt*, Vol. I, p. 232.
227. al-Raḍī, *Nahj al-Balāghah*, Sermon 83.
228. al-Kulaynī, *al-Kāfī*, Vol. I, p. 200.
229. al-Majlisī, *Bihār al-Anwār*, Vol. XXV, p. 199.
230. al-Kulaynī, *al-Kāfī*, Vol. I, p. 204.
231. al-Qundūzī, *Yanābī' al-Mawaddah*, p. 36; al-Tirmidhī, *Jāmi' al-Ṣaḥīḥ*, Vol. V, p. 329.
232. al-Kulaynī, *al-Kāfī*, Vol. I.
233. Sharaf al-Dīn, *Kalimat al-Ghurrā'*, p. 213.
234. al-Kulaynī, *al-Kāfī*, Vol. I, p. 203.
235. al-Majlisī, *Biḥār al-Anwār*, Vol. XXVI, p. 160.
236. *Ibid.*, p. 159.
237. *Ibid.*, p. 160.
238. al-Kulaynī, *al-Kāfī*, Vol. I, p. 255.
239. *Ibid.*, p. 222.
240. al-Baḥrānī, *Ghāyat al-Marām*, p. 514.
241. al-Khwārazmī, *al-Manāqib*, p. 390; *al-Mu'jam al-Mufahras li Nahj al-Balāghah*, p. 1407.
242. al-Muttaqī, al-Ḥindī, *Kanz al-'Ummāl*, Vol. XV, p. 113.
243. al-Kulaynī, *al-Kāfī*, Vol. I, p. 225.
244. Ḥurr al-'Amilī, *Ithbāt al-Hudāt*, Vol. VI, pp. 45-9; al-Ṣadūq, *Kitāb al-Tawḥīd*, pp. 427-9.
245. al-Majlisī, *Biḥār al-Anwār*, Vol. VIII.
246. al-Kulaynı, *al-Kāfī*, Vol. I, p. 225.
247. *Ibid.*, p. 202.
248. *Ibid.*, p. 176.
249. *Ibid.*, p. 264.
250. *Ibid.*, p. 229.
251. *Ibid.*, p. 61.
252. *Ibid.*, p. 61.
253. *Ibid.*, p. 63.
254. al-Ṭabāṭabā'ī, *al-Mīzān*, Vol. III, p. 74.
255. al-Kulaynī, *al-Kāfī*, Vol. I, p. 213.
256. *Ibid.*, p. 241.
257. al-Burūjardī, *Jāmi' Aḥādīth al-Shī'ah*, Vol. I, p. 138.
258. al-Qundūzī, *Yanābī' al-Mawaddah*, p. 22.
259. al-Burūjardī, *Jāmi' Aḥādith al-Shī'ah*, Vol. I, p. 141.

260. *Ibid.*, p. 130.
261. al-Qundūzī, *Yanābī' al-Mawaddah*, p. 83.
262. al-Baḥrānī, *Ghāyat al-Marām*, p. 518.
263. al-Muttaqī al-Hindī, *Kanz al-'Ummāl*, Vol. VI, p. 516; al-Ḥākim, *al-Mustadrak*, Vol. III, p. 122.
264. al-Kulaynī, *al-Kāfī*, Vol. I, p. 64.
265. al-Khwārazmī, *al-Manāqib*, p. 40; al-Ḥākim, *al-Mustadrak*, Vol. III, p. 126; al-Khaṭīb al-Baghdādī, *Tārīkh Baghdād*, Vol. IV, p. 348; Ibn Ḥajar, *al-Sawā'iq*, p. 73; Ibn al-Athīr, *Usd al-Ghābah*, Vol. IV, p. 22.
266. al-Qundūzī, *Yanābī' al-Mawaddah*,, p. 74.
267. al-Tirmidhī, *Jāmi' al-Ṣaḥīḥ*, Vol. XIII, p. 171; al-Muttaqī al-Hindī, *Kanz al-'Ummāl*, Vol. VI, p. 156; al-Iṣbahānī, *Ḥilyat al-Awliyā'*, Vol. I, p. 64.
268. al-Qundūzī, *Yanābī' al-Mawaddah*, p. 69.
269. *Ibid.*, p. 77.
270. al-Raḍī, *Nahj al-Balāghah*, Sermon 187.
271. al-Tirmidhī, *Jāmi' al-Ṣaḥīḥ*, Vol. V, p. 297.
272. al-Radī, *Nahj al-Balāghah*, Sermon 105.
273. al-Ṣadūq, *Kitāb al-Tawḥīd*, p. 73.
274. Ibn al-Athīr, *Usd al-Ghābah*, Vol. I, p. 391.
275. Ja'far Subḥānī, *Āgāhi-yi Sevvom*, p. 184.
276. Alexis Carrel, *Insān, Mawjūd-i Nāshinakhteh*, pp. 135 ff.
277. al-Kulaynī, *al-Kāfī*, Vol. I, p. 256.
278. *Ibid.*, p. 256.
279. al-Majlisī, *Biḥār al-Anwār*, Vol. XXVI, p. 115.
280. al-Kulaynī, *al-Kāfī*, Vol. II, p. 258.
281. *Ibid.*, Vol. I, p. 192.
282. al-Majlisī, *Biḥār al-Anwār*, XXVI, p. 110.
283. al-Kulaynī, *al-Kāfī*, Vol. I, p. 261.
284. al-Majlisī, *Biḥār al-Anwār*, Vol. XXVI, p. 27.
285. *Ibid.*, p. 110.
286. al-Kulaynī, *al-Kāfī*, Vol. I, p. 261.
287. al-Majlisī, *Biḥār al-Anwār*, Vol. XXVI, p. 141.
288. Ibn Abi 'l-Ḥadīd, *Sharḥ*, Vol. II, p. 175.
289. *Ibid.*, p. 291.
290. *Ibid.*, p. 253.

291. Ḥurr al-'Amilī, *Ithbāt al-Hudāt*, Vol. V, p. 147.
292. Abū al-Faraj al-Iṣbahānī, *Maqātil al-Ṭālibiyyīn*, p. 172.
293. Ḥurr al-'Āmilī, *Ithbāt al-Hudāt*, Vol. V, p. 266.
294. Abū al-Faraj al-Iṣbahānī, *Maqātil al-Ṭālibiyyīn*, p. 298.
295. Ḥurr al-'Āmilī, *Ithbāt al-Hudāt*, Vol. V, p. 207.
296. *Ibid.*, Vol. VI, p. 286.
297. *Ibid.*, Vol. VI, p. 213.
298. Ibn Abi 'l-Ḥadīd, *Sharḥ*, Vol. II, p. 286.
299. *Ibid.*, Vol. II, p. 294.
300. Ibn Hishām, *Sīrah*, Vol. IV, p. 308; al-Ṭabarī, *Tārīkh*; Ibn al-Athīr, *al-Kāmil*; Ibn Kathīr, *al-Bidāyah*.
301. Ibn Abi 'l-Ḥadīd, *Sharḥ*, Vol. I, p. 132.
302. Muslim, *al-Ṣaḥīḥ*, "Kitāb al-Jihād wa Sayr" Bāb Ghuzwah Badr, Vol. III, p. 1403.
303. al-Kulaynī, *al-Kāfī*, Vol. I, p. 200.

Bibliographical Index

(Name of the books and authors referred to in this book, with page numbers)

Qur'ānic Index

General Index

D

E

F

Indexes prepared by: M. Ridha